Q Ships, Commerce Raiders
and
Convoys

Q SHIPS, COMMERCE RAIDERS AND CONVOYS

By

Patrick Stearns

SPELLMOUNT
Staplehurst

British Library Cataloguing in Publication Data:
A catalogue record for this book is available
from the British Library

Copyright © Patrick Stearns 2004

ISBN 1-873376-84-7

First published in the UK in 2004 by
Spellmount Limited
The Village Centre
Staplehurst
Kent TN12 0BJ

Tel: 01580 893730
Fax: 01580 893731
E-mail: enquiries@spellmount.com
Website: www.spellmount.com

1 3 5 7 9 8 6 4 2

Typeset in Palatino by MATS, Southend-on-Sea, Essex
Printed in Great Britain by
T.J. International Ltd
Padstow, Cornwall

Contents

List of Maps and Diagrams

Foreword

The receipt of supplies by sea has always been crucial for Britain in times of war. The Spaniards, the Dutch and the French all in their time attacked our shipping lanes, challenging our wealth and even national survival. Philip II, Louis XIV and Napoleon, the Kaiser and Hitler have gone further and even dreamed of invasion.

The most serious threat to our shipping lanes during the twentieth century was posed by the U-boats. In 1917, and again in 1943, Britain stared defeat in the face owing to the huge losses to our shipping caused by the unscrupulous deployment against us of U-boats alongside, in the earlier years of the Second World War, powerful German battleships and pocket-battleships.

These World War I and World War II threats were met by the Royal Navy's Q ships in the First War and by the Convoy system in both struggles. Almost invariably, the enemy had the initiative, yet in both conflicts advances in technology and organisation eventually turned the hunters into the hunted.

This is a fascinating story that Commander Stearns has to relate. Anybody interested in British Naval history since 1914 should certainly read this book, and I am delighted to have provided this short Foreword.

David G. Chandler

Dr David G Chandler
MA (Oxon), DLitt FRHistS, FRGS

Acknowledgements

I was serving as a teenage midshipman on board the veteran battleship HMS *Warspite* when the Allies launched the invasion of German-occupied Normandy during June 1944. I returned to the invasion area with my wife for the fiftieth anniversary functions in June 1994. The idea of a book germinated during discussions with others who had been present as part of 'the Great Invasion', who had also served in World War II decoy ships and had had wartime experiences other than the maritime side of the invasion of Europe.

The present book barely mentions the Normandy Landings, but I have been an avid absorber of military and naval history and thought that it might be interesting to produce some rather 'broad brush' studies which might stimulate curiosity among readers and lead them to the fascination of digging more deeply into specific aspects of an infinitely large fund of knowledge.

I have kept notes for many years, but, until recently, never thought of turning them into a book so I have been lax about recording more than, say, the name of a book or an author without any other embellishment. If I have, in my ignorance, stepped on any toes, I can only apologise.

Statistics have been kept to a minimum, probably because I am extremely bad at remembering them; and also because I know that public libraries contain reference books which can provide a multitude of details if these should really be needed

I have been fortunate in having been sent original material (in one instance from the Antipodes); and I hope that I have 'mentioned in despatches' those who have been kind enough to help me in this respect. In particular, I am indebted to Mr A W Bennetts of Kenmore, Queensland, Australia and Mr Michael Irwin of Gosforth, Newcastle-upon-Tyne.

I have learned by experience that it takes more than one person to write a book. My wife, Gaye, and my son, Michael, have been generous with their encouragement and work with turning my drafts into legible typescript. My daughter, Amanda, was once kind enough to tell me that my handwriting was neat, but she found it difficult to decipher. To all three, my grateful thanks.

Patrick Stearns
Woking, Surrey
March 2004

Introduction

'The life and war effort of the country depend directly
upon the weight of imports safely landed.'

Winston Churchill in the House of Commons, 25 June 1951

The story of Britain, her rise to greatness and survival in periods of emergency, has revolved round the effectiveness with which the nation has had the will to remain a strong maritime power. It is all too easy to remember naval history by the details of actions fought by warships rather than the basic cause of these actions. In the great majority of cases, naval engagements were directly connected with the problems of trade warfare. Trade warfare can either be offensive or defensive, and it is difficult to imagine that the future will show any significant differences to this trend.

A distinguished military historian indicated that the causes of wars can usually be attributed to the 'criminal negligence of politicians'. In the present age it is not necessary to look very far to find examples taking place to substantiate this theory.

Whatever may be given as the causes of particular wars, armed conflicts do take place with regrettable frequency and, in the case of maritime nations, dangerous situations develop when the basic building blocks upon which sea power is normally built have been neglected.

Britain's security has been threatened a number of times over the centuries and it is interesting to study some of the causes of the occasions when the traditional shield of sea power has been lowered and the security of the country has been jeopardised thereby.

It is also fascinating to look at some of the expedients which were evolved to try to mitigate the potentially dangerous effects of hostile attempts to exploit weak points in the defence of the realm.

The great American Civil War Confederate captain, General 'Stonewall' Jackson, can be said to have adopted the three words: 'mystify, mislead and surprise' as his motto. This spells out the theories developed in a former age by the great Breton Knight, Bertrand du Guesclin. As principles go, it would be difficult to beat the above when planning strategical, or tactical, moves in any period, including the present. The use of the Trojan Horse was one of the earliest recorded examples of a deception which turned out to be tremendously successful. The expression 'Trojan Horse' is still used to describe, say, the insertion of an innocent-looking merchant vessel containing a concealed nuclear weapon into a potential enemy's harbour shortly before the outbreak of hostilities. Many other uses of the Trojan Horse principle can be imagined in sea, land or air warfare in both major, or limited, conflicts, acts of terrorism and so forth.

The morality of the Japanese carrier-borne aircrafts' assault on Pearl Harbor, which was the main United States naval base in Hawaii, early on Sunday 7 December 1941 will probably be debated for generations to come. The Japanese attack was implemented before any declaration of war had been made and while diplomatic negotiations between the two countries involved were still taking place.

There is no doubt that surprise had been well and truly achieved. The losses inflicted upon the US Navy gave a great initial advantage to Japanese maritime forces; but, mercifully, for the future American conduct of the Pacific War, no US aircraft-carriers were in harbour at the time of the Japanese attack. Perhaps, more note should have been taken of the way in which the Japanese had started the Russo–Japanese War in February 1904 by launching a surprise attack on Russian warships in Port Arthur.

It is very common in written stories or films for pirates to fly well known national colours to lull potential victims into a false sense of security, then hoist the 'skull and crossbones' immediately before the start of the attack upon their prey.

In similar manner, in the days of sail, it was not unknown for merchant ships to be decorated with false gun ports or dummy guns, in the hope that such artifices might discourage privateers or small hostile warships from attacking them. The disguising of, and the use of, decoys at sea is dealt with at greater length in succeeding chapters of this book.

The sea can be looked at in a number of ways, but the strategist probably considers it as a huge highway which is capable of carrying an almost infinite number of human beings, food supplies and munitions to required destinations. It can be thought of as a liquid desert; but it is probably one of the greatest blessings conferred by the Creator on countries whose shores its waters lap. In times of war, the two great problems facing combatants with maritime interests are how to deny the use of the sea, as far as possible, to an enemy, and how to protect one's own seaborne trade from hostile interference.

For an island race, such as the British, the outbreak of war can change what has been a convenient medium of transport into a vital lifeline. It is not unknown, when an island is at war, for opposing armies to be unable to meet. In this event, commerce can provide a world-wide battlefield.

Advances in the range and capabilities of aircraft, guided weapons and so on may modify previous thoughts on the detail of employing sea-power; but the large-scale destruction of vessels at sea must still be an aim of the highest importance.

The sole objective of a war on commerce is to carry out the campaign with an intensity, and thoroughness, which could ultimately strangle the enemy, both as regards trade and food supplies.

When the Almighty positioned the British Isles it seems that he must have put on an Admiral's hat in that Britain was placed to enable British fleets to operate on 'interior lines' vis a vis other European countries.

A quick glance at the map will show that, with the availability of an effective fleet, Britain is in an admirable position to threaten points on the European coastline from Scandinavia to Spain. She is also well placed to exercise control over the Iceland–Faeroes Gap and the Faeroes–Shetland Gap, and also the waters between Shetland and the Orkneys, and the Orkneys and north-west Scotland. Another asset of tremendous value is the stretch of sheltered water known as Scapa Flow.

In the years immediately preceding the outbreak of the First World War, the British Naval Staff worked on the assumption that the German seaboard adjacent to the North Sea was of the order of 114 miles, while the length of the coastline of the British Isles could be measured in thousands of miles with numerous port and harbour facilities. The conventional reasoning was that this geographical advantage implied that there was far more chance of British overseas trade being successfully continued in time of war than would be feasible for the potential enemy's (Germany's) maritime commerce.

With the geographical factors mentioned above in mind, Britain's use of a large Navy tended to be based on the philosophy of the blockade of European countries with which the nation happened to be at war. This, in turn, affected the strategies and tactics of the blockading nation and those being blockaded. The countries being blockaded tended to pursue the trade war by thinking in terms of blockade runners and commerce raiders, while the blockading country worked on closing loopholes and trying to bring enemy ships to action whenever they left their home shores. At the same time, it would be necessary for the blockading forces to take the appropriate precautions to protect their own merchant shipping from hostile interference.

Having had a brief look at a number of general principles and the geographical position of the British Isles, it is time to turn to two developments which were to have a profound effect upon maritime thought prior to World War II. The first of these was the refinement of submersible craft until they could be constructed, more or less, in their modern forms.

It is not generally known that an Englishman, called David Bourne, had produced a boat which was capable of achieving short spells beneath the surface of the water in 1578. This craft was demonstrated before King James I.

In 1776 an American, by the name of David Bushnell, produced a mobile submersible boat which took part in an attempt to blow up Admiral Lord Howe's flagship by attaching a delayed-action charge to the warship's bottom.

In 1801 another American, Robert Fulton, showed off a similar style of boat to the Emperor Napoleon. During the war of 1812, Fulton's craft was employed in an attempt to sink the line-of-battleship *Ramillies* which was flying the broad pennant of Commodore Hardy.

The first successful submarine attack occurred during the American Civil War when the Federal Warship *Housatonic* was sunk, in harbour, by an explosive device which had been attached to the ship's bottom.

The early experiments which were made with submersible boats did little to ruffle the current trends of naval thought. This was due to the fact that the mobility of the submersibles was severely limited and awaited the arrival of some motive power other than that which could be exercised by the circumscribed endurance and strength of human beings. In addition, the difficult evolution of attaching some sort of charge to the bottom of a motionless ship was then deemed to have its limitations, especially if the vessel concerned was keeping an alert watch. Damaging a ship in motion presented even more difficult problems to the very early submarines.

The evolution of electric motors, which could be powered from storage batteries, provided the means of achieving submerged locomotion.

In the late 1860s a weapon was being developed by an Englishman called Whitehead, who was then employed by the Austrian Government. By about the year 1868 Whitehead's torpedo could transport an explosive charge weighing some eighteen pounds at six knots for approximately four hundred yards. The torpedo could run at a depth of between five and fifteen feet. After the passage of a further two years, the torpedo's performance had been increased to give it a speed of eight knots and a range of seven hundred yards. The Austrian Government, at this time, failed to appreciate the revolutionary new weapon which was being handed to it on a plate and decided to cancel its financial backing of Whitehead's project. How often has this failure to see the merits of inventions, with military applications, occurred in the history of the last thousand years?

The British Admiralty eagerly seized the opportunity to invite Whitehead to bring his torpedoes to England and to continue developing the devices under the umbrella of HM Forces.

The torpedo gained in size, speed and range. Also, in its ability to carry a higher weight of explosive material. The Royal Navy now had a mobile underwater weapon which could damage a ship where it really hurts, that is below the water line.

At about the time submarines were becoming truly sea-going, the torpedo was available to them, and the marriage of the two had resulted in the birth of a formidable weapon system.

Discussion on the future potential of the submarine became more intense as the outbreak of World War I approached, even though most people could not visualise the outbreak of hostilities on a truly vast scale before the declarations of war were actually made in 1914. Writers, pre-World War I, such as Erskine Childers in *The Riddle of the Sands* (1903) often showed considerable prescience.

An extract from a publication called *Truth*, dated 4 February 1914, stated that:

> Intelligent discussion of our naval requirements is rendered almost impossible by party politics and popular ignorance of the subject. Whether on the side of spending or the side of saving, all arguments are addressed to the gallery and the gallery is more easily moved by its sentiments than by its brains. But for this, one of the points on which we should have heard much during the last few weeks, but on which we have heard next to nothing, is the future of the modern battleship. Battleships absorb by far the largest portion of our naval expenditure. Yet many tacticians are now asserting that submarine and aerial craft – not to mention long range torpedoes – have reached a stage of development when they can effectively dispute the supremacy of the ship-of-the-line.

Those of us who are alive in the early stages of the twenty-first century can judge the foresight displayed by the remark of the Right Hon. the Lord Fisher of Kilverstone, GCB, OM, GCVO, Admiral of the Fleet, who once said at a Spithead Review, pointing to a submarine: 'there goes the battleship of the future.'

Pre-World War I statements that the submarine was the coming type of military vessel for sea fighting met the usual chorus of derogatory remarks from conservative sea officers who 'sounded off' against the submarine. However, a number of the more far-seeing reminded their colleagues of the following record of exploded ideas:

> An ancient Admiralty Board Minute described the introduction of the steam engine as fatal to England's Navy.
> Another minute vetoed iron ships, as iron sinks and wood floats!
> The Navy objected to breech-loading guns and consequently disaster was close for a number of years.
> There was virulent opposition to the water tube boiler (fancy putting

the fire where the water ought to be and the water where the fire should be!).

Wireless was voted damnable by armchair sailors when the first aerials were placed on the roof of the Admiralty building.

'Flying machines were a physical impossibility,' a great scientist remarked only a comparatively few years before aircraft began to become plentiful.

The coming of the submarine really meant that Britain's traditional maritime strategy, which had served her so well, had to be broken down. For generations, the nation's naval strategy was founded upon the concept of blockade. The fleet did not exist just to win battles, which important activity was really only a means, not an end. The ultimate purpose of the fleet was to make a state of blockade possible for Britain and impossible for her enemies. The ideal was to set up a situation where the British could basically do what they liked at sea, and, despite a state of war, the country could grow steadily richer. The advent of the long-range, ocean-going submarine seemed to prejudice all the dearly-held doctrines of the past. Surface ships would find it increasingly difficult to either maintain, or even prevent, blockade and all the consequences, direct or indirect, which formerly flowed from it.

The old strategic ideas had to be thrown in the melting pot. Naval staffs were faced with many new problems to study.

The British got in first with the submarine and this type of war vessel, combined with the nation's geographical position, seemed to have a great advantage. However, few would wish to dispute the effective use which Germany made of submersible fighting craft in World Wars I and II.

Academic studies are necessary; but, like staff assumptions, campaigns have been lost due to slavish adherence to what may appear to be logical conclusions. It is fascinating to consider such (pre-World War I) ideas as that which stated that two countries with approximately the same length of seaboard and an equal number of submarines facing each other across a comparatively narrow sea would find the central sea areas to be equally dangerous to both combatants.

The case of Germany at war with Britain was deemed to be somewhat different. The sea area surrounding the coast of Germany is much smaller than the equivalent case for Britain. This means that considering the British exits in the North Sea from, say, Dover to Dundee, and those in Germany from Emden to the Skaw, the proportion would be somewhere about 5 to 1, and that proportion, for equal danger to accrue, must obtain in the relative number of submarines. Assuming both countries to possess an equal number of relatively large submarines, the central open waters of the North Sea could be taken to be equally infested and dangerous to both countries. On approaching the German exits, however, the area is diminishing rapidly and the danger to German craft increasing proportionately, while on approaching British ports the reverse is the case.

That is to say, the difficulties of a close investment of the British North Sea ports compared with those of investing the German exits should be about five to one in Britain's favour. Britain also has some pretty significant ports on the West Coast so, in general, the country is not so dependent upon its North Sea ports. Perhaps, similar arguments are being used at present to justify defence cuts in view of recent happenings in the formerly Soviet-dominated communist world.

It would be wrong to embark upon any study involving aspects of sea power without acknowledging the debt which all students of naval history must owe to a then unknown American naval officer, who in the years 1888 and 1889 was engrossed in the sometimes soul-destroying task of attempting to find a publisher for a book. The aspiring writer submitted his manuscript to firm after firm, only to be met with a series of rejections. By the closing months of 1889 he had become extremely despondent and was on the point of giving up when Messrs Little, Brown & Company of Boston offered to accept the manuscript. This publisher was, thus, destined to be sponsor of nineteenth- and early twentieth-century naval theory.

The book, entitled *The Influence of Sea Power upon History*, became a success story of the first magnitude; but perhaps, not in the first instance in the land of its birth, where it appeared in 1890. In the United States the book's reception was favourable, but not enthusiastic. It was read by a few clear-sighted persons in high places such as Theodore Roosevelt, who was marked out to be President of the United States in the not very distant future, and who understood the work's message. He wrote to the author, Captain A T Mahan, a letter of congratulation and stated that the book would become a naval classic.

In Britain, which was then the world's foremost maritime nation, *The Influence of Sea Power upon History* received a more passionate welcome. Fulsome reviews and favourable opinions greeted its publication. The timing could not have been more appropriate in Britain. During the 1880s the Royal Navy had been suffering from one of its all too common periods of neglect and the country's naval might had been allowed to decline. This sad state of affairs had caused anxiety in a number of naval and even political circles, which had resulted in public agitation from a small group of commentators and politicians for a bigger fleet.

Shortly before the publication of Mahan's book, this clamour had succeeded in achieving the adoption of the 'two-power standard' as the frame of reference of British naval policy. This meant that the Royal Navy had to be at least as powerful as the second and third largest world navies combined. *The Influence of Sea Power upon History* came as manna from heaven to the Big Navy Group in Britain and provided a wealth of arguments and quotations to support their cause. Mahan became their natural ally and guru, and his writing was doubly welcome in that so much of his championship was founded upon the glorious past deeds of the Royal Navy.

Mahan's book made a great impression upon the section of the British Naval Officer Corps who indulged in the habit of serious reading. It is difficult, however, to find signs of great intellectual activity in the Royal Navy during the previous three-quarters of a century. For many years, British sea officers basked serenely in the warm afterglow of the Battle of Trafalgar. They maintained a service which was second to none in smartness, seamanlike efficiency and pride of performance; and they seemed all too happy to assure themselves that to 'engage the enemy more closely' was the master key with which to unlock the solutions to nearly all the warfare problems which might be encountered at sea.

In the 1860s the spirit of enquiry was beginning to re-establish itself. The Navy was, against all opposition, changing from sail to steam; and officers were beginning to speculate how this shift in the means of propulsion might affect traditional methods of waging sea warfare.

Deliberations were taking place in the forum of the Royal United Service Institution and in the recently founded *Brassey's Naval Annual*; and also in the more popular journals which dealt with service matters. The discussion was, in general, competent on technical and tactical aspects; but the higher levels covering strategy and general war policy were sadly neglected. It would probably not be unkind to come to the conclusion that naval officers were not disposed to think much further than the naval battle. Royal Navy officers knew how to conduct a fleet action, but only had somewhat hazy ideas on how to manage the broader aspects of a war.

Perhaps the greatest problem was that, in the past, naval warfare as a whole had not been properly studied. Before Mahan, there had not been any in-depth study of the philosophy of it. There was no shortage of naval histories, but these were mainly in the form of narratives which told of the brilliant exploits of the Royal Navy and of how they took place. What remained unexplained was why they happened and whether the thought processes and policies which brought them about were well, indifferently or poorly conceived. There were those who realised that this unhappy gap in the then state of naval knowledge existed; but it was left to Mahan to produce a book which many in Britain had been eagerly awaiting for years. A comprehensive, analytical study of naval warfare would provide not only the military, but also discerning civilians with a good groundwork for an understanding of sea power, its attributes and possibilities in many fields of endeavour.

Sea power and its potential should be well understood by the politicians who are alleged to have some say in the national security, and world influence, of maritime powers.

It might be a little simplistic, but not inaccurate, to state that Mahan sought to do for the study of maritime warfare what General Carl von Clausewitz's *On War* and Baron Antoine Henri de Jomini's *The Art of War* had done for predominantly land warfare. Mahan did not hesitate to refer to these two authorities, one German and the other Swiss, who had made much of their respective experiences as staff officers during the Napoleonic Wars, and whose writings are still today the subject of study by the military on a worldwide basis.

At the same time that the *Influence of Sea Power upon History* was animating thought in naval and political circles in Great Britain, Captain Mahan was busy preparing a second book which, like the first, was based upon lectures he had been delivering at the US Naval War College. *The Influence of Sea Power upon History* was, in general, based upon a survey of naval warfare in the period 1660 to 1783. In his later lectures, Mahan progressed to an examination of the next period; and two years after the publication of his first book, the lectures appeared in two volumes entitled *The Influence of Sea Power upon the French Revolution and Empire*. This book caused an even greater stir than its predecessor. The author had gained a reputation and was now dealing with that striking period which covered the glittering Nelsonian victories; and it was rich in material to suit the purpose of interpreting the nature and merits of skilfully displayed sea power. Full use was made of this golden opportunity. Mahan closely examined the long series of Revolutionary and Napoleonic wars and showed that they developed into a stark contest between the predominant land power and the supreme sea power. The sea power had emerged the winner. The theme, as treated by Mahan, provided a striking illustration of the power of the naval weapon. This made a great impression in many quarters, and not only in Britain.

In most maritime countries, Mahan's interpretation of naval history excited lively discussion; but in one European country his doctrines were subject to especially close attention. To the military authorities in Germany, Mahan's teachings seemed to be replete with meaning; and on no one did they make a greater impression than the nation's supreme head. The young Kaiser Wilhelm II was captivated by the entrancing seascape which Mahan had painted in words. The Kaiser wrote: 'I am just now, not reading but devouring Captain Mahan's book; and am trying to learn it by heart.'

The Kaiser was already in possession of the world's most powerful army; but at sea Germany was, and always had been, weak. Compared to that of Britain or France, the German fleet had little significance. Bismarck and his predecessors had not seen much need for naval strength. Their land forces had been quite capable of defeating the Danes, the Austrians and the French, in succession, on dry land. However, the German states had now been united into the German Empire in 1870 and the German rulers were dreaming dreams of potential achievements which might be open to the Greater Germany which had come into being. At this particular moment, Mahan's books, with their startling revelation of the force of sea power, had arrived on the scene. To a military country, with an eye on expansion, a powerful fleet as well as a powerful army should assure the Fatherland a place in the sun.

The direction in which Germany's policy was being pointed was announced in a speech by the Kaiser in which he used the celebrated phrase that 'Germany's future lies on the ocean.' The Royal Lieutenants were quick to elaborate the theme. Captain von Luttwitz of the General Staff floated the concept that Germany had been too late to take part in the general partition of colonial territories which had taken place during the previous century and stated that an effective fleet was required to enable advantage to be taken of a forthcoming grab for colonies. It was clear that this type of utterance was pointed in the direction of the British who duly took note of the sentiments expressed. The German outbursts could be said to have played a significant part in the laying of the 'keel plate' of World War I.

As far as Germany was concerned, words were soon converted into action. The Kiel Canal was opened in 1895, which provided a sheltered passage between the North Sea and the Baltic. The first German Navy Law was passed in 1898 which authorised an increase in the size of the Fatherland's fleet. This was followed, in 1900, by a second law which approved a considerable extension to the expanding size of the German Navy. An open challenge had been made to British sea power and Britain took alarm at once as she always should, and formerly did, in the face of such a threat. Britain also began to enhance the size of the Royal Navy. The result was a naval race between the two countries which continued, with increasing tempo, until the outbreak of war in 1914.

On a number of occasions, commentators have aired the thought that the doctrines propounded by Mahan gave an early push to a movement which led to the world catastrophe of 1914–18. History, which delights to puzzle its students, may cause many arguments to be floated for and against this proposition. It can at least be doubted whether, without Mahan to lure the Kaiser and his advisers on to bold maritime ambitions, World War I, when it came, could have taken the form that it did. It is conceivable that, without the challenge to her naval position which arose from the Kaiser's brag that Germany's future lay upon the ocean, Britain might have taken a more distant view of the situation in Europe. The British had not interfered to save the French from defeat in the Franco–Prussian War (1870). It was also not beyond belief that Britain might not have intervened to assist the French against Greater Germany in 1914. The conclusion can, therefore, be reached that the advent of Mahan's treatise on sea power must have played a part in fostering the conflict between Germany and Britain.

From the point of view of the British, the maintenance of a powerful fleet gave the feeling of security that potent land powers could do what they liked without, necessarily, affecting the integrity of the British Isles.

A number of readable books were published shortly before, or at the beginning of, the Second World War whose object was to keep the subject of the importance of sea power in the mind's eye of the British public. Examples are: *Sea Power* by T124 and *Modern Naval Strategy* by Admiral Sir Reginald Bacon and Francis E McMurtrie. These books give an insight into the thought processes prevailing in the late 1930s and early 1940s.

The use of air power became more and more important as the First World War progressed; and by 1939 sea power had become, to a great extent, dependent on its air equivalent. With hindsight, it is easy to say that the extent of the danger posed by hostile aircraft was not appreciated and that this lack of understanding tended to be reflected in the inadequate anti-aircraft defences of warships in general.

The American and Japanese navies produced large naval air arms and were ahead of the British in the development of fast carrier groups which had an effective offensive capacity. These groups had the potential to secure command of the air, in particular areas, and to provide commanders with a long reach with which to attack enemy naval forces.

At the beginning of World War II, the Royal Navy tended to use aircraft carriers singly on services such as the provision of anti-submarine patrols and, in conjunction with powerful surface ships, to detect surface raiders and to keep the disposition and movements of the same under surveillance.

It is hoped that this brief overview of the fascinating subject of sea power might help to provide a useful framework to the more specialised sections which follow.

PART ONE

Q Ships

CHAPTER I
Decoy/Q Ships
Masters of Deception

Shortly before the outbreak of World War II I had made up my mind that I would like to join the Royal Navy when the time came to leave school. I was given a book about Q ships for Christmas 1938; but, my mind being so filled with mental pictures of majestic battleships and battle cruisers, aircraft carriers, sleek cruisers and dashing destroyers, Q ships seemed to be rather a dull subject for a book about the Navy.

During the next few years, the Battle of the Atlantic unfolded and the consequences of U-boat attacks on British shipping became abundantly clear. Growing boys and girls suffered from pangs of hunger, particularly if they had to spend the greater part of the year at a boarding school. The level of nourishment at times has been described as 'dangerously low' by members of the medical profession.

Before the end of World War II, I had experienced sea-time in both merchant ships and Royal Navy vessels and began to understand that the U-boat menace had to be countered by as many means as possible and that subterfuges, if they worked, were a legitimate weapon. It also became clear that many valiant deeds and effective operations were carried out by fighting men out of uniform and without the back-up of the usual 'panoply of war' in the form of conventional warships, armoured fighting vehicles or military aircraft. In this context, the activities of Q ships, particularly during World War I, must have earned a special place. It is interesting to note that the wife of the late Nicholas Monsarrat added an addendum to her husband's book *Darken Ship – The Master Mariner Book 2*. One of the entries indicated that a Q ship was being planned as the setting for a future book in the series. The ambience of such a vessel, disguises, 'panic parties' and a wide range of adventures and operations in which these units had been, or may have been involved, could provide the background for many plots.

A Q ship is a 'decoy' ship. Admiral of the Fleet Viscount Jellicoe of Scapa GCB, OM, GCVO nearly always wrote of decoy ships in his books which were published shortly after the end of the First World War, for example, *The Crisis of the Naval War*. This said, individual ships were sometimes mentioned by their particular designation, such as Q22.

3

There is nothing new about the concept of decoy ships, as has been mentioned in the Introduction. A specific example could be the employment of armed vessels, disguised as innocent merchant ships, which were deployed around the British coast with the aim of surprising the many privateers which infested these waters in about 1806 to 1810 and which were acting to assist Napoleon's Continental System and other schemes designed to interrupt Britain's maritime trade.

Perhaps not surprisingly, the French used decoy ships in the La Rochelle area, at about the same time, with the aim of counteracting the activities of British privateers which were disrupting Gallic maritime traffic and earning a profit for their owners.

During World War I the great British public and the Admiralty tended to be at odds over what to call Q ships. Whitehall favoured special service ships; the public preferred mystery ships as alternatives to the more prosaic Q ships.

The label 'mystery ship' tended to add an air of secrecy and romance which could fire the imagination, but was, perhaps, not needed in official documents or offices directly concerned with naval activities.

There is some doubt about the reason why the designation of the letter 'Q' should have been chosen. More than one explanation has been floated. The fact that many mystery ships were operated from Queenstown (now Cobh) in Ireland, where the World War I equivalent of the Commander-in-Chief, Western Approaches had his headquarters is a nice thought. Q being the first letter of the word 'question' might be tied in with the mysterious employment of Q ships. Another more mundane thought is that the letter Q was vacant when, in modern parlance, the 'hull numbers' of this type of ship had to be determined.

In the First World War, the letters QQQ... were used to designate 'unknown merchant ship' in sighting/alarm signals.

Q ships or decoy ships could come in many sizes, shapes and types. In World War I, when Q ships reached the zenith of their importance, at least until the convoy system was re-invented, sailing ships of various descriptions, fishing vessels, colliers, and three island tramp steamers* were enlisted. Even Royal Navy 'Flower' class sloops were imaginatively altered so that they could give the appearance of being smallish merchant ships. However, the fine lines of a converted sloop tended to give the game away to an experienced observer on board a German U-boat. It was proposed that oilers should be used as decoys; but upon mature consideration it was decided that tankers were too precious a commodity to be risked in this role.

---

* So called because they had three raised sections: the bridge at the stern; loading equipment in the centre, and a raised bow section, separated by the lower deck.

Those responsible for controlling and deploying Q ships needed to ensure that any vessel being used in a particular operation would be the type of ship to be expected to be going about its occasions in the sea area concerned.

For long periods during the First World War, the Grand Fleet was to be found at moorings in the large expanse of Scapa Flow, like a resting giant. The demands of this giant naval force for coal, oil and many types of provision were incessant and had to be satisfied by a constant stream of colliers and ships designed to carry the loads of stores and munitions which were needed by the hungry warships and the crews who manned them. A Q ship, disguised as a collier, ostensibly bound for the Orkneys would, therefore, not seem to be out of place approaching the Pentland Firth, or tracking north off the west coast of Scotland. Other types of merchant ship might arouse the immediate suspicion of a well-trained German submarine officer. German U-boats frequently, and with intent, numbered among their complement officers who had served in the mercantile marine. These gentlemen were wise in the ways of merchant shipping and would have seen large numbers of ships of many nationalities as they travelled the world's shipping lanes.

Anything which did not fit into the 'frame of reference' of these veteran seafarers could cause mental alarm-bells to start ringing; and the reasons for provocation of suspicion would be reported to the U-boat command.

A small number of 'made to measure' Q ships were ordered by the Admiralty during the course of the First World War. HMS *Hyderabad* was an example. These ships were constructed to look like three island tramp steamers; but there were significant differences. The purpose-built Q ship would have a top speed of about fifteen to sixteen knots, which was significantly faster than that of their merchant counterparts. They were designed to appear as though they were in a half-laden state and comparatively low in the water. In fact, the ships had an extremely shallow draft of only four or five feet.

The aim of this exercise was to try to ensure that missiles fired by a U-boat would have assumed that a deeper depth-setting would be needed for the torpedoes to achieve maximum effect. Hopefully, the U-boat commander would imagine that the torpedoes had not run according to plan and would be tempted to surface to try to sink a gun on the forecastle and another on the poop. She would also be fitted with a four-inch gun abaft the funnel on the midships superstructure. These guns would be suitably concealed.

Four torpedo tubes were mounted under the superstructure and four bomb-throwers were in the forward and aft holds. An unwary attacking submarine might, therefore, receive somewhat more than she bargained for.

CHAPTER II
The Manning of Q Ships
Discipline and other Considerations

Once the decision to use decoy ships has been taken, it will be necessary to enrol seafarers to form the ships' companies of these highly specialised vessels. It will also be correct to point out, at an early stage, that in the past the Q ship service included all sorts of conditions and specialisations of seafaring men among its members. There would be officers and ratings from both the active and retired lists of the Royal Navy, of the Royal Naval Reserves, of the Merchant Navy and Fishing Fleet. Precise manpower needs obviously depended, to a great extent, upon the type of ship being commissioned; for example, during World War I it was beginning to be more difficult to obtain officers with a deep knowledge of large sailing ships, than had been the case in their fathers' generation. The advent of steamships made the recruitment of trained engineers of paramount importance.

Men were sucked in from other types of warship, Royal Naval barracks, yachts which had been built for pleasure, ocean liners, fishing vessels, tramp steamers, sailing ships, overseas possessions, offices and many other places of employment. These mariners were called upon to serve in, generally speaking, slow, lightly armed hulls to perform as bait for relentless enemy submariners. It was an achievement which needed bravery of a high degree, good seamanship and professional skills and a lively imagination. The successes accomplished by Q ships in both World Wars can be attributed to the satisfactory mix of the qualities listed above. This implied that both officers, in particular commanding officers, and ratings needed to be specially selected. The impulsive, dashing individual who might display an excess of gallantry and, equally, the slow-thinking, hesitating type of person could be equally out of place if called upon to serve in a Q ship.

To start at the top, it is worth directing a spotlight at the commanding officer. It would be hard to beat E Keble Chatterton's description of the ideal Q ship captain, as given in his book *Q-ships and their Story*:

> In the ideal Q ship captain was to be found something of the virtues of the cleverest angler, the most patient stalker, the most enterprising

7

big-game hunter, together with the attributes of a cool, unperturbed seaman, the imagination of a sensational novelist, and the plain horse-sense of a shrewd business man. In two words, the necessary endowments were brains and bravery.

It is probably relatively simple to find one or two suitable commanding officers for Q ships among hundreds of officers, but it could be no easy task to find an intrepid fighter, with a high intellect, among the many who volunteered for duty in special service ships.

It is fortunate that training at sea tends to make both officers and crew members learn to think and act rapidly without, hopefully, doing silly things too often. The ship-handling problems to be met in stormy weather, strong tides, going alongside a jetty, etc. tend to develop instinctive reactions. But an 'x', or something plus, factor was required in the Q ship environment.

It is easy to forget that a Q ship might be called upon to cruise for weeks, months, or even years in the submarine zones of, say, the Atlantic or the North Sea without ever getting a glimpse of a U-boat. All of a sudden a look-out might report a torpedo's track charging straight at his ship.

The officer-of-the-watch would have to react instantaneously to give the necessary wheel orders to enable the ship to evade the torpedo; and to bring the ship's company to the necessary 'active state'. Never failing vigilance and prompt assessment of the situation could be a matter of life or death, when a live submarine attack suddenly developed from nowhere.

The initial contact would, probably, only have been the beginning for the commanding officer of a Q ship. The next phase of the proceedings, as likely as not, would require the captain to use his own ship as live bait to coax the submarine to make further attacks and show itself. A submerged submarine could invisibly shadow a low speed merchant vessel for an hour or two, or for several days. The hours of anxiety could be very trying for the crew of the decoy.

Watches changed and nothing seemed to happen. Weather conditions changed and it was necessary to guess when the enemy might make his next move, for example, would he choose dawn, or dusk, or wait until the moon was high, or had he given up in disgust due to shortage of fuel or some serious mechanical defect?

When, unexpectedly, shells come screaming past and one's own ship sustains a hit is the sort of moment when it would be possible to see the low-lying U-boat firing his guns as rapidly as possible while trying to keep out of range, or clear of the arcs of fire of the target's guns. This was the type of situation in which a captain had to decide whether to continue the charade of being an innocent merchant ship, or to hoist the White Ensign, unmask the concealed guns and to engage the enemy as soon as he appeared to come within range.

On occasions, when a Q ship was sinking, the captain had to decide whether she could be kept afloat long enough to deliver the submarine a mortal blow if the curious adversary made as to come alongside, for example. There were instances when a decoy ship could be called upon to be offered up as a sacrifice in the interests of killing an enemy submarine.

Finding volunteers of a suitable calibre to man decoy ships was not the only problem. Royal Navy officers and ratings had to dress and behave like merchant seamen. This involved wearing clothes other than uniform, forgetting the 'spit and polish', saluting of superiors, maintaining a ship in the high state of cleanliness to be expected of a warship, the falling in and smartness of movement, which had become second nature to naval personnel. A naval signalman had to disguise the smartness of his semaphore and the speed of answering; and the impeccable procedures which he had laboriously assimilated when exchanging messages on a warship to warship basis.

Strict discipline of, perhaps, a somewhat different kind than that to be expected of a naval vessel was essential in the operation of a Q ship. There would be times when a number of the crew had left the ship in the guise of the 'panic party' the evolution of which will be covered in more detail in due course. Those remaining would be directed to remain concealed, possibly, in a prone position in strategic parts of the ship, for example, in close vicinity to one of the hidden guns, or as invisible lookouts. Nothing gives a position of concealment away more readily than movement,or, at close quarters, uncalled for noise. Crew members might be required to remain, as long as the situation demanded, in uncomfortable attitudes possibly suffering from wounds of differing severity, from the 'chill factor' of wintry winds and occasional dollops of spray with a minimum of movement and without breaking silence until such time as the command ordered the next move in the game of, sometimes deadly, chess which was being indulged in by the commanding officers of the Q ship and enemy submarine. Fortitude and great self-discipline had to be exercised by individuals who had to endure the rigours of this type of situation, to say nothing of the strain of controlling feelings such as fear or excitement to which it can be all too easy to succumb in a position of peril.

Career naval officers have been brought up to ensure that a warship is, as far as possible, kept in a high state of cleanliness and smartness. As the military historian Liddell Hart has put it, regular service officers and non commissioned officers, in all three armed forces, can suffer from a 'totem complex'. That is to say that, in times of peace, their ship, armoured fighting vehicle, gun or aircraft must be kept assiduously painted, polished and cleaned so that it is a credit and, even, object of beauty to those who are responsible for it. In times of war, it can be difficult to shift attitudes and to appreciate that even the most expensive and sophisticated weaponry or weapon platform might have justified its existence should it be obliterated in achieving major damage, or destroying, a hostile target to which the attention of its crew has been directed. In like manner, it is no use a decoy vessel impersonating a 'scruffy' tramp steamer, or collier, if the ship has attained a state of smartness because it has been recently painted.

A Q ship, due to the need to man its outfit of weapons and to fight, when the occasion arose, would have a markedly larger ship's company than the type of merchant ship which she was simulating. A watchful eye had to be kept on the number of men who might like to be sunning themselves in the open air on a balmy summer's evening, for example. A tramp steamer, or a collier, with an unusually large number of men relaxing on the upper deck would arouse misgivings in the mind of an observer watching the scene through the periscope of a hostile submarine. Men serving in a Q ship were never allowed upon deck for exercise except when darkness had fallen; and then only for a circumscribed period of time.

The minor luxury of being able to have a smoke on the upper deck was a pleasure in which it was difficult for members of the ship's company of a Q ship to indulge except on rare occasions.

The organisation of lookouts required strict attention. Extra lookouts were usually positioned at dawn and dusk and this development could be combined with the ritual of dawn and dusk 'action stations'. The gun which could normally be expected to be sited in a defensively armed merchant ship might be manned by a couple of ratings who could be found leaning over the gun, or walking to and fro in the general vicinity of the weapon. These individuals had been charged with the duty of keeping a sharp lookout.

Lookouts were, in general, kept at their posts for a maximum of about one hour. It is pretty nigh impossible for anyone to keep an effective lookout for a longer period. In a Q ship a man would, probably, be placed in each corner of the bridge, or lolling against a rail. Each man would be responsible for covering a specific arc, no more no less, and it was the lookout's job to keep his eyes constantly upon the arc which had been allocated to him. Immediately anything was seen the lookout reported it to the officer-of-the-watch.

When a lookout was relieved, the relief went to the opposite side of the bridge. The individual being relieved was not permitted to leave until his successor was in position. This might seem to be obvious; but the object of the exercise was to minimise the very human tendency for one man relieving another to have a little gossip before the latter set off down below. The efficiency of the process of looking-out tended to deteriorate markedly during a 'gossip gap'. Believers in 'Murphy's Law' will, no doubt agree that a periscope may be elevated above the sea's surface, or some other emergency may be likely to occur, during a 'gossip gap'.

In many of the accounts written shortly after the conclusion of the First

World War, much is made of the problems of security which arose in the operation, refitting and manning of decoy ships. For those who experienced service in World War II, and subsequent periods of conflict, some of the remarks on security may appear to be a little naive. Pictures of young officers of the three fighting services 'chatting up' a gorgeous girl with the caption 'keep mum, she's not so dumb' and jokes such as 'burn before reading' abounded and the state of the art concerned with the maintenance of operational security reached a high level. However, some of the skills were learned the hard way during the 1914–18 struggle.

The great Duke of Marlborough had an Oxford don on his staff who was experienced and skilled in the breaking of codes and who could be let loose on messages, which might be encoded, and in the possession of a courier who had had the misfortune to be captured by an alert British patrol.

The remark 'if I thought that my coat knew my plans, I would take it off my back and burn it' was attributed to Frederick the Great; but similar aphorisms have been placed to the credit of other great commanders. There is nothing really new, and as Napoleon once remarked, 'On the field of battle, the happiest inspiration is often but a recollection'.

In the specific subject of Q ships, it is worth remembering that many of their operations were based upon Queenstown. The Sinn Féin, or 'Ourselves Alone' Irish Republican party had been founded in 1902 and became potent during the commotions of 1914, and later the unavailing 'Easter Rising' in 1916.

The implications of the activities of Sinn Féin added another dimension to security problems in the vicinity of Haulbowline, the base which had been constructed to service Royal Navy and, later, US Navy vessels which were operating from the Queenstown area. Periods of rest and recreation also suffered as RN personnel walking in the hinterland to enjoy the scenery and the sensation of having dry land underfoot could be given a far from rapturous welcome by some of the local inhabitants.

From the American viewpoint, the situation is very well described in Rear Admiral Sims' book *The Victory at Sea*, which was published in 1920. How little things have changed. The US Admiral wrote:

> During the nearly two years which the American naval forces spent in Europe only one element in the population showed them any hostility or even unfriendliness. At the moment when these lines are being written, a delegation claiming to represent the 'Irish Republic' is touring the United States, asking Americans to extend their sympathy and contribute money towards the realization of their project. I have great admiration for the mass of the Irish people, and from the best elements of these people the American sailors received only kindness. I have therefore hesitated about telling just how some members of the Sinn Féin party treated our men . . .

11

The people of Queenstown and Cork received our men with genuine Irish cordiality. Yet in a few weeks evidence of hostility in certain quarters became apparent. The fact is that the part of Ireland in which the Americans were stationed was a headquarters of the Sinn Féin. The members of this organization were not only openly disloyal; they were openly pro-German. They were not even neutral; they were working day and night for a German victory, for in their misguided minds a German victory signified an Irish Republic. It was no secret that the Sinn Féiners were sending information to Germany and constantly laying plots to interfere with the British and American navies. At first sight it might be supposed that the large number of sailors – and some officers – of Irish extraction on the American destroyers would tend to make things easier for our men. Quite the contrary proved to be the case. The Sinn Féiners apparently believed that these so-called Irish-Americans would sympathize with their cause; in their wildest moments they even hoped that our Naval forces might champion it. But these splendid sailors were American before they were anything else; their chief ambition was the defeat of Germany and they could not understand how any man anywhere could have any other aim in life. They were disgusted at the large number of able-bodied men whom they saw in the streets, and did not hesitate to ask some of them why they were not fighting on the Western Front. The behaviour of the American sailors was good; but the mere fact that they did not openly manifest a hatred of Great Britain and a love of Germany infuriated the Sinn Féiners. And the eternal woman question also played its part. Our men had much more money than the native Irish boys, and could entertain the girls more lavishly at the movies and ice-cream stands. The men of our fleet and the Irish girls became excellent friends; the association, from our point of view, was a very wholesome one, for the moral character of the Irish girls of Queenstown and Cork – as indeed of Irish girls everywhere – is very high, and their companionship added greatly to the well-being and contentment of our sailors, not a few of whom found wives among these young women. But when the Sinn Féin element saw their sweethearts deserting them for the American boys their hitherto suppressed anger took the form of overt acts.

Occasionally an American sailor would be brought from Cork to Queenstown in a condition that demanded pressing medical attention. When he regained consciousness he would relate how he had been set upon by half a dozen roughs and beaten into a state of insensibility. Several of our men were severely injured in this way. At other times small groups were stoned by Sinn Féin sympathizers and there were many hostile demonstrations in moving-picture houses and theaters. Even more frequently attacks were made, not upon the

American sailors, but upon the Irish girls who accompanied them.

The importance of another incident which took place at the cathedral has been much exaggerated. It is true that a priest in his Sunday sermon denounced the Americans as vandals and betrayers of Irish womanhood, but it is also true that the Roman Catholics of that section were the most enraged at this absurd proceeding. A number of Roman Catholic officers who were present left the church in a body; the Catholic Bishop of the diocese called upon Admiral Bayly [the British Admiral] and apologized for the insult, and he also punished the offending priest by assigning him to new duties at a considerable distance from the American ships.

But even more serious trouble was brewing, for our officers discovered that the American sailors were making elaborate plans to protect themselves. Had this discovery not been made in time, something like an international incident might have resulted. Much to our regret, therefore, it was found necessary to issue an order that no naval men, British or American under the rank of Commander, should be permitted to go to Cork. Ultimately we had nearly 8,000 American men at this station; Queenstown itself is a small place of 6,000 or 7,000 so it is apparent that it did not possess the facilities for giving such a large number of men those relaxations which were necessary to their efficiency. We established a club in Queenstown, provided moving pictures and other entertainments, and did the best we could to keep our sailors contented. The citizens of Cork also keenly regretted our action. The great majority had formed a real fondness for our boys; and they regarded it as a great humiliation that the rowdy element had made it necessary to keep our men out of their city. Many letters were printed in the Cork newspapers apologizing to the Americans and calling upon the people to take action that would justify us in rescinding our order. The loss to Cork tradesmen was great; our men received not far from $200,000 to $300,000 a month in pay; they were freespenders, and their presence in the neighbourhood for nearly two years would have meant a fortune to many of the local merchants. Yet we were obliged to refuse to accede to the numerous requests that the American sailors be permitted to visit this city.

A committee of distinguished citizens of Cork, led by the Lord Mayor, came to Admiralty House to plead for the rescinding of this order. Admiral Bayly cross-examined them very sharply. It appeared that the men who had committed these offences against American sailors had never been punished. Unless written guarantees were furnished that there would be no hostile demonstrations against British or Americans, Admiral Bayly refused to withdraw the ban, and I fully concurred in this decision. Unfortunately the committee could give no such guarantee. We knew very well that the first appearance of Americans in Cork would be the signal for a renewal of hostilities, and the temper of our sailors was such that the most deplorable consequences might have resulted.

But the Sinn Féiners interfered with us in much more serious ways than this. They were doing everything in their power to help Germany. With their assistance German agents and German spies were landed in Ireland. At one time the situation became so dangerous that I had to take experienced officers whose services could ill be spared from our destroyers and assign them to our outlying air stations in Ireland. This, of course, proportionately weakened our fleet and did its part in prolonging the war.

From time to time, a Q ship might be directed by the British Admiral at Queenstown to make for the rugged places on the shores of the west coast of Ireland in case the Germans made efforts to land men and arms in one of the wild spots with the aim of assisting the Sinn Féin movement and fanning the embers of insurrection into a potentially dangerous flame. One of these deployments was described by Lieutenant Commander Harold Auten VC, RNR, in his book *Q-Boat Adventures*. No doubt, it can be argued that such distractions diluted efforts which might otherwise have been directed towards the aim of counteracting the U-boat peril.

It may be fascinating to speculate on historical 'ifs'; but, perhaps, this is not necessarily a productive exercise. Sinn Féin seemed to think that a German victory in either of the World Wars would result in Ireland being able to achieve independence. It would, also, be attractive for the Germans to encourage this concept when they were locked in a struggle in which one of the major aims was to defeat Great Britain. However, it is not beyond the bounds of possibility that the extremist Irish elements would have been ruthlessly dealt with if they had incurred the displeasure of occupying German forces.

'Panic parties' have been briefly mentioned, and could also be described as 'abandon ship parties'. The objective of the 'panic party' was to give a very realistic impersonation that the Q ship, acting as a harmless merchantman, had been abandoned. This, it was hoped, would allay the suspicions of an attacking U-boat commanding officer, cause him to surface and to close the apparently derelict vessel. The attacking submarine might then present an attractive target to those of the Q ship's company who remained concealed on board their ship.

'Panic parties' needed to be well thought out, and thoroughly drilled in order that maximum realism could be attained. The 'panic party' invariably needed to be made up of the same number of men as would have been on board to man the ship in its role of merchant vessel. The aim was that no suspicion should be aroused in the mind of the submarine commander as to the number of men he could observe in the boats. The whole of this miscellaneous rabble was generally taken charge of by the navigating officer who acted the part of master of the ship, even grabbing the captain's cap and being the last to get into one of the boats.

The drill for the 'panic party' would normally be that the men who had been loitering about the upper deck would rush to the boats and be joined by others who came scrambling up from the stokeholds and machinery spaces, or running from the forecastle. A general picture of pandemonium would be generated flavoured with shouts for help. Even if shouts and cries could not be heard in the submarine they were likely to add vividness to the charade which was being enacted by the Q ship's 'abandon ship' troupe of performers.

A stampede would be made for the boats and one of the boats would often be let go 'with a run', and add to the confusion. Captain (later Vice-Admiral) Gordon Campbell, who gained a reputation as being the 'beau ideal' of Q ship commanding officers, arranged for a stuffed parrot in a cage to be kept in the saloon to be collected by the navigating officer as he played the part of master and of being the last into the boats.

I am a little sceptical about the potential efficacy of this particular 'realistic touch' which appears in a number of books which feature Q ship operations.

After the boats, which contained circa thirty men and would include a representative 'mixed bag' of officers, seamen, engine room personnel, cooks and stewards, etc., had left the ship's side, a ploy could have been a grimy stoker appearing from the stokehold giving a one-man act of panic-stricken shouting, yelling and waving his arms. One of the boats would go through the motions of returning to the ship to collect him.

The boats would then lay off to see what happened to their ship which would now, to all intents and purposes, be deserted; but, in reality, gun crews would be stationed by their weapons. The Chief Engineer and a party would be in the boiler and engine-rooms, the Captain and Quarter-master would be concealed on the bridge and a signal rating would be standing by to break out the White Ensign.

In the earlier stages of the U-boat war, U-boat commanders were reluctant to expend expensive torpedoes. They favoured surfacing to sink unescorted merchantmen by gunfire or placing timed explosive charges on board their victims. This tactic would also place the submarine in its most vulnerable position, which was on the surface in full trim and gave rise to a Q ship's desire to tempt U-boats to close them and then to surface.

Different 'alarms' could be given on board a Q ship to indicate whether a submarine, or periscope, had been sighted to port or starboard. This procedure was carried out to enable any men who were employed on the upper deck to move to their action stations on the offside (side away from

15

the sighting). Should an individual's station be on the bridge, he would ascend via the offside ladder. No one was permitted to run to his action station, nor was any crowding tolerated. This was basically achieved by limiting the number on the upper deck at any one time. An alarm started guns' crews, who were not already in position, to their weapons and anyone else to his particular station. The resulting movements took place, as far as possible, unseen by making maximum use of alleyways and hatches.

It should be noted that if a torpedo had been discharged by the submarine, the order 'torpedo missed' or 'torpedo hit' would be given by voice-pipe. In the first case, all went on essentially as before maintaining the illusion that the wake of the torpedo had not been spotted or those concerned did not know what it might be. In the second instance, the 'panic party' could be triggered off to go through the motions of abandoning ship. The order to 'abandon ship' would also be given in the event of the Q ship coming under shellfire from the U-boat.

The developments mentioned above had to be well thought out and perfected by regular practice. Gordon Campbell summed up the situation well when he wrote in his book *My Mystery Ships*: 'In fact, we combined an outward appearance of slackness with an inner soul of strict discipline.'

Should a Q ship be totally destroyed, it could be a headache to explain away the large number of men the ship had on board. Towards the end of World War I, U-boat commanding officers were given directions to do their best to obtain information about the name, tonnage, destination and so forth of all the ships which they had sunk. They, therefore, became concerned to contact the crews of boats which had recently left a stricken ship. The Germans did not lack discernment. They would tend to go to one boat and, if there should be more than one, visit the next boat and so on, question the occupants and check whether the replies received from the various boats conformed. A number of Q ship personnel had been 'caught out' by the skilful use of this technique.

Resulting from the above, it became mandatory that the ship's company of a Q ship should be taught one simple story. The aim of this exercise was to try to ensure that when a submarine captain surfaced his boat and asked questions he would receive similar answers from all those questioned.

One solution to the problem was to keep what the crews of Q ships tended to call 'The Board of Lies'. This was essentially a blackboard with headings such as those listed below, and the current answer written in white chalk. The board was usually kept up-to-date by the navigating officer and three similar boards might be placed in three positions, say, one in the forecastle, one amidships and one in the stern to facilitate the task of ensuring that the fictitious details were digested three times a day, in a similar form to that shown:

SHIP'S NAME
OWNER'S NAME
CAPTAIN'S NAME
TONNAGE
PORT OF REGISTER
PORT LEFT
DATE/TIME OF LEAVING
PORT BOUND
CARGO
No. OF CREW

A Q ship cruising day after day in the same sea area, perhaps, steaming north one day and south the next would soon become an object of suspicion. In the early days of the First World War, merchant ships displayed their own funnel and company marks. Q ships could, therefore, build up a useful supply of various shapes, for example, triangles, diamonds and various coloured paints so that they could change markings pretty well daily if so desired. Circa 1916 the convention was that British ships should be painted alike and, not necessarily, fly an ensign. This complicated the problem of disguise.

For hundreds of years, the *ruse de guerre*, of flying 'false' or 'neutral' national colours, has been used and is considered legitimate. This meant that a supply of foreign ensigns needed to be carried, plus large boards painted to represent neutral colours for fitting over a ship's side. The expansion of submarine warfare against merchant vessels meant that the flying of an ensign could make the process of recognition difficult for a submarine. Neutral ships, therefore, frequently resorted to the expedient of ensuring that their colours were displayed on the ship's side.

The flying of 'false' colours may be legitimate; but armed ships, such as Q ships, are required to display their national ensign before opening fire.

There are a number of other ways in which a ship's disguise may be altered in almost any modern decade, for example, empty crates can be assembled to provide make believe arrangements of deck cargo, and 'dummy boats' can be placed in different positions and removed if and when required. Spare ventilation, or ventilator cowls can be carried to be rigged in various positions to suit the 'disguise of the day'. Derricks can be stowed in a number of diverse postures, and lightweight 'samson-posts' can be positioned, or taken down, with comparative ease. Q ships were known to have telescopic top masts so that they could appear to be vessels with a stump-mast or to be fitted with more lofty top masts. While on the subject of masts, a portable crow's nest could be erected or taken down and spare trestle trees and yards could easily be carried on board.

Minor alterations could include changes in the position of life-belt racks, stanchions or the siting of navigation and side-lights. Dummy donkey-boiler funnels could be used to some effect and be moved to a position just before, or aft of, principal funnels. Many ingenious ploys to disguise their ship could be left to the imagination and ingenuity of ships' officers and men.

Perhaps one of the most effective disguises could give, say, a three island tramp the appearance of being a flush-deck ship. A 'well deck', often to be found between the bridge superstructure and the forecastle, could be built up to look like the ship's side. This could be achieved by simply stretching suitably coloured canvas tautly laced to a length of wire rope. This particular evolution was not suitable in foul weather though, as movement of the canvas sheeting could easily give the game away.

During periods of suspense, officers and ratings needed to maintain a high degree of alertness as the charade in which they were engaged to deceive any potential observer watching through a periscope had to continue inexorably lest a moment's slip spoil the entire act. Any 'breakdowns' which occurred could be attributed to the tension which might build while operating during extended periods, unrelieved by any form of action and the associated excitements.

The sight of a torpedo's wake rapidly closing a Q ship could be an almost agreeable sight, after a long period of inactivity. The torpedo passing ahead or astern of the ship could be distinctly disappointing. If such an emergency occurred, the genuine merchant vessel would exert every possible effort to avoid the torpedo; but the helmsman of the decoy ship would do all he could to ensure a 'hit'. This, seemingly suicidal, manoeuvre needed to be executed with consummate skill as no one in their right mind would be likely to seek to collide with several hundred pounds of high explosive. Too obvious an attempt to achieve the unthinkable would betray to the attacking submarine the target ship's real role. It was quite likely that a number of the crew might be killed or seriously wounded when contact was made with the torpedo; but that would all be part of the deadly game which was in progress. Sadly, achieving the prime objective of the ship could be more important than the lives of a number of men. If the ship could remain afloat long enough to give the guns' crews a good opportunity to mortally injure the submarine, honour would be satisfied and the main aim achieved.

Decoy ships were frequently loaded with wood, in every accessible cargo space. This would provide adequate buoyancy for the ship to have a fair chance of surviving considerable punishment before it foundered, or enable it to stay afloat for a profitable time. Long enough to effectively engage an attacking submarine, if the U-boat could be coaxed to the surface.

When a Q ship had been ostensibly abandoned, the placing of the lifeboats could present another nice problem. If the submarine did, in fact, surface it would, more often than not, close the boats, searching for the ship's documents or looking for worthwhile prisoners. Lifeboat crews, therefore, were directed to take up a position between their ship and the U-boat, whose bearing would give the ship's guns the optimum chance of engaging the submarine most effectively. This exercise could involve great risk to the boats' crews; that consideration had to be accepted in the interests of killing a U-boat.

As World War I progressed, the above performance was simply the torpedoing of a hapless merchant ship; but German submarine commanding officers became very wary of accepting the situation as such an obvious interpretation. The commander concerned would have no intention of approaching either the ship, or its lifeboats, until he was absolutely certain that he was not dicing with one of the decoy ships; the Germans tended to call them 'trap ships' which they had learned to treat with great circumspection. Probably the best way for the U-boat to satisfy itself that all was as it should be was to shell the merchant ship so inexorably that if any human beings remained on board they would be killed, seriously wounded or only too thankful to surrender. The submarine would aim to surface at a distance of two to three miles. It would be possible for a well-aimed, or lucky, shot to hit the U-boat at such a range, but the odds were against it. The firing of such a shot would, of course, indicate that a gun's crew remained on board and that the vessel could be a decoy. This would cause the submarine to submerge, approach under water and treat the Q ship to another torpedo or more.

However great the urge and temptation, those on board the decoy had to play 'dead' and not by so much as a twitch allow the U-boat to suspect that there were any living creatures left. This feat of endurance required bravery of the most majestic proportions. Gun crews would lie prone beside their weapons waiting and waiting the order to open fire. The captain lay on the screened bridge, watching proceedings through a peephole, with voice tubes close at hand through which he could talk to his men. At times, these positions would need to be maintained for hours. Not a finger could be raised in defence, while the U-boat, from a safe range, rained large numbers of shells upon the ship. The horrible projectiles would scream overhead, land on decks, wound men and, at times, wipe out entire gun crews, even if parts of the ship might turn into large quantities of blood, and broken remnants of human bodies would lie with infinite stoicism until the *moment critique* at last arrived. This was the type of evolution which was required to persuade the submarine that its victim was what it purported to be, a hapless merchantman, that no living persons were on board and that it would be safe to come near. The ever cautious German would eventually decide to submerge and to close within a few hundred yards. The watchful captain's eye, at the peephole, could only see the periscope as it progressed around the ship, sometimes at very close range. No chances were being taken with the tortured victim

19

which was being examined inch by inch for the slightest sign that the vessel might be a decoy.

After close inspection, the submerged submarine might well move off in the direction of the drifting lifeboats. The periscope would be stuck up close to the faces of the anxious boats' crews to see if any traces of naval personnel could be detected under the merchant vessel disguises.

However, the burning question would remain: 'Could the submarine appear from the surface of the sea?' The men of the decoy ship were helpless until the moment the U-boat showed itself. It is a waste of time and ammunition to fire at a submerged submarine as shells barely penetrate the water and are more likely to ricochet off the surface. Those on board the Q ship would know that the German officer would be agonising over the same problem. He would know that to surface in the vicinity of a mystery ship could mean the loss of his submarine and death to some, or all, of her company. On the other hand to slink away underwater could mean that the injured ship, if a genuine merchant vessel, might remain afloat for long enough to be salvaged. It would also mean that the submarine commander could not prove that he had achieved anything worthwhile with the expenditure of a valuable torpedo. Had the derelict been shelled sufficiently intensely that no living person could possibly have survived? Had the target ship been examined in the microscopic detail which would ensure that nothing could go amiss? In the year 1917 a submarine would go through a similar procedure with every surface ship which did not sink soon after it had fallen victim to a torpedo. Almost invariably, it would be discovered that a real merchant ship had been the victim. The U-boat would have squandered hours of time and large stocks of ammunition on vessels which were not decoy ships but harmless freighters. These false trails tended to make submarine commanders short of patience and careless. Perhaps, it was a case of 'it was trying which got the Greeks into Troy'; but, in the majority of cases, the Q ship captain knew the merits of biding his time and that his hidden opponent would eventually rise.

The captain, on the Q ship's bridge, would notice the preliminary disturbance of water which heralded the fact that the submarine was about to emerge from the depths and would trigger a softly articulated 'Stand by!'

This order would come blandly through the speaking tubes to alert the gun crews.

In a short while, the submarine would be floating on the surface, and officers and members of the crew would climb out on deck. This within a short distance of several hostile guns.

If all went according to plan, the command 'Let go!' would come in a loud voice, for the time for concealment was past. The Q ship's ensign would be fluttering from the mast, bulwarks would fall down, sides would drop from the deckhouses, hen coops, other innocuous-seeming structures, and some lifeboats would collapse and guns would be revealed. The apparently stricken merchantman billowed flame and smoke; and numerous shells would descend upon the U-boat, punching holes in the hull, hurling German sailors in the air, decapitating them or blowing off limbs. This grisly scene would not last long before the hapless vessel would take its final plunge.

The physical conduct of Q ships has been discussed in some detail and it cannot be stressed too strongly that every submarine which was sent to the bottom of the ocean in 1917 added up to the saving of thousands of tons per annum of merchant shipping and valuable supplies that would have been sunk by a U-boat if the submarine had been left unhindered to pursue its death-strewn course. Decoy ships, therefore, provided a valuable contribution to the various systems, which were developed by the Allied navies, for hunting enemy submarines. It was important to observe strict secrecy over methods used and the public at large heard nothing of the special service vessels which came to be known as 'mystery' or 'Q ships' until the end of World War I, even though decoy ships had been operating for some three years. Perspicacious members of the public had worked out that something must be afoot when they saw announcements that certain RN officers had received the Victoria Cross. No citations explained why the recipients had gained these most desirable awards which, somewhat aptly, became known as 'mystery VCs'.

It would probably be of interest to say a few words about several of the characters who commanded First World War Q ships.

Captain Gordon Campbell must rank highly among commanders of decoy ships even though this officer was considered to have been adept at publicising himself through the written word and public presentations. Once again it is fascinating to turn to Rear Admiral W S Sims, US Navy who met Captain Gordon Campbell and wrote a useful third party description of the encounter:

> On one of my visits to Queenstown Admiral Bayly showed me a wireless message which he had recently received from the commanding officer of a certain mystery ship operating from Queenstown, one of the most successful of these vessels. It was brief but sufficiently eloquent.
>
> 'Am sinking,' it read, 'Good-bye, I did my best.'
>
> Though the man who had sent that message was apparently facing death at the time it was written, Admiral Bayly told me that he had survived the ordeal, and that, in fact he would dine at Admiralty House that very night. Another fact about this man lifted him above the commonplace: he was the first Q-boat commander to receive the

Victoria Cross, and one of the very few who wore both the Victoria Cross and the Distinguished Service Order; and he subsequently won bars for each, not to mention the Croix de Guerre and the Legion of Honour. When Captain Gordon Campbell arrived, I found that he was a Britisher of quite the accepted type. His appearance suggested nothing out of the ordinary. He was a short, rather thick-set, phlegmatic Englishman, somewhat non-commital in his bearing; until he knew a man well, his conversation consisted of a few monosyllables, and even on closer acquaintance his stolidity and reticence, especially in the matter of his own exploits, did not entirely disappear. Yet there was something about the Captain which suggested the traits that had made it possible for him to sink three submarines, and which afterward added other trophies to his record. It needed no elaborate story of his performances to inform me that Captain Campbell was about as cool and determined a man as was to be found in the British navy. His associates declared that his persistence knew no bounds; and that the extent to which his mind concentrated upon the task in hand amounted to little less than genius. When the war began, Captain Campbell, then about thirty years old, was merely one of several thousand junior officers in the British navy. He had not distinguished himself in any way above his associates, and probably none of his superiors had ever regarded him as in any sense an unusual man. Had the naval war taken the course of most naval wars, Campbell would have probably served well, but perhaps not brilliantly. This conflict, however, demanded a new type of naval fighter. To go hunting for the submarine required not only courage of a high order, but analytical intelligence, patience and a talent for preparation and detail. Captain Campbell seemed to have been created for this particular task.

While talking of courage, it is worth mentioning the distinction between 'fearlessness' and 'courage'. No doubt there are fearless animals; but in his *Laches*, Plato made Nicious state: 'I do not call animals . . . which have no fears of dangers, because they are ignorant of them, fearless, courageous, but only fearless or senseless . . .' There is no particular connection between fearlessness and courage. Thoughtful courage is a quality with which only a very few are endowed. However, fearlessness, boldness and rashness can be displayed by many humans, perhaps due to a lack of imagination.

Before I went to sea in World War II, I was advised by a senior RN Officer to take firm control of my imagination before going into action. However, a proviso was made that an officer should have imagination as one of his attributes. In this context, Napoleon said, 'imagination rules the world'.

Disregarding the 'fearless man', it is probably true to believe in the great majority who acknowledge fear but appreciate that they must act positively in spite of it.

The thoughts aired must apply to the commanding officers of Q ships as also must what Naploeon called 'two o'clock in the morning courage', a time when human metabolism tends to be at a low ebb. Captain Gordon Campbell undoubtedly scored high in most of the qualities which go to make up 'reflective courage'.

Another officer who seems to have attracted attention as a World War I Q ship captain was Lieutenant Commander Godfrey Herbert, RN. Herbert seems to have been a laid back, colourful officer with, at times, a somewhat bizarre sense of humour. The pre-World War I Navy offered too humdrum an existence for Godfrey Herbert who proferred his talents to the submarine service in 1905. He was duly accepted into this youthful branch of the Royal Navy.

The young officer's career as a submariner had more than its share of ups and downs. A high spot was that Herbert, as commanding officer of the C-36, together with two other British submarines, participated in a trial ten-thousand mile deployment to Hong Kong. The sea voyage occupied eighty-three days, and in 1911 this was the longest journey undertaken by submarines.

It was during this commission that the jester in Herbert's make up caused him to concoct his 'walking on water' performance. His act would involve him hanging on to the periscope while the submarine dived beneath him until sea water lapped his boots. This caused consternation among superstitious local fishermen who plied their trade in the waters off Hong Kong. A gala performance saw Herbert enfolded in a white sheet and disguised behind a painted face as his submarine returned to harbour on a balmy, calm evening with the performer lashed to the upper six feet of the submerged submarine. Perhaps unfortunately the spectacle of an apparently messianic figure was witnessed by the Admiral commanding the Far East Fleet. Herbert was duly sent for and admonished for his irreverant prank and bad taste.

Herbert's career as a submarine officer did not flourish during the early stages of the First World War, despite the fact that he had had several years' service in submarines. Some seventeen days after the declaration of war on 21 August 1914, Herbert spectacularly missed a German cruiser while both he and the hostile surface vessel were operating off Denmark. Two torpedoes were discharged from a range of about six hundred yards and passed well beneath the cruiser. The reason was that the operational torpedoes were, due to their warheads, about forty pounds heavier than the dummy practice torpedoes which had previously been fired. Not unnaturally, the torpedoes used in anger ran too deep as allowance had not been made for the change in weight.

Not long after the above incident, Herbert's submarine was directed to make contact with the three German battle cruisers which had been despatched to bombard Yarmouth. No opportunity of engaging the hostile surface ships was given as the submarine detonated a British mine and virtually disintegrated. Herbert and four men who had been on the conning tower with him were the sole survivors and were retrieved by a trawler.

In December 1914 Herbert was sent to a French submarine, *Archimede*, in the role of liaison officer, spent some time in the submarine depot ship at Harwich, and was then directed to a new form of anti-submarine weapon in the form of a Q ship, or trap-ship as the Germans preferred to designate it.

The first British Q ship was the SS *Vittoria* which had all the looks of a commonplace merchant vessel; she was commissioned in November 1914, but was unarmed and sent to patrol in a location in which hostile submarines had been reported to have been operating. Despite the excellence of the concept, *Vittoria* had no luck as a hunter of submarines and was paid off in early 1915 without ever having sighted a German submarine.

The idea of using decoy ships had, however, caught on as far as a number of naval officers were concerned, and their proposals had percolated through to the Admiralty as the year 1914 drew to its close. It thus came to pass that a second decoy ship was commissioned on 27 January 1915. This was the Great Eastern Railway steamship SS *Antwerp* (originally the *Vienna*).

Antwerp was placed under the command of Lieutenant Commander Godfrey Herbert. The choice of a trained submariner definitely had its merits because a submarine officer would be aware, if anyone was, of the strengths of his opponent and the limitations with which the commanding officer of an enemy submarine was faced during the tracking and attack phases of an encounter with a surface ship convoy.

Numbers of vessels of various types, including sailing ships, trawlers, colliers and tramp steamers, were enlisted to act in the decoy role during the course of 1915; but it would be fruitful to stay with Herbert a while longer to obtain a feel for typical Q ship activities.

The German submarine campaign's centre of gravity was transferred to the Western Approaches and the English Channel. Herbert was directed to work the waters off Le Havre, based on Southampton; but he gained no contacts. Later he was ordered to adopt Falmouth as his base of operations, and it was then that he had his first confrontation with a hostile submarine.

Kapitän Leutnant Otto Weddingen, who had become Germany's first U-boat ace when he sank the three British cruisers *Aboukir*, *Hogue* and *Crecy*, within the space of an hour some six months previously, had started to hound Allied merchant ships in the Western Approaches in his new command, U-29. He had achieved some success in administering the *coup de grâce* to three ships and seriously damaging a fourth. Radio messages were received at Falmouth and *Antwerp* was sailed. In the vicinity of the Scillies, Herbert approached a large sailing ship. The U-29 slipped astern as the decoy ship closed and Herbert ordered his gun crews to unmask their weapons and to range on the submarine. Weddingen's suspicions were aroused when a Great Eastern Railway ship suddenly turned in his direction. The German submarine dived and eluded its would be attacker. However, it could be said that Herbert played some part in Weddingen's demise. It was here that U-29 was noticed by the battleship *Dreadnought*, was rammed and sent to the bottom leaving no survivors.

The brush with U-29 taught Herbert that a slow, rather ungainly vessel such as *Antwerp* left much to be desired in the decoy function and his opinion was transmitted to the Admiralty. Herbert was sent for and had a highly confidential discussion with Admiral Fisher, the First Sea Lord.

Herbert's next command was a three island tramp steamer which became known as HMS *Baralong*. Three island tramps were ordinariness personified, and could be found all over the world pursuing their trade in any of the seas which blanket such a large proportion of the globe. These ships seemed to set the standard for being an ideal candidate for employment as a decoy ship.

Some of *Baralong*'s vital statistics were that the ship had been built about a year after the turn of the century, she weighed a little over 4,000 tons, had a speed of ten knots and was armed with three twelve-pound guns which were mounted on the poop.

Herbert 'won' between two and three thousand empty casks while the ship was at Devonport. Half the casks were stowed forward in number one hold, the other half were loaded in number four hold. Coal was carried in number two and number three holds. The disposition of coal and casks was arranged so that, with a modicum of luck, *Baralong*'s trim would not be shifted too markedly whenever the ship might sustain a hit.

It would probably be true to say that the British Admiralty were not overly convinced about the efficacy of decoy ships at this stage of the First World War. They remained to be persuaded of the potential worth of what was still a novel idea. To stay with *Baralong*, and her commanding officer, for a little longer is to be privy to an episode which was so successful that it succeeded in achieving that most difficult of tasks, a change in official thought processes.

Baralong had fruitlessly steamed thousands of miles; but during the afternoon of 19 August her chance came to play a major part in the submarine battle. In the area between the south-west coast of Ireland and the western extremity of the English Channel, eight British merchantmen were sunk. This number included the White Star liner *Arabic,* of over 15,000 tons. It appeared that more than one U-boat had been operating in the area in question and the Germans had reaped a rewarding harvest. *Baralong*, with the aim of detecting one of the hostile submarines, was steaming on an easterly course about a hundred miles south of Queenstown. She was disguised as an American cargo ship and was displaying United States colours, painted on boards, on her flanks. The boards were to be rapidly retrieved, and the ensign staff dropped, the moment she was due to go into action with the White Ensign flying.

At 1500 *Baralong* sighted a steam ship acting in an unusual manner and at about the same time a wireless 'distress message' was intercepted from her. *Baralong* immediately altered course and steadied on an interception course. Next a submarine was observed, about seven miles away closing the steamer, whom she was engaging with gunfire. The crew of the freighter, which turned out to be the Leyland passenger ship *Nicosian*, had taken to the ship's boats and were rowing about in the general area. The enemy submarine, U-27, which boasted a twenty-two-pounder gun forward of the conning tower and a twin weapon aft of it, steered to come close to *Nicosian*'s port side and towards the latter's boats with the object of preventing *Baralong* from contacting and rescuing the men in the boats.

When the U-boat was wooed by *Nicosian*, *Baralong* assumed her true colours and trained her guns on the bearing which would enable fire to be opened as soon as the submarine became visible, clear of *Nicosian*'s bows. As soon as the enemy came in sight, she was given an unwelcome shock in the form of a storm of twelve-pound shells mixed with rifle fire. The submarine was penetrated on the waterline below the conning tower before she could make any reply. To cut the story short, some frightened Germans leapt into the sea and soon afterwards the submarine heeled over and began her descent to the bottom.

The engagement had happened extremely quickly and *Nicosian*'s company were as surprised as they were thankful at the turn of events. *Nicosian*, with her important cargo of mules for the army, was taken in tow by *Baralong* and eventually entered Avonmouth under her own power.

The Germans made some bitter accusations about the *Baralong* incident, which smouldered on for a long time, and the fact that Herbert had used the US flag. That Germans were fired on when trying to climb up *Nicosian*'s side threatened to encourage the American population to think that the British could carry out as uncalled for actions as the crews of U-boats. The *Baralong* Affair is covered in detail in *Slaughter at Sea* written by Alan Coles.

Baralong's tactical handling had been simple and effective and this success in the middle of a sad narrative of shipping casualties probably played a major part in convincing the British authorities of the potential efficacy of the Q ship as an anti-submarine system. Despite the serious shortage of seagoing tonnage at this time, because ships were needed to transport every description of stores and munitions (to say nothing of mules) to British armies from the USA, and supplies to meet the wartime logistic requirements of the Russian army, the decision was taken to requisition more merchant vessels to be converted to decoys. The tramp steamer *Loderer* was among this number, and under the command of Gordon Campbell, she made history as the most famous of all decoy ships under the aliases of *Farnborough* and Q5.

When the Germans initiated an unrestricted phase of submarine warfare in early 1917, they had triggered off an increase in the number of decoy vessels being used by their British opponents. By late May 1917 these were of the order of eighty steamships and sailing vessels employed as, or being converted to, Q ships. Most of the large Q ships were serving under the command of Admiral Bayly from his headquarters at Queenstown. Others of the larger types were based on such places as Longhope, Portsmouth, the south-east of England and Malta.

When the year 1917 was approaching its end, the decoy ship had had its time. The introduction of the convoy system, which is dealt with in more detail later, meant that the vast majority of merchant ships were sailed in convoys. A decoy ship cruising alone in, say, the Atlantic would probably arouse suspicion by the mere fact that it was acting as a loner. How would such a vessel be able to convince a vigilant and mistrustful submarine commanding officer that she was a genuine straggler from a convoy?

The increase in the number of decoy ships was accompanied by a fall in the success rate, as measured by the number of U-boats sunk or damaged – a form of diminishing returns. This was primarily due to the fact that the use of Q ships was becoming more widely known, so the element of surprise was far more difficult to achieve. Captain Gordon Campbell also mentioned the fact that the introduction of camouflage techniques made it harder for a decoy ship to change its appearance at frequent intervals.

The history of warfare has the habit of teaching its devotees that when mankind develops a new weapon, often during a difficult stage in a conflict, it will be well-nigh impossible to refrain from using it at the first possible moment. The new weapon will, on these occasions, be deployed in 'penny packets' when the exercise of a little patience might have enabled the build-up of an overwhelming force. The commitment of a new form of armament in driblets may also destroy the secrecy surrounding the device and enable the enemy to begin studying antidotes at an early stage. Modern examples of the above tendency might include the first British use of tanks in World War I and the German introduction of airborne 'V' weapons in World War II. In short, when a country has a surprise weapon system, or a new invention, it can be a mistake to use it until ready to do so on a large scale. World War I decoy ships were only used in small numbers in their early stages. In hindsight, it should have been clear that in due course an unsuccessful operation would take place which would mean that the secrecy surrounding this type of ship would leak out. This, in turn, would make their chances of success more difficult to achieve. This, in fact, is what occurred.

Over a hundred and eighty decoy ships of all sorts and conditions were employed during the First World War. The number of U-boats sunk by these vessels was eleven.

It may be thought that a great amount of effort went into the sinking of a rather small number of enemy submarines. However, it should be remembered that only two hundred German submarines were sunk in World War I and, of these, only one hundred and forty-five were sunk by direct actions, such as ramming by surface warships.

The anti-submarine effort, controlled by the Royal Navy, involved of the order of five thousand auxilliary craft, guns, large quantities of depth charges, mines in their thousands, miles of nets, and later, a convoy system of huge proportions and many other devices to attain the number of a hundred and fifty-five submarine victims. To entrap and kill a hostile submarine is not such a straightforward task as it may appear to the uninitiated.

The great achievements of the Q ships were centred on their effect on enemy morale. To the German submariner it must have come as a mosty unwelcome shock to the nervous system to be dealing with a seemingly innocuous tramp steamer and to suddenly learn that he was taking on a well-armed warship with an impressive outfit of lethal weapons.

Critics of the Q ship have argued that they enticed an attacking submarine to make use of torpedoes, rather than gunfire. The argument continues to air the view that it was, in general, easier to escape when attacked by a gun than it was from the more lethal wound, below the surface, inflicted by a well-aimed torpedo.

The counter-argument was that the submariner would have fewer opportunities to attack with torpedoes, and when he had expended his complement of these expensive weapons he would need to return to Germany often using the circuitous route around the north of the British Isles. Chancing a passage via the extremely well-protected Straits of Dover was not an attractive option. In its train, the trip round the British Isles would imply a useful reduction in the number of U-boats available for operations at any one time.

A fact which stands out clearly is that, apart from the actual direct sinkings of U-boats by decoy ships, their employment had a significant effect upon the crews of German submarines. The Q ships also forced the commanding officers of hostile submarines to approach potential victims with noticeably increased caution in case they might be 'walking into a trap'.

Books written about decoy ships in the aftermath of World War I tended to end with speculation on the possible use of Q ships in any future war.

On the whole, it seems to be considered that Q ships were unlikely to be used again; but history, which delights to puzzle its students, would be repeated in the Second World War.

Before closing this chapter, it is interesting to air a few thoughts on the use of early electronic warfare techniques which were employed in the World War I campaign against German U-boats. British ships would monitor transmissions made by hostile submarines and sometimes valuable intelligence was gleaned as a result.

Bearings could be taken of enemy radio transmissions made by hostile submarines and experienced operators could give an estimate of range from gauging the signal strength of intercepted transmissions. Distress messages, initiated by Allied merchant vessels which were under attack by a submarine, would provide a datum upon which a hunt for the U-boat concerned could be based.

Techniques for fixing the position of a submarine using the bearings of the U-boat's radio transmissions, as received simultaneously by two or more surface ships, were known and could be used by the hunters.

CHAPTER III
World War II Q Ships

The years following the end of World War I saw the customary post-war run-down of the British Armed Services. Pruning the military seems to have a fatal attraction for politicians. War is not a great 'vote catcher' for obvious reasons; and other targets for public expenditure are adopted without any regard for the old Roman adage: 'If you wish for peace, prepare for war.'

There was not a great demand, post 1919, for eccentric naval officers who had spent a proportion of the war years wandering about the ocean in disguised merchant vessels whose main aim in life was to attract, disable or, better still, sink an enemy U-boat. Gordon Campbell endured a number of somewhat mundane appointments during these 'dog years'; but he did have the satisfaction of being promoted Rear-Admiral in April 1928, even though he was smartly placed on the retired list the next day.

Admiral Campbell was elected MP for Burnley in the General Election of 1931, which saw the formation of a National Government which, it was hoped, might do something positive to deal with the desperate economic crisis which had descended like a threatening cloud upon the United Kingdom and other countries in the developed world.

The Admiral failed to hold his Parliamentary seat in the next election, and in the year 1935 he faded into private life; but, as the future was to show, he was not entirely forgotten.

The international scene was looking increasingly gloomy by the middle of the summer of 1939 and the prospects of Europe becoming involved in another war were moving from the category of 'possible' to that of 'probable'. The deteriorating international scene triggered a number of conferences and meetings in Whitehall government offices, including the Admiralty. One of the topics discussed in deliberations chaired by the Assistant Chief of Naval Staff was the possible use of Q ships in the war which those present were becoming convinced was inevitable. It was decided that an experimental vessel should be acquired for conversion into a decoy ship. However, before this decision could be executed, Hitler's Germany had attacked Poland, and a couple of days after the assault on the Poles had been launched, Britain and France were at war with Germany. Just before the outbreak of the Second World War Admiral Gordon Campbell had been recalled for duties in the Admiralty.

A short time after Mr Winston Churchill had taken over the distinguished office of First Lord of the Admiralty, Gordon Campbell was summoned to his presence and informed that he was being given a virtually free hand to take over a number of merchant ships and to convert them for service as decoys. The Admiral lost no time in setting off on a tour of British ports to earmark ships which were, to his mind, suitable Q ship candidates.

It was clear that the conditions in which sea warfare would be fought had changed since the end of World War I. Campbell was aware of the different circumstances. For example, merchantmen would rapidly be defensively armed; the convoy system would be implemented from the very beginning of the war; enemy submarine commanding officers would hesitate to surface to attack their victims with gunfire if there was any danger of attack from the air. The capabilities of military aircraft had progressed in leaps and bounds during the twenty years of peace.

As a matter of interest, the German Admiral Doenitz had a bit of a complex about decoys, and at the beginning of World War II, had warned the captains of German submarines that Q ships should be expected, and the U-boat captains must never get too close to merchant ships unless their boats were submerged; also, that stragglers which had dropped astern from convoys should be treated with suspicion in case a trap was being set for an unsuspecting submariner.

A major complication, as far as the new generation of Q ships was concerned, was that Adolf Hitler's navy had not been built up with a confrontation with the Royal Navy's surface fleet, of Jutland-type proportions, in mind. The Führer's capital ships, and in particular the much-publicised 'pocket battleships', had been created for the lesser function of commerce raiding. This role is covered in a later section of this book. Suffice it to say, for the moment, that Campbell's new look decoys should be capable of playing a part in countering this potential threat as well as playing 'hide and seek' with hostile submarines.

British government departments responsible for War Transport were, not surprisingly, loath to give up any of the fast, modern ships which formed part of the nation's merchant fleet. This meant that Gordon Campbell had to try to do the best he could with what he could get.

In the final event, nine ships, from those available, were selected. Six vessels were destined for deep sea cruising and three for working in coastal waters. Brief details of the larger ships are:

Name	Tonnage	Length (feet)	Beam (feet)	Fuel used	Date built	Approx. speed
King Gruffydd	5,072	400	52	oil	1919	8.5 knots
Cape Howe	4,443	375	53	coal	1930	9.5 knots
Cape Sable	4,398	375	53	motor/diesel	1936	9.5 knots
Botlea	5,119	400	53	coal	1917	10 knots
*Williamette Valley**	4,702	401	54	motor/diesel	1928	10.5 knots
City of Durban	5,850	379	53	coal & oil	1921	12 knots

A Constructor Officer was given a place among Admiral Campbell's small group of staff officers. His role was to oversee that conversion work was efficiently implemented and that the highest security standards were maintained. This was no easy task as Campbell had strong views on such matters as the concealment of Q ship armament; and guidelines had been formulated by the Admiralty Committee which had earlier studied the reintroduction of decoy ships

It had been decided that 4-inch guns should be mounted as these would have the punch to penetrate the pressure hull of a submarine. It was also stipulated that these weapons should be hidden behind hinged flaps in the ships' sides, rather than use the more ingenious and mysterious trick devices that had been dreamed up during World War I. It was also determined that torpedo tubes should be fitted. Small arms in the form of Lewis guns were carried, as were 100 depth charges per ship. Four of the new Q ships were blessed with the installation of asdic, or sonar, equipment. These were *Cape Howe, Williamette Valley, City of Durban* and *Cape Sable*.

A common practice during the First World War had been to fill the holds of Q ships with timber with the aim of maximising their buoyancy. This practice was repeated. Internal passage-ways were cut between decks so that crew members could deploy to their 'action stations' without being seen by observers outboard of the decoy ship.

It was necessary to rename the selected vessels whose new titles were chosen by Admiral Campbell: the *King Gruffydd* became the *Maunder*; *Cape Howe* the *Prunella*; *Botlea* the *Lambridge*; *Williamette Valley* the *Edgehill*; *City of Durban* the *Brutus* and *Cape Sable* the *Cyprus*.

During the time which was spent in converting the Second World War Q ships to meet their needs and become effective decoys, Gordon Campbell had to arrange for the manning of his 'brain children'. Officers were selected by the process of interviewing prospective candidates; but

---

*For a ship to have borne the name of a valley in Oregon seems to be unusual; but, perhaps there was some reason I have yet to discover.

33

ratings were drafted as seen fit by the drafting authorities at the Port Divisions of Chatham, Portsmouth and Devonport with no mention of what their future was to hold in store. Perhaps the old jingle, 'I wonder, oh I wonder if the "jaunty" made a blunder when he made this draft chit out for me', held a special significance for ratings who found themselves serving their country on board decoy ships. The lucky lads concerned came from the customary mix of Royal Navy personnel and reservists.

The captains were all regular or retired Royal Navy officers who were personally picked by Campbell from the roll of those who had the temerity to volunteer for 'hazardous service'.

Earlier lessons had not been forgotten and the complements of Q ships were of the order of three times those to be found in a 'run of the mill' merchantman. This was, of course, necessary to cater for convincing 'panic parties' that they could abandon their ship and still leave adequate men on board to man the weaponry.

As had been the case in the First World War, officers and ratings had to wear Merchant Navy style clothing, often civilian attire, dungarees and a motley selection of head gear. A grateful government gave naval personnel a small addition to their pay to help cover the purchase of the necessary plain clothes. Officers and ratings were in receipt of four shillings (20p) 'Special Service' allowance.

Merchant ships serving as decoys were obliged to fly the Red Ensign at sea except when they had adopted a neutral disguise. When entering harbour, Q ships hoisted the Blue Ensign. In the event of their over-generously sized ship's companies being queried, the explanation of transporting a naval draft to a foreign port was to be used.

After they had been commissioned, decoy ships were directed to the Beaulieu river, not far from Southampton, where in comparative privacy, they could be given a work-up of several weeks during which the ship's companies could be intensively examined to train them to cope with a range of the situations they might be expected to meet on active service. No leave was granted during this 'work-up' period.

In World War II, unlike in 1914–18, the convoy system was activated from the very beginning. This said, it obviously took some time to put the well-prepared plans into effect. Briefly, it took time to organise escorting forces; and British merchant shipping was dispersed on a worldwide basis and needed to be co-ordinated.

Admiral Gordon Campbell believed that, during the rather chaotic early stages of the war, the optimum use of decoy ships could be made by deploying them widely abroad to cover focal areas such as those to be found off major South American ports, the South Atlantic, West Indies, Sierra Leone, Aden and the Indian Ocean to name but a few. It was in such areas that hostile raiders, of most types, might reasonably be expected to operate. However, he discovered that he was not able to employ the freedom of action which he believed that he had been led to anticipate.

It is amazing how human weaknesses can affect important (and unimportant) events. At the time in question, considerable leverage was wielded in the Admiralty by Rear-Admiral T S V Phillips, who was later to perish when the *Prince of Wales* and *Repulse* were sunk by Japanese torpedo-bombers, off Malaya, in1941. Phillips had commanded a sloop on the South Atlantic Station where Campbell was ensconced as the Captain-in-Charge of Simonstown Dockyard. Phillips had developed a firm, and lasting, dislike of the heavily decorated former Q ship star. Enough said, Campbell's proposals were overruled and the decoy ships were directed to patrol in the south-west approaches to the British Isles, off Cape Finisterre and around the coast of Ireland. Perhaps a promising opportunity had been missed. It would probably be true to say that the full potential of Campbell's World War II brain children, in the form of decoy freighters, would never be achieved.

A significant number of German merchant vessels were known to be sheltering in various neutral harbours in the early stages of the Second World War, awaiting opportunities of 'making a break' for home. A number of these ships were taking cover at Vigo in Spain. In due course, intelligence became available that a break-out from Vigo was imminent. A large Allied naval group was assembled to intercept the enemy merchantmen. The British contribution included a significant detachment from the Home Fleet plus Coastal Command sorties. The Royal Navy ships consisted of a battle cruiser (*Renown*), an aircraft carrier (*Ark Royal*), a cruiser and escorting destroyers. Possibly this was the birth of what was to become the famous Force H.

In due time, six German merchant vessels emerged to attempt to run the gauntlet. Only one survived to reach safety. It was, no doubt, possible that if a number of decoy ships had been deployed to cruise off Vigo, and other ports in which German commercial ships were known to be skulking, greater and more economic successes could have been achieved.

The British World War II decoy ships remained on active service until Winston Churchill directed that the then remaining six vessels should be withdrawn. Despite all their efforts, the British Q ships had not managed to sink a single German submarine. Perhaps, this particular *ruse de guerre* was over twenty years out of date. The commanding officers of U-boats tended to shoot first and ask questions afterwards when it came to attacking lone merchant vessels; and, as mentioned previously, they had been instructed not to approach merchantmen too closely unless their submarines were submerged.

The ship's companies of World War II Q ships were drawn broadly from the same sources as their forebears in the First World War. The men were, in every way, as brave and resourceful as their predecessors and they faced similar dangers, hardships and casualties. The part they played in the Second World War is worthy of remembrance. The next chapter describes incidents involving decoy ships between 1939 and 1945. I believe that this cocktail may provide a feel for Q ship operations without dwelling too deeply upon technicalities.

CHAPTER IV
Adventures of World War II Q Ships

This chapter seeks to take a look at adventures and incidents involving the Q ships which were deployed during World War II. Where possible, the words used by personnel who were closely involved are included as it is very difficult to surpass eyewitness accounts.

The *Maunder*, ex-*King Gruffydd*, was the first of the decoys to set sail with Commander Edward Masterman Loly in command. Loly was an ex-submariner. His second-in-command was Lieutenant Commander Joseph Gabbett, who had previously been serving as the First Lieutenant of the Royal Naval Barracks, Devonport.

Maunder joined an outward-bound convoy as far as Land's End, on completion of the statutory work-up period. For approximately a week she loitered about in the mouth of the Channel, attaching herself to diverse west-bound convoys, then dropping astern, no doubt to the chagrin of escort force commanders, who, ignorant of her true function in life, must have wondered what on earth she was playing at. Of the order of thirty-nine merchant vessels were sunk by enemy submarines in the south-west approaches during the first eight months of the war; but no German U-boat commanding officer showed any temptation to close this particular straggler.

The German pocket battleships were known to be operating in the Atlantic Ocean during October 1939. Allied hunting groups were formed to search for the hostile raiders which, among other things, stripped valuable escort vessels from convoys. While these excitements were in progress, *Maunder*, with a keen, well-trained ship's company which was enthusiastic to prove itself, was kept fruitlessly trifling about in the English Channel.

A minor incident occurred on 17 December 1939 when *Maunder* was boarded by an officer from a French destroyer. Shortly before he left, the Frenchman asked to see the ship's poop and from this point of vantage he noticed two of the after guns. Commander Loly realised that the game had to end and disclosed his ship's true role. The boarding officer expressed approbation at the manner in which the armament was concealed and *Maunder* was allowed to proceed. Engine defects made it necessary to return to harbour where the ship remained until late February 1940.

Maunder carried out another unavailing stint of patrolling off the south-west coast of Ireland. The ship had no lucky breaks even though a number of U-boats were performing in the general area, laying mines and sinking merchant vessels. To give credit where credit is due, morale in *Maunder* remained at a high level which says much for the qualities shown by her officers and senior ratings. An incentive must have been provided by the usual decoy's knowledge that the ship could be torpedoed at any time in a twenty-four-hour day; and the anticipated games with a U-boat might begin at any moment. Commander Loly was completely confident that his ship could assimilate up to five torpedoes, due to her timber-filled holds, without foundering and still be able to engage her assailant.

Eventually, and after more lingering in the areas to the south-west of Ireland, *Maunder* was directed to steam sedately down the coast of west Africa, stopping at Sierra Leone and various other ports of call on the way to Durban. With Durban as her base, *Maunder* was to cruise in the Indian Ocean with the idea of stumbling across an armed merchant raider, or even a German pocket battleship.

Two hostile merchant raiders were making their way in the same general direction. This was a development which was unknown to Commander Loly. One of the enemy ships was the *Atlantis* which had left the Baltic in late March 1940, passed undetected through the Denmark Strait and 'crossed the Line' by the month of May, disguised as a Japanese vessel. Closing the normal trade route between Sierra Leone and the Cape of Good Hope, *Atlantis* sank the British ship *Scientist*, which had taken this course independently.

Atlantis laid a number of mines off Cape Aghulas and subsequently entered the Indian Ocean. She was patrolling in the triangle broadly bounded by lines connecting Madagascar, Mauritius and Rodriguez Island in which area she captured, or sank, five Allied merchantmen.

The German raider *Pinguin* negotiated the Denmark Strait with the aim of sailing to the South Atlantic. She put paid to a British merchant ship off the small island of Ascension, rounded the Cape of Good Hope and followed *Atlantis* into the waters which surround Madagascar. Three more merchant vessels were rapidly dealt with by her guns; but all contrived to transmit warnings that they were under attack. This alerted the local naval authorities before their radio equipment was put out of action. *Maunder* toiled after the raiders at her best speed of eight and a half knots; but the prospect of action remained frustratingly out of reach of the raiders who had an appreciably faster turn of speed.

The dogged *Maunder* had covered more than 43,000 nautical miles by December 1940 and the disposition of both officers and men had changed for the worse. In the days before air-conditioning, life in the metal box, to which can be likened the hull of a ship, could become insufferably hot and result in a number of irritating minor ailments such as 'prickly-heat'. In a vessel, like *Maunder*, which was a coal-burner and into which the larger complement of a decoy had been crammed, the discomforts of the tropics were magnified. Breakdowns of the propulsion machinery occurred with increasing regularity to say nothing of other defects.

Illnesses became prevalent, the ship's doctor developed habitual ear trouble and Commander Loly fell victim to tuberculosis from which he later died. Command was assumed by the First Lieutenant, Gabbett, who achieved what was once cynically called 'the greatest event in a naval officer's life', his first stomach ulcer. The ship's company were also plagued by a surfeit of dental problems.

Despite its manifold problems, the modified freighter perversely continued with her quest. She steamed as far as the Sunda Strait, between Java and Sumatra, the place where Captain Ahab brought the Great White Whale, Moby Dick, to bay, and as far to the north as the island of Ceylon. Reports of enemy operations relayed via the Admiralty were frequently some days out of date and consequently of scant help in deciding in which area of her huge hunting ground *Maunder* should place herself to the optimum advantage.

Not once during the slow-moving, overpowering, heat-laden months did she come across a single suspect ship. This was despite the fact that at least three hostile merchant raiders were deployed in the Indian Ocean, their speeds of the order of twice that of which *Maunder* was capable. The pocket battleship *Admiral Sheer* also showed itself in the general area for a limited period.

In April 1940 the 'phoney war' in Europe burst into a ferocious explosion. Denmark was overrun and Norway invaded by the Germans. An Allied expeditionary force was rapidly got together and despatched to help the Norwegian forces who were opposing the Nazi assailants of their native land. The Germans had captured the major airfields and Allied ships were the victims of pitiless attacks from the air.

It was at this juncture that the inevitable collision between Admirals Phillips and Gordon Campbell took place. From his lofty perch as Vice-Chief of the Naval Staff, Phillips sent for Campbell and directed him to recall two of his Admiralty freighters which were 'trailing their coats' in the Atlantic and to deploy them to Norwegian waters. Gordon Campbell 'dug his toes in' and objected that the ships would be useless off Norway as their anti-aircraft armament was virtually non-existent; and that their real function would be jeopardised. Phillips persisted; but the exasperated Campbell went back to his office and took no further action.

The First Sea Lord, Admiral Pound, became involved and 'read Campbell's horoscope'. Campbell resigned and was relieved by Rear-Admiral G W Taylor, who had retired from the Royal Navy in 1934.

Taylor proposed more aggressive employment for the decoys, whose activities were reported weekly to the First Sea Lord; but his viewpoints carried even less weight than those of his illustrious predecessor. Churchill also seemed to have lost interest in the World War II Q ships and, in late 1940, was implying that their role might well be coming to an end.

The next decoy to be studied is the *Lambridge*, formerly *Botlea*, which was another coal-burner. *Lambridge* was built for the British Prince Line and named *African Prince*. She was transferred to Greek ownership during the late 1920s and her name was altered to *Pentridge Hill*, which did not have a very classical ring to it. The ship came into the British Government's orbit in 1939, when she was purchased by the Ministry of War Transport.

The bearded Commander Thomas Bennett Brunton was appointed as her commanding officer. Brunton had served for a short time in a sailing vessel and joined the Royal Naval Reserve during the First World War. He later managed to transfer to the Royal Navy where he became a submariner.

Lambridge was the oldest, and was even more of a lame duck than her sisters. She was converted to decoy ship at HM Dockyard, Chatham; but sadly, her engines failed only about forty-eight hours after the dockyard had worked on them. Not unnaturally, they had to be refitted again. *Lambridge* got away from the dockyard in mid-December 1939 and, after working-up,she sailed in early January 1940. She was directed to patrol in the area between the south-west of Ireland and the Azores; and then to base herself on Freetown.

Grim weather marked the first winter of World War II and this highlighted many of the ship's failings. *Lambridge* was light despite the weight of her timber cargo to which should be added the weight of her weapons, including torpedo tubes, depth charges and ammunition. This caused Commander Brunton to arrange a false Plimsoll Line. The ship was difficult to handle and in a seaway outdid a three badge able seaman who had had a glass or two too many, by developing a rapid twenty degree roll. This would have made it impracticable to fight the guns in anything like bad weather.

Lambridge had a number of adventures, including near misses with German raiders; but it is not intended to go into detail as this could overlap the subsequent section of the book.

Commander Brunton had been relieved by Commander Scott-Bell for the last part of *Lambridge*'s life as a decoy ship. In late January 1941 *Lambridge* steamed into the Indian Ocean on what turned out to be her last cruise in the role of Q ship. During early March 1941 Commander Scott-Bell received a signal from Admiral Taylor ordering *Lambridge* to hoist the White Ensign and head for Colombo.

The next decoy to be examined is *Brutus*, formerly *City of Durban*. The previous owners of the *City of Durban* were Ellerman's City and Hall Line. The ship could burn coal as well as oil fuel and had a best speed of twelve knots, which made her the fastest of the Second World War Q ships, even though the higher speed was only relative to that of her sisters.

The commanding officer of *Brutus* was Commander Humphrey Hopper whom I knew through periodic contact in the Ministry of Defence during the early to mid-1970s. Hopper was then a captain and was nothing if not a character. He was an ex-'Springer', which means that he had completed a long course in physical training. He was a powerfully built man with an attractive sense of humour. He had been awarded the Silver Medal of the Royal Humane Society in July 1918 for saving the lives of six soldiers from a French troopship which had been torpedoed in the Mediterranean. About four years later he won a clasp to the medal, for gallantry, when the cruiser HMS *Raleigh* was wrecked off Labrador in August 1922.

Mr A W Bennetts, who now lives in Queensland, Australia sent me some vivid notes about *Brutus* which are given virtually verbatim as they provide a wonderfully lucid picture of a World War II Q ship.

SS *City of Durban* was a 5,900 ton merchant ship belonging to the Ellerman Hall Line of Liverpool. She was coal burning and was built in 1921. After war started on 3 September 1939, she was taken over by the Admiralty, and the Merchant Service crew sailed her to Devonport for conversion into a Q ship.

The holds were filled with timber to keep her afloat in case of being torpedoed. The space between the upper deck and the next deck down was known as 'between decks', and housed the crew (except officers) and all the main armament. Four 4-inch guns and two 21-inch Fixed Torpedo Tubes were installed on each side (port and starboard) of the Between Decks. Two depth charge rails were fitted in the stern. The guns and torpedo crews manned either the port or starboard weapons as required and their accommodation was between their respective port and starboard weapons.

The guns could be brought into action by dropping sections of the ship's side, and training the guns outboard. In the case of the torpedo tubes and depth charges, the flap was hinged at the top and swung upwards away from the ship's side. In addition, one false cabin was built to the existing ones each side on the upper deck, and this contained a depth charge thrower plus depth charges. When a lever was operated, the outside rail (bulkhead) of the cabin collapsed, allowing the thrower to be fired.

A 4-inch DEMS (Defensively Equipped Merchant Ship) gun was installed on the poop, but if the *City of Durban* was playing the part of a neutral or Allied ship, a locker on wheels mounted on rails could be pushed over the gun. When concealed, the gun's crew could man the gun inside the after superstructure by a locker, and when instructed, push the locker forward clear of the gun and bring the gun into action.

In the wings of the bridge, small holes had been cut to enable ranges to be taken using a hand-held range finder, whilst keeping out of sight.

Every manned position was inter-connected by magneto telephone and gunner control could be made from any position, but normally from the bridge. An Asdic set was installed in the bows. The A/S (anti-submarine) office was above the set and was connected by a magneto telephone system to the bridge, although this was in addition to being on the general system.

Twin Lewis guns were available on the bow, stern and bridge, although later on, when with convoys in the North Atlantic, the water-cooling cases of the Lewis guns on the bridge were stripped off to allow the gun to be fired at aircraft without being mounted.

To complete the RN atmosphere, a cell was built Between Decks, and in the tropics this steel box became a hell hole. If there was a prisoner, the door was left open to enable him to get what fresh air there was.

The Commanding Officer was Commander H D Hopper, RN, known to the lower deck as 'Slapsy'. Humphrey Hopper was a long-term RN Officer and had been on the China Station as Physical Training and Recreation Officer. He was an ex-boxer and had a broken nose and cauliflower ears, hence the nickname.

There was the 'Fake Master', a retired Merchant Service officer who would assume command on entering and leaving harbour and deal with the Pilot and Port Authorities. He was given the rank of Lieutenant Commander RNR, and was Lieutenant Commander Fitzpatrick. He had served his apprenticeship on the sailing ships to the Far East and Australia. Other experienced deck officers were Royal Naval Reserve, and came from the British India Line and Union Castle Line. Other officers, including the doctor, were RNVR and were responsible for torpedoes, etc.

The five Engineer Officers came with the ship and four had signed the T124 agreements for their contract with the RN. The Second Engineer joined the RNR. The Marconi Radio Officers also signed T124 articles.

The fighting of the ship was to be done by RN personnel, who also provided the ratings for the stokehold and engine room. Men not required in the stokehold and engine room at times of action became part of the 'Panic Boat Crew' if we were stopped by a U-boat. This number was increased by cooks, stewards and crew not required to fight. Cooks and stewards were Merchant Service and had signed T124 contracts.

There were three or four RFR (Royal Fleet Reserve) men, ex-Navy and then Merchant Service, who were the Quartermasters, and were used to steering by magnetic compass and also used to the Harbour Pilots' orders when entering or leaving harbour.

Recruitment of the crew in Royal Naval Barracks, Devonport was made by calling for 'Volunteers for Special Service', type unspecified. The volunteers were then interviewed by Commander Hopper who made his selection.

We were moved from Royal Naval Barracks into a Nissen Hut, and we went into the dockyard each day to familiarise ourselves with the ship and to organise our own little piece of the deception. In my case I had quite a job persuading the Naval Dockyard Stores that I required Merchant Navy Ensigns of various countries,without giving the game away. These ensigns were to be flown according to the nationality we were supposed to be. We even had a German Merchant Navy ensign which we used in 1941.

The dockyard painted the ship externally with a magnificent camouflage design which was supposed to fox any U-boat commander, and to make it difficult for him to assess our course and speed. This was the last thing we wanted him to do.

After the crew shook down, we sailed from Plymouth and proceeded up the English Channel and into the Solent, and anchored off Beaulieu to do our working up. We painted the whole of the ship over the camouflage, hoisted a Blue Ensign with the gold anchor of a Royal Fleet Auxiliary, and became RFA *Brutus*. We then sailed for our first patrol which was into the Atlantic and eventually to Bermuda.

After sailing from the United Kingdom, Commander Hopper cleared the lower deck and we assembled on the quarterdeck which in our case was on top of number two hold, but 'Between Decks' and out of sight.

We were then told that in addition to our naval pay (mine was three shillings and three pence per day – about 17p), we were getting an extra four shillings (20p) per day 'danger money', and that this had been backdated to our Commissioning date, 1 January 1940. In 1940 this was riches to us and, funnily enough, the fact that the Merchant Service personnel on board were getting Merchant Navy rates of pay, plus ten pounds per month Merchant Navy danger allowance, plus the four shillings per day RN danger allowance, did not worry the RN types.

From Bermuda we went up the oil tanker route to the United Kingdom, but ran into foul weather and finished up in Halifax, Nova Scotia, for repairs. It was decided that the weather was too cold to work on the steel and we were sent back to Bermuda. Whilst in the North Atlantic, we had only our one Naval Issue blanket, but on our return we were issued with another blanket each. We never went into cold climates again.

For most of 1940, we wandered the Atlantic, spending quite a time steaming northwards and southwards off the coast of Spain and France. This meant changing our silhouette every few days and painting the ship in the dark. For this operation, everyone was involved: engine room, cooks, stewards, doctor; everyone not on essential watchkeeping. Sometimes the hull had to be painted and stages were hung over the side in complete darkness. The drill was to feel the steel plates with your left hand, and, if dry, paint it. If wet, it had already been painted.

The colour of the superstructure was changed, Samson posts (small masts) erected, the funnel had a different colour band painted on it or painted out, or sheet metal letters or flags or moons etc., hoisted up and bolted onto the funnel. All this in case we had been seen previously on a different course.

Conditions 'Between Decks' were not good. To retain our disguise as a merchant ship, only the watch on deck were allowed to be seen and other crew members had to stay below decks in daylight. After dark it was permissable to go on deck freely, but no smoking was allowed on deck after dark.

There was no fan ventilation between decks, and the only fresh air coming into the area was from bell mouth deck ventilators, and if there was a following wind, there was no fresh air. Water was extremely short and the condensate from the boilers went into the fresh water tanks. This water was far too hot to have a shower, so the routine was to draw a bucket of water from the cold water tap and leave it in the bathroom to cool down before use. The boiler water was also used for drinking and when it had cooled to atmospheric temperature (which was warm) we used to add a couple of teaspoons of Eno's to give it some life, otherwise being condensed steam, it tasted flat. Our stomachs became used to the Eno's, but new crew members suffered until becoming used to it.

Normal life at sea in the *City of Durban* was four weeks, with a few days in harbour. We had a ration of one bottle of beer per man per week. This was issued on Saturdays. It was decided before leaving the dockyard that a canteen would be required to sell duty free cigarettes, biscuits and other goodies. The NAAFI were not interested and a volunteer was found in the crew to man it; the management to be the responsibility of the Purser.

It was necessary to raise capital to purchase stocks for our weeks at sea, so every member of the crew put in an equal amount of money. Stocks were sold at a profit to pay the volunteer and also to increase the range of goods stocked. On arrival in port the value of stock in hand at cost was ascertained, and added to the cash in hand. The value of each pound invested was declared and crew leaving the ship were given their investment plus profits. The replacement was offered these shares at the enhanced price, and they usually took them.

The days at sea were very boring, although when well away from U-boat routes, gun and boat drill was carried out and every day before daybreak 'action stations' was sounded and everyone closed up at their stations until after dawn. In the messes, Bridge was played every day and, eventually, the better players were playing for five shillings per 100 points.

We had a radiogram which, if security permitted, was used for news and BBC programmes, and anyone was permitted to play their own gramophone records. Loudspeakers were in all messes and in the Wardroom.

Able Seaman Murphy, from Southern Ireland, played his favourite record 'Sure a little bit of heaven dropped from out the sky one day . . .' on every possible occasion, until one crew member could take it no longer. He walked into our mess where Spud Murphy lived and asked him how much the record cost. Spud told him, whereupon the visitor placed the amount on the mess table, produced the record and broke it in half – then all hell broke loose.

I found myself assisting the Navigating Officer in taking sun and star sights. I was then designated 'Navigator's Yeoman' and received the allowance of two pence (1p) per day. I corrected the Admiralty charts from the amendments received whilst in harbour, and was taught how to calculate the ship's position from the sights. This helped to cut down the boredom. I was also lent books covering the syllabus for Merchant Navy Officers.

Boxing was encouraged by Commander Hopper, and occasionally, in the Dog Watches, the Bosun's Mate would come along between decks piping 'The Captain is on the upper decks with the gloves on. Anyone wishing to have a go, hop up top.' That would be the signal for Jerry Lane, an AB from Cornwall, to say, 'the punch drunk B . . . , lace up my gloves.' He would get a pair of boxing gloves from his locker, put them on and go on to the upper decks to pummel the Captain.

On arrival in port, the Captain would report to the senior Naval Officer, then come back and clear the lower deck. We would then be told which port we had come from and what ships we had seen. It was completely incorrect, but spreading false information was part of our job. This could lead to awkward situations. On one occasion in Gibraltar, a group of our Officers were spreading the information as instructed, and a security-minded person called the police. They asked the group, 'what ship?' and the reply was, 'RFA *Brutus'*. They asked the Doctor what he did on board and he replied that he was the Doctor. The Police knew that an RFA ship did not carry a naval doctor, and they put the whole lot inside jail. Word got back to the ship and arrangements were made with Naval Security to get them out. If the Doctor had only looked at his dockyard pass, he would have seen that he was a Third Engineer. We were issued with Merchant Navy lapel badges to wear with our civilian clothes.

In March 1941 our status was changed from Q ship to Armed Merchant Cruiser and we patrolled the Atlantic and Indian Oceans, looking for German Merchant Raiders. I can't remember that the change made a big difference in our lives except that our four shillings per day danger money was, in any case, cut back to one shilling per day 'hard lying' allowance. But on patrol, our guns were still behind the shutters and we did not fly the White Ensign as a warship does.

In September 1941 we sailed with a convoy from Freetown to the United Kingdom. Our position was astern of the convoy and we did not fly an ensign until in St George's Channel, when we were instructed by the Commodore of the convoy to escort the Clyde-bound ships to the Clyde. We then hoisted a White Ensign and a flag signal telling them to follow. The other merchant ships must have thought it funny, because nearly everyone signalled to us saying, 'thank you for your protection'. We thought it a big joke, as our maximum speed was about ten knots and we had not acted as a naval ship during the voyage.

We had previously trailed Freetown to United Kingdom convoys, acting as a straggler, twenty-five miles astern of the convoy, with the object of attracting a U-boat pack to attack us so that we would be able to warn the convoy, but we were not attacked, although the convoy was.

This seems to have been the story of the *City of Durban*'s naval career. After returning to the United Kingdom, she made one more trip from the Clyde around the north of Scotland (as Commodore of a convoy) and down to the Thames. When nearly into the Thames, the convoy was attacked by German aircraft. One bomb hit the *City of Durban* on the Chief Engineer's cabin and did not explode. The bomb disposal squad subsequently removed it.

After the war, the *City of Durban*, which had looked after us so well, was scrapped, and a new bigger and better namesake built. I saw her in Durban in 1970, flying the same house flag as her predecessor.

In August 1939, with the outbreak of war imminent, the Admiralty were concerned with the threat that Germany's U-boats would pose to Britain's sea lanes. They had experienced exactly the same problem during the First

World War and their attention was inevitably drawn to one of the counter-measures used quite successfully during that conflict – Q ships.

These were ordinary merchant vessels that were armed with concealed weapons hidden behind hinged shutters, false lifeboats and tarpaulins. Their aim was to have unsuspecting U-boats surface where the Q ship's guns could be brought to bear on the enemy. Eleven U-boats were sunk in this way during the Great War and it was hoped that they would prove of similar usefulness during the forthcoming conflict.

A number of merchant ships were subsequently requisitioned and brought to naval dockyards around the country to be refitted and armed. One of the vessels was the SS *Cape Howe*, a 4,443 ton steamer owned by the Lyle Shipping Company.

During the winter months, work got underway to transform her into an unlikely fighting ship. She was armed with six 4-inch guns which were concealed behind hinged shutters. Four torpedo tubes were fitted, two on each beam, and a hundred depth charges were in the aft section. The *Cape Howe* was also fitted with Asdic (Sonar) equipment to enable her to hunt submarines.

Commander Eric Langton Woodhall was appointed as Captain. He was an experienced submarine hunter who had won the DSO in November for operations against U-boats in the south-western approaches.

The *Cape Howe*'s crew also began arriving and they comprised many reservists from the Royal Naval Reserve, Royal Fleet Reserve and Royal Naval Volunteer Reserve; but they also included regular naval personnel and some from the Merchant Navy.

By April 1940 the ship, now re-named *Prunella*, was ready for operations against U-boats and was deployed as a straggler to incoming and outgoing convoys in the Western Approaches. However, she encountered no U-boats as most had been recalled to support the German invasion of Norway. *Prunella* was duly recalled and re-assigned to Norwegian waters, but again her mission was abortive as no enemy vessels were encountered. Commander Woodhall then ordered the vessel to sail south to the North Sea. Whilst nearing the Orkney Islands, the ship was stopped and boarded by two officers from a Royal Navy trawler. The Captain and crew had an anxious wait as they proceeded to study *Prunella*'s log – which was a fake one kept for just such circumstances. Satisfied with the entries in the log, the officers left none the wiser that they had just been on board one of His Majesty's Q ships.

June 1940 saw the U-boats tighten their grip on Britain's maritime supply lines and nowhere was this more apparent than in the south-western approaches. Dozens of merchant ships had been sunk in the area, including six by U47, commanded by Prien, known as the 'Bull of Scapa Flow'. The Admiralty ordered *Prunella* to the area in the vain hope of enticing a U-boat to the surface.

47

In the small hours of 21 June, *Prunella* received a distress call from the *Otterpool* which had been torpedoed some eighty miles south of the Scilly Isles. Woodhall immediately set a course to intercept the U-boat, calculating that *Prunella* would arrive at the stricken ship at about 0900.

Prunella was steaming at full speed to the area when at 0750 a torpedo slammed into her hull, killing one man and injuring several others. Some of the crew immediately began to abandon ship in 'panic parties' which rowed away from the seemingly sinking ship. Meanwhile, those left on board secretly manned the concealed 4-inch guns and lay in wait for the U-boat to surface. The ship began to list to port but was in no danger of sinking as she was being kept afloat by the timber packed into her hold for just such an eventuality.

Beneath the waves, Kapitän Leutnant Gunter Kuhnke in U-28 scrutinised the scene briefly through his attack periscope. He thought he had just torpedoed an ordinary merchantman, which he estimated at between five and six thousand tons. Kuhnke had no idea she was a Q ship but he was not going to surface; instead he fired another torpedo thirty minutes after the first, which hit *Prunella* just below the bridge causing more damage and further casualties.

Slowly *Prunella* began to sink, but the men manned the guns until the water was lapping at their feet. Eventually Woodhall ordered the crew to abandon ship which they did in two lifeboats, two carley floats, a jolly boat and a raft. At 1250, exactly five hours after first being hit, *Prunella* finally sank.

Everyone was in good spirits as a distress signal had been transmitted, the sea was calm and they were only a hundred miles from Land's End. Rescue, it seemed, would come almost certainly later that day. However, during the evening a storm blew up, causing the boats to drift apart and out of sight of each other. It was three days before the first survivors were rescued; twenty-eight in one lifeboat were picked up by the French ship SS *Casamance*, outward bound from Bordeaux. Six days after *Prunella* went down, twelve men were rescued from the raft by the destroyer HMS *Versatile*. Of the remaining boats with fifty-six officers and men aboard, including Commander Woodhall, nothing was ever heard again. They succumbed to man's oldest adversaries – the sea and the weather.

Only eight days later another Q ship, *Edgehill*, was torpedoed in the South Western Approaches, again with heavy loss of life.

PART TWO

Commerce Raiders

CHAPTER V

Commerce Raiders: Threats of Attack

In the present day and age, submarines are arguably the most deadly enemies of merchant ships to be found in the expanses of the ocean. Aircraft, too, can be particularly lethal if merchant ships come within their range of operation. But over the centuries surface raiders have had an impressive history, and a heavily armed surface warship can still inflict a great deal of damage in a short space of time if it can get within range of a group of merchantmen, for example when these are formed into a convoy. The Allied invasion of Normandy in June 1944 saw one of the tasks of major Allied warships to be the provision of flank protection in the event that the remaining German capital ships might mount an assault on the seaborne landings and the huge array of shipping which had been deployed in support.

The two main aims of attack against a maritime country with an effective navy and, in particular, an island nation such as Great Britain, are its territory and its trade. As regards Britain, sea power has so far provided an adequate safeguard against both threats. The general lesson of history would seem to be quite clear: direct attacks on commerce by a navy which has not struggled for, and gained, command at sea should never be fatal. These attacks can be upsetting and tie down valuable resources, but if the necessary counter-measures are taken, such as warfare against the trade of the predominant naval power, they should not be decisive. As a means of disruption and pillage the *'guerre de course'* may be fulfilling. However, it has so far always failed as a means of overwhelming a strong antagonist.

In this section, the aim is to take a 'broad brush' look at commerce raiders with the emphasis on surface ships. Only a few examples will be examined in any detail to illustrate the general principles and to whet the appetite of readers towards studying books which deal with the subject in greater detail and put the adventures of individual vessels under a magnifying glass.

My attention was drawn to the problem of commerce raiders at the tender age of 5 in the early 1930s, when my parents took me, and my younger brother, to Hong Kong in the P & O liner RMS *Comorin* for what was to be a three-year 'tour' in the colony.

My mother had first travelled to Hong Kong with her parents in 1914 when she was in her early teens. Mother was adept at making the best of a good story and gave vivid details of the need to 'darken ship', and she implied that the liner in which her family were embarked was chased by the famous German cruiser *Emden* which, at that time, was causing varying degrees of panic amongst shipping in the Indian Ocean.

A year or two after my arrival in Hong Kong, an early film of the cruiser *Emden* was shown and I was duly taken to see the movie in question. In hindsight, it is believed that the last thing that the chivalrous Kapitän von Muller would have wanted to interfere with would have been a passenger liner. Had anything unpleasant happened to women and children, the gallant commanding officer of *Emden* would have had to stand by to receive a 'bad press' from the world's media. On the whole, captains of German surface raiders tended to be somewhat shy of tangling with passenger liners due to the problems of coping with female and very young prisoners.

When I was serving in the Royal Navy South Atlantic station, based at Simonstown, I grew interested in the Confederate raider *Alabama* and became extremely fond of the catchy song, 'Der Kom die Alabama' which seemed to be a 'standing dish' among the lively coloured bands which performed in the Cape Town area. *Alabama* had obviously made a great impression on southern Africa when she transferred her activities to the waters of the South Atlantic in 1863.

The long history of commerce raiding has involved ships of many types ranging from oriental junks, armed merchant ships and privateers to warships, including aircraft carriers, whose activities may have been diverted to this form of nautical activity. A powerful surface warship which has been let loose in the great open expanses of the ocean can exert great influence on all the armed ships which have been deployed to find her and, in the final event, to fix and destroy her.

The adrenalin must flow at a higher level when, say, the Escort Force Commander and Convoy Commodore know that a major hostile warship is operating in their general vicinity.

Naval battles are not engaged in with the object of conquering vast numbers of square miles of salt water. The aim is to obtain control of the seas in order that friendly ships may sail in them without hindrance, and that their use may be denied to the enemy. In the present age the dominion of sea areas cannot be complete if it does not work hand-in-hand with control of the skies. In earlier centuries pirates and other forms of predator, which have been mentioned previously, would lie in wait on major sea routes and in focal areas, rather like the shore-based footpad or highwayman, to sink or capture merchant ships.

Two exponents of the art of being a corsair, a slightly more polite word than pirate, were the English Sir Francis Drake in the sixteenth century, and the French Admiral Jean Bart in the seventeenth.

In 1570 Drake acted as a 'loner' and with two small vessels exploited a weakness in the Spanish system of using coasters and mules to bring gold, silver, jewels and other valuable commodities to 'collection points' in the Caribbean where they would be picked up by 'flotas' which were normally escorted before beginning the sea voyage to Spain.

In the seventeenth century Jean Bart, with a mere five frigates, managed to keep over fifty British and Dutch men-of-war at sea to counter his activities. Not a bad leverage to exert upon the navies of two acknowledged sea powers – one of whose principal objectives was to protect their seaborne trade. It is, possibly, thought-provoking to wonder whether Jean Bart's early service in the Dutch Navy might have encouraged exercises in 'lateral-thinking' when he had transferred his loyalty to the French.

In the days of sail, ships could remain at sea for very long periods. The limiting factor was the need for victuals and water for the subsistence of their crews. The effectiveness of the human being has to be sustained by food and drink. Without these requirements, the human body, all too rapidly, begins to descend the efficiency curve. The problems of survival in an open boat or upon a life-raft have provided too many examples of the physical frailty of men and women whose ships had to be abandoned in the two World Wars of the last century. The means of enhancing the probabilities of survival in abnormal circumstances have been the subject of study for many years and will continue to need to be addressed for many years to come.

Nuclear propulsion methods can enable ships and submarines to remain at sea for prolonged periods; but, once again, the humans who sail in these vessels need to be supported in time-honoured ways.

The digression on the subject of the sea-keeping qualities of ships is applicable to commerce raiders which need to avoid detection, to be far-ranging in their influence and to exploit the element of surprise whenever possible. To return to the sixteenth and seventeenth centuries, it is appropriate to mention the 'privateers' which flourished during the period between, say, 1520 and the late 1640s/early 1650s. People often ask for an explanation of what a privateer was. It can best be described as a ship used by quasi-legal freebooters whose employment consisted of attacking Spanish shipping and settlements in the Caribbean area at the time in question. In a number of cases privateers were pirates, but others were issued with 'letters of marque' by their own governments. 'Letters of marque' basically authorised the captains of privateers to attack Spanish treasure ships (and towns) as tools of war during the periods of strife with Spain. Drake and Hawkins from England in the late 1500s and the Dutchman, Piet Heyn, in the 1620s fall neatly into the category of privateers. There were also some disreputable French corsairs active at about the same time.

The port of Liverpool has a venerable and diverse maritime history which can be traced back to the reign of King John (1199–1216). By the middle of the eighteenth century, Liverpool had become the second seaport in Britain and enjoyed a virtual monopoly of trade in the Irish Sea. It had also built up a very large maritime trade which extended to the Continent, Africa, America and the West Indies. The slave trade, too, formed a lucrative branch of Liverpool endeavour until it was abolished in 1807 by Act of Parliament. Incidently, the last 'blackbirder' (slave trader) sailed from the Mersey in May 1808. The ship was called *Kitty Amelia*.

Another slightly disputable maritime venture in which Liverpool became involved during the Napoleonic Wars was that of privateering against the seaborne commerce of the French and the Americans. No fewer than a hundred and twenty privateers were fitted out by Liverpool shipowners at that time.

In last hundred years it may be difficult to comprehend that the merchants of civilised nations were permitted to steal their neighbours' belongings in time of war; but it happened. Firms engaged in this type of venture operated under 'letters of marque' and were permitted to fly their colours at the fore!

In general, privateers featured prominently in the ranks of commerce raiders. From the point of view of governments, they provided an economical instrument of attrition when participating in a *'guerre de course'*. They could also be a profitable investment for the merchants who fitted them out.

The American Civil War broke out in 1861 and will serve for a short study of the arts of commerce raiding and blockade running in the interim phase between the 'age of sail' and the wars of the twentieth century.

In the middle of the nineteenth century, the United States mercantile marine was carrying the star-spangled banner to most corners of the world and was of impressive size. However, the United States Navy was still small and bore scant relationship to the magnitude of the country's merchant fleet.

The southern states laboured under the burden of having practically negligible naval forces. When war did break out, common opinion had it that the struggle would have to be fought out on terra firma; but events proved this to be a false assumption. The northerners had a preponderance of industrial power and a great superiority in naval strength. Despite these obvious advantages, they were unexpectedly exposed to the depradations of privateers and the activities of southern blockade-runners which, for a period, seriously threatened the northern sea communications. When Virginia went over to the side of the Confederates, the frontier between the warring sides was drawn in the area of Chesapeake Bay; and the great arsenal at Norfolk, which is still of world-class proportions, fell into the lap of the Confederates.

One of the first incidents of the Civil War involved a ship and took place when shore batteries sited at Charleston engaged the Federal *Star of the West*.

The strange thing was that the northerners seemed to make not the slightest effort to hinder the Confederates from building up a modest naval force which would later prove to be a 'thorn in the flesh'.

Captain Raphael Semmes, who was to prove to be one of the south's most successful naval commanders, was still serving with the US Navy in February 1861. He resigned before going over to the Confederates, but continued to move freely about the northern states. President Davis had given him the mission of placing orders for munitions and machinery, for the Confederates, with factories situated in the north. He was even empowered to work with state arsenals if this should prove to be possible.

In April 1861 the Confederates acquired their first warship. This was the *Merrimack,* a heavily armed,steam-powered frigate and prototype of a new class of fighting ship which was being re-fitted in the naval dockyard at Norfolk. The northerners were planning to have her towed to Philadelphia before the state of Virginia declared for the Confederacy. They were overtaken by events as the Virginians made their decision to join the south while *Merrimack* was still in the hands of Norfolk dockyard. She was scuttled by a demolition squad which arrived in the USS *Pawnee* and tried to carry out a 'scorched earth' exercise directed at the arsenal's workshops and installations in general.

The southerners later managed to raise the frigate, clad her with armour-plating and renamed her *Virginia*. In this guise she became a powerful addition to the Confederate naval forces.

The Federal Navy was, in the meantime, doing its best to maintain an effective blockade of southern ports. The Confederate States had insignificant industrial potential and were obliged to import the bulk of their arms and munitions. Of equal importance, they needed to export their cotton to cover the cost of their essential imports. Trade was the lifeblood of the Confederate war effort.

During the first two years of the American Civil War, some eight hundred and fifty blockade-runners were reported as having been captured by Union ships. This was no small number.

The principal centre of the blockade-running activity was Bermuda; and the vessels used tended to be lengthy, lean paddle-steamers which were capable of attaining speeds of circa seventeen knots. Interestingly, these craft burned anthracite which produced less smoke than coal. They were painted grey which helped them to be less conspicuous when at sea. The colour grey is generally used to paint warships to this day and for the same reason.

It was not only cargo to satisfy the logistic requirements of war that blockade-runners embarked at Bermuda. Luxury goods, spirits and pretty well anything that was in short supply in the war-torn southern states was worth loading. This side of the Civil War is vividly covered in Margaret Mitchell's brilliant novel *Gone with the Wind*.

The blockade-runners used their speed to outrun the Union ships. They would make port at night, rapidly discharge cargo and put to sea again, loaded with cotton, before blockading ships, which might be at anchor off the port of discharge, had time to be alerted, weigh anchor and get under way. A hard night's work but, no doubt, remunerative.

Blockade-running was undoubtedly a dangerous business; but the rewards could be highly profitable. It has been said that freight charges were such that three auspicious voyages could pay for the cost of a suitable ship. The captains of blockade-runners could make several thousand dollars per month as opposed to their normal peacetime wages which could be somewhere on either side of, say, one hundred and fifty dollars a month.

The Confederates had an answer to the blockade. This was to divert commerce raiders to make inroads into the Union's seaborne trade. Even though comparatively few privateers were engaged in this counter-attack, results exceeded the most optimistic hopes. During the first six months of the struggle, some sixty Union merchantmen were seized. These early successes, with ships which had been fitted out in their poorly equipped yards, raised Confederate morale and caused them to look elsewhere. Orders placed with British shipbuilders followed. The British Government was technically neutral, but it seemed to have no qualms about extending assistance to the Confederate States,whose ships were permitted to use British harbours as ports of call and to allow them to place orders for new ships.

Once again, trade (or the lack of it) gave strong economic roots to the growth of British lack of enthusiasm for the north. The Union blockade was responsible for the loss of money to British shipping interests. The menace of curtailed deliveries of cotton to the mills of Lancashire resulted in deep resentment in the British commercial circles affected. Despite the threat of unemployment and the consequent hardships, the majority of the British working classes tended to stand by the north as they favoured the anti-slavery ticket.

The extent of the assistance given to the south can be estimated by the fact that a Neutral Commission, convened in Geneva in 1869–72, called upon Britain to pay the United States of America the then considerable sum of fifteen and a half million dollars in compensation for damage caused by Confederate privateers which had been fitted out with British connivance.

The privateer (commerce raider) which was most frequently cited during the course of the judicial proceedings was the *Alabama*, which had a score of seventy-one seizures of Union ships to her credit. A short study of *Alabama*'s exploits should give a worthwhile glimpse into commerce raiding in this period of history.

The ship had been laid down in the Laird Shipbuilding Yard, Birkenhead and was designated by the number 290. She was basically a three-masted barque with an auxiliary engine which could give a maximum speed of about thirteen and a half knots. At this stage in her career, no armament had been supplied.

The officer appointed to command *Alabama*, as it would be convenient to call the ship from now on, was the Captain Raphael Semmes who has been briefly mentioned earlier. Incidentally, *Alabama* was one of three ships to be built at Birkenhead for the Confederacy whose agents made no attempt to hide the aim that the ships would ultimately be armed and employed in the role of privateers.

The British Government had announced its neutrality and the proper form had to be kept up. Consent clearly could not be given for warships to be built in English yards for one or other of the warring sides. The contracts for the ships were alleged to be on behalf of the Government of France, or of the Khedive of Egypt. However, one day a ship's company arrived to take over the *Alabama*. When Captain Semmes wrote his *Memoirs*, he described his crew as 'a hundred and ten of the most reckless boozers from the Liverpool pubs'. They were a tough outfit and, no doubt, tested the leadership skills of their officers to the utmost.

Alabama's trials took place quietly under the command of a Captain J Butcher who had been 'induced' to leave Cunard, his parent company, to act as a stand-in until Semmes could join the ship. No doubt, Butcher had been tempted by the offer of a substantial sum of money to leave Cunard for a short, but possibly, risky engagement with the Confederacy, the aim being that he should take the ship to a foreign port.

One evening, during the trials period, Butcher omitted to return to port, probably having gained intelligence that the ship was likely to be seized by the port authorities on directions received from the British Government who were being pressurised by the Federals.

A convivial party had been arranged on board, the guests having been invited to act as 'cover' for preparations being made to get the ship ready for sea. A tug had been organised to take off the visitors, male and female, before the ship had progressed very far.

Some days later *Alabama* reached the Azores. On 18 August 1862 the barque *Agrippine* of London joined her, bringing the weapons and ammunition, which had been clandestinely loaded, and a large supply of coal.

During the conversion of the ship to armed raider, the Portuguese authorities turned a 'blind eye' to the proceedings. A couple of days later, Captain Semmes arrived to take over his command. On Sunday 24 August Captain Semmes took his ship to sea and read out to the ship's company his commission from the President of the Confederated States to the command of the steam-sloop CSS *Alabama*.

The length and breadth of the Atlantic Ocean was *Alabama*'s oyster and during the course of the next two months she apprehended twenty enemy ships and burned them, as there was no means of securing the vessels whose crews were taken prisoner.

A further rendezvous with *Agrippine* had been organised in Martinique; but an intruder arrived in the shape of the USS *San Jacinto*, which was larger and fitted with a heavier armament than was *Alabama*. Fortunately for the latter, the US warship was not so fast and *Alabama* managed to give her the slip during the hours of darkness. Before they parted company, *Alabama* had arranged to meet with *Agrippine* in Venezualan waters. All went according to plan, and as soon as *Alabama* had replenished, the raider again put out to sea where she soon added another 'scalp' to her collection. On Sunday 7 December a very large side-wheel steamer came into sight, heading southward. It could only be a Californian ship bound towards the isthmus with passengers, not from there with gold. The *Alabama* set course to cross the track of the stranger who was wearing the flag of the Union. The *Alabama* was flying the same flag and was, understandably, assumed to be an American ship. However, as the two vessels came within range, the *Alabama* exchanged the Confederate flag for the Stars and Stripes and fired a blank round to indicate that the other ship was required to stop. The warning was ignored and the target proceeded on her way at speed. A live round discharged by *Alabama* struck the foremast of the other vessel which then came to and surrendered. The large prize turned out to be the Californian ship *Ariel* which had some five hundred passengers on board and a hundred and forty Federal marines who were on their way to join the US Pacific squadron.

The *Alabama* was embarrassed by the sheer size of this prize. *Ariel* was carrying much that was of value, for example, three boxes of specie, weapons and thousands of rounds of ammunition. Semmes would have liked to make a bonfire of this captive ship, but could not contemplate this until the large number of prisoners had been dealt with. Apart from anything else, the narrow deck of his ship could not even provide standing room for more than about half of the captives. The earlier prisoners taken by *Alabama* were already having a far from comfortable passage.

Captain Semmes kept his prize in company for two days in the hope that he might chance upon a Californian ship which was homeward-bound, transfer his prisoners and then make a bonfire of *Ariel*. This wish was not fulfilled.

The next plan was to close Kingston, Jamaica, land the prisoners in boats and then set fire to *Ariel*. However, when Semmes learned that a yellow fever epidemic was raging in Kingston, he had not the heart to put a crowd of men, women and children ashore in a plague-ridden harbour. He came to the decision that his only option was to regretfully release *Ariel* upon bond.

Perhaps, to date, *Alabama* had run no great risks; but the situation changed when off Galveston on 11 January 1863 she met a division of Union ships which was intended to support a landing of northern troops. The raider, at this time disguised as a British ship, the *Petrel*, knew of the proposed Union expedition against Galveston, but was not aware that the place had been recaptured by Confederates and that the Union exercise had been delayed. Several vessels were observed lying off the bar. One of these, the gun-boat *Hatteras*, caught sight of *Alabama* in the distance and stood out to investigate. Semmes edged slowly seaward and succeeded in drawing the Union vessel some twenty miles away from her consorts. The rate at which *Hatteras* approached indicated that she was no match for *Alabama* as far as speed was concerned. The latter could be confident that she could make her escape if it became evident that she was involved with a more powerful opponent.

Soon after dark, *Hatteras* had approached within hailing distance. There was an exchange of hails when suddenly *Alabama* revealed her real identity, unmasked her guns and put paid to the smaller vessel. *Hatteras* went down in flames very shortly after the last of her company were taken off.

Alabama had suffered some damage, but nothing which could have been claimed to have in any way disabled her. Two of her ship's company were slightly injured.

On board *Hatteras* two were killed and five were wounded. The boat's crew, which put off shortly before action was joined, pulled the twenty miles to shore: a longish pull, but perfectly feasible. All the remainder, over a hundred strong, became prisoners and were taken to Kingston where they were landed.

Alabama prowled among the West Indian islands for two months. In about mid-March she tracked southwards along the coast, taking a significant number of prizes on the way. The ship reached Bahia in Brazil by the middle of May. Here she met the *Georgia*, a fellow Confederate raider, and embarked coal and received repeated warnings from the Brazilian authorities that she was not a welcome visitor due to Brazil's fear of giving offence to the northern Americans.

Alabama's next move was to steam across the South Atlantic heading for the African coast. She made port in the Cape on 5 August and loitered in these waters for over a month.

Alabama's eventual departure from Simonstown was hastened by the knowledge that the Union steamer *Vanderbilt*, of superior strength, had been despatched to search for the raider and was operating not far from the Cape.

Alabama sailed at night, to give *Vanderbilt* the slip, and into the teeth of a gale. The Cape of Good Hope was once known as the 'Cape of Storts' and, on this occasion, lived up to its early name. Perhaps, it was ships seen battling against the elements as they tried to work their way round the Cape which helped to add verisimilitude to the legend of the 'Flying Dutchman'.

The activities of *Alabama* were shifted to the Indian Ocean and the China Sea. It is interesting to observe that her score of prizes increased markedly more slowly than had been the case in previous months. This was partly due to the fact that Union merchant ships were transferring to foreign flags at a startling rate because their owners were growing shy of sending them to sea under their own flag.

Semmes brought the *Alabama* back to Europe in the summer of 1864 after twenty months of cruising the world's ocean routes and having had a myriad of experiences and adventures which are beyond the scope of this scrutiny. Two more ships were captured in the Atlantic which brought the raider's total up to seventy-one. On 11 July *Alabama* was off Cherbourg where permission was requested to enter harbour for a much-needed refit.

The news of the raider's arrival 'set the cat among the pigeons' among Union representatives stationed in Europe. Semmes had, hitherto, always contrived to elude his pursuers because communications at that time tended to be slow and inadequate. However, good telegraphic communication systems had been implemented in Europe and the United States consul managed to pass a message to the USS *Kearsage* which was then at Flushing. The *Kearsage* put in an appearance three days after *Alabama* had secured in Cherbourg.

The *Kearsage*'s commanding officer Captain John A Winslow, had been a colleague of Semmes in the less complicated days of the Mexican War, but his mind could not dwell on thoughts of former friendship in the current situation. *Kearsage* passed close to the *Alabama* almost in an act of defiance, then proceeded to patrol beyond the harbour mole. Semmes did not keep him waiting for very long.

The French Minister of Foreign Affairs had ordered *Alabama* to leave. Semmes would be obliged to face up to *Kearsage* whether he wanted to or not. The only other options seemed to be internment or to desert the ship, which would have involved Semmes, and the Confederacy, in an unacceptable 'loss of face'. Another consideration was that, if *Alabama* delayed too long, other Federal vessels might have time to appear upon the scene.

Semmes decided to play the knightly part of sending a challenge to his adversary. Word of this gallant challenge spread like wildfire throughout Europe. A British yacht, *Deerhound,* chanced to appear in the area, before the day of the battle. Cherbourg hotels and boarding houses soon filled to capacity and an excursion train conveyed some twelve hundred Parisians to watch the spectacle from the heights of Cherbourg.

Alabama got under way at about 1030 in the forenoon of Sunday 19 June and sailed past the considerable French fleet which was occupying the harbour at that time. The ship's company of the line-of-battle ship *Napoleon* manned the rigging and gave three cheers as *Alabama* glided past, to the astonishment of Semmes and his crew.

The two ships were pretty evenly matched. The USS *Kearsage* had a ship's company of a hundred and sixty-three to the CSS *Alabama's* one hundred and forty-nine, and *Kearsage* had seven guns to the latter's eight. *Kearsage's* broadside was marginally (about seventy pounds) the heavier of the two. The weather was excellent with light airs and only a very few clouds to deface a predominantly blue sky.

The Union ship was accompanied outside territorial waters by a French warship which then acted as a guardian of the three-mile limit during the entire engagement.

Alabama opened fire first at two thousand yards, as soon as she was outside French territorial waters. The Confederate ship had been fitted with British-made rifled guns which somewhat outranged *Kearsage's* armament.

The engagement was rather an unusual one. Each ship tried to rake its opponent and they moved in concentric circles as dogs might when chasing each other's tails. The circling exercise went on for about an hour or so, with each vessel firing at the other and drawing closer together until they were of the order of six hundred yards apart. The shooting from *Kearsage* was the more effective, which was perhaps understandable in view of the somewhat hotchpotch make-up of Alabama's ship's company. Captain Winslow had thoughtfully achieved some protection for his engine room area by spreading chain cable over the sides of his ship.

Alabama discharged about three hundred and seventy shots of which only fourteen are said to have achieved hits on the *Kearsage*. Not a very impressive rate of striking.

After the ships had been enjoined for about a quarter of an hour, *Alabama* contrived to lodge a hundred-pound percussion shell in *Kearsage's* quarter, near her propeller, but this projectile did not explode. This shot might have had a critical impact upon the course of the battle, had the round functioned properly. A case of 'for want of a nail, a shoe was lost'.

Towards the end of the hour's steaming in circles, a fortuitous eleven-inch shot from *Kearsage* put the privateer's engines out of action. Semmes attempted to make more sail; but it was of no use. His ship was foundering, he struck his colours and hoisted a white flag almost simultaneously. The ship which had dispatched so many other unarmed vessels was at last being sunk herself. Soon after 1220 the *Alabama* was going down by the stern and the water was filled with struggling men who were trying to swim clear before they were caught in the suction of a sinking ship. Wounded men were the only persons who had been catered for in *Alabama*'s few remaining boats. Finally, the doomed ship's bow was thrown high in the air and she then slipped under the waves.

Captain Semmes and about forty of his ship's company were rescued by the British yacht *Deerhound,* and some French craft which had rapidly put out from Cherbourg. With the exception of about a dozen killed, the remainder were taken prisoner on board *Kearsage.* Included among those who met their fate on board *Alabama* was the ship's doctor, a Welshman named David Herbert Llewellyn, who gallantly refused to abandon the remaining wounded and accompanied them down with the sinking ship.

Alabama was not the last of the Confederate commerce raiders. The *Shenandoah* was fitted out in October 1864, and succeeded in destroying thirty-six Union ships, most of which were engaged after hostilities had been terminated. News of the end of the Civil War, in those pre-radio days, took a long time to reach the raiders. *Shenandoah* created such havoc among the whaling fleet in the North Pacific that tradition has it that it has never been fully restored to its former importance.

The *Alabama*'s career has been covered with a minimum of detail; but the ship's exploits do provide a good picture of a commerce raider's operations and the effect that this can have on a more powerful navy. The American mercantile marine suffered gravely from the attentions of the Confederate privateers; but these failed to have an overwhelming effect upon the course of the war.

A plus point for the Union Navy was that the Civil War produced unique opportunities for the northern officers and naval engineers to develop new armaments and to play a leading role in the evolution of sea warfare, which was being subjected to great changes with the introduction of steam propulsion and the growth of more modern forms of seaborne ordnance. The advances in question were all leading towards the development of modern navies.

CHAPTER VI

The Gentle Guile of German
Sea-raiding in World War I

The First World War provides a chronicle of German sea-raiding on the surface which is of fascinating interest both in terms of detailed and careful planning, and the daring and determination with which the plans were transformed into effective operations.

The policies that determined the German submarine campaigns tended to be carried out with great persistence and resulted in a wearing-down process which came uncomfortably close to success as far as Britain and her Allies were concerned.

In contrast, surface attacks on Allied shipping resulted in a series of glittering achievements and adventurous successes which add up to one of the more exciting fragments of the history of naval warfare.

In the First World War, this particular phase of the struggle was more intermittent than the pressure of the U-boat campaign, yet the scope of operations was more wide-reaching. It also required an organisation that had to be in place and in working order before the war in Europe broke out. This meant that reliable officials had to be deployed overseas who could maintain a highly confidential system during times when communications with Berlin might be unreliable or even impracticable. As has been the case in most maritime conflicts, the German pre-war aim, as regards merchant ships, must have been twofold, that is to preserve her own maritime property and to destroy as many as possible of her enemies' vessels.

In the context of World War I, how could the above two aims be achieved and what were some of the problems which could be anticipated for the Germans to meet while carrying out these aims?

In the final event, it would be seen that the carrying out of well-laid plans was adequately rewarded. The vast organisation for assaulting ocean commerce was put into operation with surprising speed, and it functioned extremely well. The same energy, farsightedness and shrewd cunning which had built up the German Mercantile Marine in the order of three score years and ten, managed to arrange that rivals should suffer from the moment when peaceful competition came to an end. Germany, in 1914, was second only to the British Empire when it came to owning steamships; but, perhaps, the Germans displayed greater cohesion when it came to managing its shipping.

Approximately sixty per cent of German shipping was in the hands of ten companies. This added up to one powerful association which was ready to act in the government's service. The big ten were the Hamburg-Amerika, the North German Lloyd, the Hamburg South American, the Hewsa, the German-Australian, The Kosmos, the Roland, the German East Africa, the Woermann and the Hamburg-Bremen-Africa lines. This huge conglomerate represented 3,194,000 tons and there was also the German Levant line of some 155,000 tons. Monetarily subsidised by the Government, the whole of the German Mercantile Fleet was, to all intents and purposes, a potent national combine.

The British Honourable East India Company had been the largest ship-owner in the history of the world until the nineteenth century. In August 1914 all this had changed, and the Hamburg-Amerika Line with its fleet of some five hundred vessels, seventy-five services serving four hundred ports and carrying over four hundred thousand passengers per annum, had become the largest shipping corporation ever. This had been achieved from its founding in May 1847 with three smallish sailing ships. By the eve of the First World War, it owned well over a million tons of steam ships.

A similar story could be told of the North German Lloyd Company whose first Atlantic steamer was the *Bremen* built by Laird of Greenock in 1858. The wealth of the company's passenger trade was such that in the year 1897 they were able to launch the twin-screw *Kaiser Wilhelm der Grosse*. This ship had a speed of over twenty-two knots, was able to outrun the *Campania* and *Luciana* and, for the first time, take the blue riband of the Atlantic from Britain. This four-funnelled liner was, later, to play a noteworthy part in the story of commerce-raiding.

It is worth recording that, at this time, the German Merchant Navy's policy was to rely principally upon liner trades. Germany was able to build costly mammoth passenger steamers, often quite capable of breaking records, because she had attracted a considerable share of the emigrant traffic from the continent of Europe, rather as Holland had built up an imposing mercantile fleet in the seventeenth century, based upon herring fisheries. Two hundred years later, Germany created a superb commercial navy on the backs of poor emigrants from Russia. At one period there was an average yearly emigration of about a 113,000 Germans to the United States of America; but this figure had declined by about two thirds in the decade which ended in 1914. To compensate, the stream of emigrants wishing to change their homes in Russia for habitations in North America steadily increased from an average of two thousand per annum in the decade which ended in 1874, to the best part of 200,000 per annum shortly before the outbreak of the First World War.

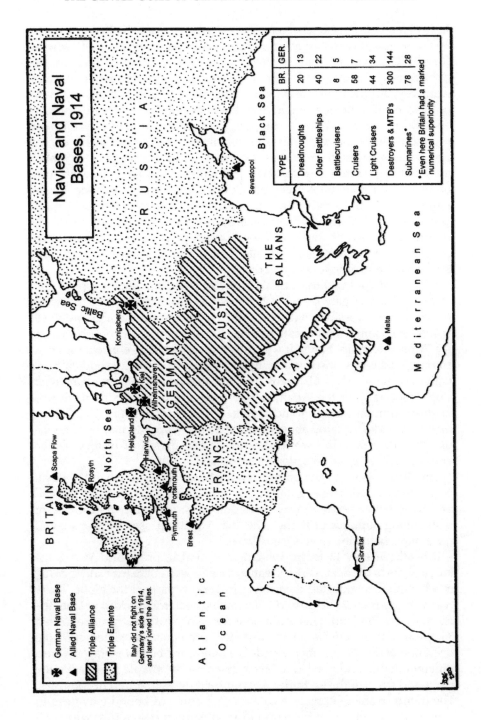

Navies and Naval Bases, 1914

TYPE	BR.	GER.
Dreadnoughts	20	13
Older Battleships	40	22
Battlecruisers	8	5
Cruisers	58	7
Light Cruisers	44	34
Destroyers & MTB's	300	144
Submarines*	78	28

* Even here Britain had a marked numerical superiority

German Naval Base
Allied Naval Base
Triple Alliance
Triple Entente

Italy did not fight on Germany's side in 1914, and later joined the Allies.

In 1894 the German Government, in its wisdom, established what were to be known as control stations at various positions along the frontier with Russia. The original aim of these stations was purported to be the prevention of the spread of cholera by Russian emigrants passing through Germany, but the interesting point is that the building and management of the control stations was placed in the hands of the Hamburg-Amerika and North German Lloyd shipping companies, arguably a form of privatisation. Be that as it may, the companies used the stations in such a profitable manner that it was extremely difficult for any potential emigrant to get through unless he expressed the intention to travel by one of the two shipping lines involved. Government legislation made it even more difficult and costly for emigrant passengers to reach the United States except in German ships. Facilities such as through rates over the continental railways and the geographical position of German ports contrived to steer hordes of travellers into German-American ships and thus ensure a steady flow of revenue.

By way of contrast, the British Isles depended for their supplies and overseas trade largely on what is known as the tramp steamer, a name which scarcely does much justice to the many beautifully built and well-found steamships of moderate tonnage which made their contribution to the British Merchant Navy. It was these vessels which were keeping their country's factories, institutions, finances and actual living bodies from withering away, while Germany concentrated on ocean-going passenger ships, especially in the Atlantic. Sixty per cent of British tonnage was made up of tramp steamers and a mere forty per cent of liners. This 'loose', mobile superiority came about because British shipping had become the principal carrier of the world, just as, at one period of history, Dutch vessels were the great 'waggoners of the sea'.

The British Tramp Fleet amply demonstrated its value when the Royal Navy demanded large numbers of auxiliaries after July 1914; and extremely heavy pressure was exerted upon cargo-carrying steamers for maintaining supplies at home. The fast Atlantic passenger ships could never have had enough space available.

It is all too easy to forget the extent to which, pre-World War I, the movements of the fleet were traceable to the seasons of nature and the way in which they manifested themselves in various parts of the globe. There was a steady trade to be carried out in taking coal from Cardiff or from the north-east of England. This continuous movement of coal from the United Kingdom had its effects on the logistical problems associated with the operation of hostile commerce raiders. Homeward-bound voyages were a different matter and needed to be modified for the simple reason that the crops and fruits of the earth ripen at different times in different countries. The tramp steamer acting as a collier when outward-bound may need to wander from one part of the world to another in order to return with such commodities as corn, rice, wheat, sugar, jute, wool or cotton to name but a few. It is difficult to plan such movements to anything like a strict timetable; the tramp steamer tended to have to go where she was wanted and when required. In the month of January, the Burma rice crop would be waiting to be shipped before the monsoons broke; the Calcutta jute season opened in August; the Australian wheat trade began in December; the United States grain trade in July, and so on.

It is not to be denied that there was a steady flow of cargoes borne in British ships which also carried passengers, even though these would not have been the fastest vessels. Some liners had to give priority, not to the transport of human beings, but to commodities which were needed with both regularity and despatch. A collier could saunter along at slow speed; but the delivery of, say, foreign meat, bananas and various other products should not be delayed. In the event of war breaking out, it would be strategically sound for Germany to conceal her liners in the most opportune harbours, and to deploy cruisers to harass vessels transporting cargoes to the British Isles. It was not wise to attack purely passenger liners or even those which carried half cargo and half people for reasons which have been touched upon. Perhaps, the most cost-effective achievement would be to intercept a large freighter conveying, say, meat from South America, or grain from North America; or any other supplies which were needed for the prosecution of the war or for the continuance of life in the enemy country.

It followed that raiders would have to reach the trade-routes along which important seaborne traffic must pass. For the few sailing ships which survived into the 1914–1918 War there were recognised routes across the face of the oceans, based upon the direction of the trade winds. The tracks for steam ships were as obviously delineated, subject to navigational hazards, as a road stretched across any length of country. The meeting point of two, or more, sea routes implied a potentially lucrative patrol station for any raider. For example, the waters in the vicinity of the Canary Islands are an area of convergence through which a vast quantity of shipping passes. It is not surprising to see that this part of the ocean, off the north-west coast of Africa, was a popular hunting ground for German raiders.

Another self-evident position was the north-west shoulder of Brazil near Cape San Roque, for here the seaborne traffic divides into that which can be seen proceeding north-west to the West Indies and the Atlantic seaboard of the United States, and that flowing north-east to the Canaries. It was, therefore, no great surprise that German raiders should be found operating off the cape and the adjacent Roca Reef. The North American route from the United States and Canada to Europe was, without much doubt, the most precious of all. At the same time it did present problems for a raider.

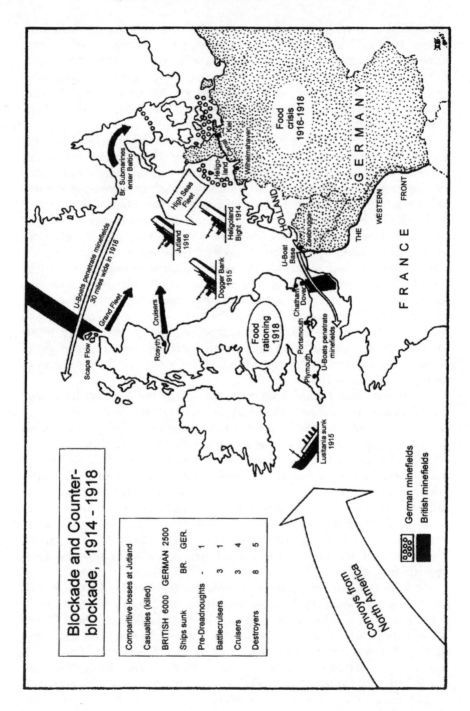

Blockade and Counter-blockade, 1914 - 1918

Comparitive losses at Jutland

Casualties (killed)

BRITISH 6000   GERMAN 2500

Ships sunk	BR.	GER.
Pre-Dreadnoughts	-	1
Battlecruisers	3	1
Cruisers	3	4
Destroyers	8	5

German minefields

British minefields

Convoys from North America

Food crisis 1916-1918

Br. Submarines enter Baltic

Heligo- land

Canal Kiel

Wilhelmshaven

HOLLAND

U-Boats penetrate minefields 30 miles wide in 1918

High Seas Fleet

Jutland 1916

Heligoland Bight 1914

Dogger Bank 1915

U-Boat Base

Zeebrugge

Grand Fleet

Cruisers

Scapa Flow

Rosyth

Food rationing 1918

Chatham

Dover

Portsmouth

Plymouth

U-Boats penetrate minefields

GERMANY

THE   WESTERN   FRONT

FRANCE

Lusitania sunk 1915

The aim of a surface raider was to destroy; but, simultaneously to conceal both his whereabouts and his very existence, if possible. If he cruised much over the North Atlantic routes, the chances were that he would be seen, sooner or later, by some fast passenger liner which would, by superior speed, have every opportunity of escaping, and of reporting the raider's position. For this reason, there was little North Atlantic raiding in World War I except, later, by submarines, and on those somewhat rare occasions when a surface raider happened to cross a traffic lane while proceeding to, or from, her designated operational area.

The last four centuries saw whatever sea route which was being used to India become an enticing passage to tempt the enemies of merchant ships. In various ages the rich commerce being conveyed to European destinations from the Orient has been ambushed as close to its place of origin as the Indian Ocean and as near to its journey's end as the Bay of Biscay or the English Channel. The completion of the Suez Canal in 1869 opened a more modern, and direct, Eastern route via the Mediterranean and the canal. This seemed to imply that the obvious areas in which to deploy raiders should be in the approaches to the Strait of Gibraltar or to the east of the Red Sea. The German cruiser *Emden*, of which more anon, chose the latter, and during a meteoric spell of activity caused noteworthy mayhem in the Indian Ocean.

Thinking in terms of the First World War era, the factor of speed had to be reckoned with. If the raider was slow, but economical in fuel consumption, she would obviously have been no match for the then state of the art fast cargo ships, and she could not hope to overhaul any vessel which had achieved a fair start before the onset of nightfall. Nor should the raider, necessarily, have been capable of achieving especially high speed, for that would mean immoderate consumption of fuel and require frequent access to fuel supplies. Further complications could be incurred when, thanks to a special emergency, the engines might be driven beyond their normal limits which would invite mechanical failure and even the destruction of propulsion units.

At the time under consideration, four facts regarding commerce raiding would seem to stand out. First, when a raider had reached a regular trade route, only very bad luck could prevent her from inflicting a vast amount of damage on enemy shipping. Second, the series of captures and sinkings can go on for months at a time. Third, a raider had to rely, for fuel, upon her own colliers being examples of reliability when it came to arriving at classified rendezvous at the specified times or upon feeding from enemy colliers which first had to be detected and then captured along the traffic routes; of these two options, the first could be risky, and advisable only as an extemporary measure until prizes had begun to be made of enemy vessels. Fourth, with few exceptions, the raider, however lucky and aggressive, was not able to avoid being eventually destroyed herself, provided that she was hunted down by an efficient cruiser force. The chase could be drawn out for weeks, or months, but sooner or later she would become a victim, hopefully as certainly as it was believed that a criminal would discover that crime does not ultimately pay.

A problem which has bedevilled surface raiders throughout the years is that of what should be done with prisoners. World War I raiders were no strangers to this dilemma. When several victims had surrendered, the raider could collect a considerable party of prisoners and would be keen to put the captives ashore as soon as reasonably practicable. This was often done by transferring the accumulated prisoner crews into one of the vessels which had been taken captive. When the disgruntled mariners had been landed, smarting from their internment, it is well-nigh impossible to think of any way in which they could be obliged to keep their mouths shut. It would not be very long before the press, representatives of owners, consular authorities, etc. would be informed that the raider had been encountered in a particular position, on a certain date. In certain circumstances, and if the information was not too out-of-date, the intelligence gained could give searching forces a useful datum upon which to work.

During the American Civil War it is understood that the officers of the *Shenandoah* questioned Captain James Waddell's decision when he arranged for the Danish brig *Anna Jans* to take their prisoners to the neutral port of Rio de Janeiro. It was argued that once the captives were ashore they would give the American consul valuable details of the *Shenandoah*, including her last known location, course, speed, size of ship's company, state of armaments, and so on. There is not much that has not been thought of before.

The use of the Pacific Ocean as a hunting ground for raiders in World War I has scarcely been mentioned. In general, the Pacific was not given the same attention as the Atlantic and for a very good reason. The Panama Canal had not been opened to shipping when war was declared. There was some interest in the five-thousand odd mile tracks between the Far East and Vancouver or San Francisco; in the routes between western America and Australia; in the localised shipping between Sydney and New Zealand. There was an even greater chance of a raider's cruise in the Pacific being a rewarding exercise after the United States had entered the war. In due course German raiders of both the regular and ad hoc variety used lonely Pacific islands and unfrequented channels with lofty disregard for international law; but with important benefits to themselves. Colour and drama were introduced as if to show that the dull-coloured North Sea with its vast grey battle-fleets was not the sole theatre of the maritime war.

In general, it was not the Pacific Ocean, with its vast distances and, perhaps, somewhat scarce number of ships which became the most seductive region for attacks on commerce, but that portion of the South

Atlantic where the ocean is narrowest and where the greatest concentration of valuable cargo-carriers sailed. The navy did not exist which could expect to station protecting cruisers to ensure that merchant shipping proceeding on its lawful occasions might escape from interference all of the time. This on the basis that 'he who tries to protect everything, protects nothing'. The best that might be attempted was to ensure that friendly naval units might be on hand in carefully chosen areas, such as the Canaries or Cape Verde. Visits to these lonely islands and reefs, which were suspected of providing rendezvous for replenishment, could be fruitful, as was the surveillence of areas in which it was known that captures had taken place.

Defensive measures such as those already mentioned were more involved than might be thought at first glance. The commanding officers of ships entrusted with the task of harassing the overseas trade of their opponents tended to be specially selected and would try to take advantage of every possible occurrence, actual or anticipated. They were adept at using clever stage management to create a sense of uncertainty, by taking care to see that between their operations and the news of the same becoming a commonplace a sufficient time-scale should have elapsed to allow their raider to have moved a significant distance from the scene of their latest action. Matters were further complicated, for hunting warships, by the dissemination of unsubstantiated and frequently worthless rumours. An elusive game was, in the meantime, being played which could become tantalising when the hunters never seemed to be able to catch sight of the pursued.

Some of the problems and possibilities in a campaign for striking severe blows against the British Mercantile Marine have been looked at. Privateering was no longer permissable at the time of the First World War. Probably, the nearest approach to the actions taken when letters of marque were granted in former years was to be seen in the activities of armed merchant cruisers against lightly-armed non-combatants. It would be interesting now to take a look at how the Germans devised their pre-1914 plans and how the plans were converted into action.

CHAPTER VII

Early First World War German Raiders

As the start of the First World War approached, Germany was nominally inferior to Great Britain as regards naval strength. However, this inferiority in warship numbers could, to a certain extent, be offset by the fact that the Germans owned a large fleet of fine ocean liners. These vessels, with the help of assiduous organisation, could be rapidly transformed into armed merchant cruisers. The external alteration needed was negligible and could basically be achieved by the application of black paint. The more they looked like ocean liners, the less likely they were to excite suspicion when they were encountered at sea. Once they had replenished their stocks of fuel and taken provisions on board, they could be fitted with guns and sent to sea to intercept the merchantmen whose efficacy was vital to the existence of those who inhabited the British Isles. In certain regions there had to be arrangements for the availability of fuel, in those days predominantly coal, and a proportion of this supply needed to be mobile. This implied that a number of well-laden colliers had to be deployed to suitable centres, at reasonably short notice for steam, so that they could sail for assigned rendezvous with a minimum of delay.

On the credit side for the Germans, some three-quarters of Britain's exports was made up of coal. This meant that Germany's armed ocean liners could always rely, with some confidence, upon being able to help themselves to an adequate stock of seaborne coal as they went along.

With teutonic thoroughness, the Germans had issued instructions to the masters of their liners about six years before the onset of hostilities in 1914. Very briefly, these directions ordained that if a ship was lying in a neutral port, and hostilities appeared to be imminent, the ship was to remain where she was. If she was on passage, she must head for the nearest neutral port and await further instructions. The orders were supplemented as late as February 1914. Every captain of a North German Lloyd vessel, equipped with radio equipment, received a classified document which informed him that, in order to announce the outbreak of war, news would be transmitted by the Nordreich wireless station. All German ships were to set listening watch at 0700, 1300 and 2310 GMT. In April 1914 it was directed that radio communication was to be initiated between German merchant vessels and men-of-war.

The German Admiralty had produced a 'Cruiser Handbook'. This included a number of classified rendezvous where liners, so directed, could proceed without delay to be fitted with guns and supplied with ammunition. One of the localities was close to the Bahamas, another was off the lovely island of Trinidad in the South Atlantic, another was a most unfriendly spot several hundred miles east of Brazil whose reputation was infamous for its horrendous land-crabs, high seas and for futile visits by optimistic treasure seekers who could be certain of discovering one thing, its barrenness. To give a few examples, it was off the Bahamas that the *Kronprinz Wilhelm* was changed into a raider; Trinidad was the rendezvous where *Dresden* and *Cap Trafalgar* both topped up with fuel taken from German colliers during the early weeks of the war; but, perhaps most interestingly, it was here that the German steamship *Navarra*, with supplies for cruisers, was found on 11 November 1914 by the British armed merchant cruiser *Orama*. After a chase, *Orama* sank the *Navarra*, but rescued her crew.

It was indicative of Germany's thoroughness that great attention had been paid to ensuring the availability of supplies in the Atlantic. This, being the most affluent ocean area, would undoubtedly be the prime region when it came to targeting raiding effort. The Atlantic, therefore, was dotted with a number of supply centres, each of which was under the jurisdiction of a Supply Officer.

Main supply centres were situated at New York, Las Palmas, Havana, Rio de Janeiro and Buenos Aires; that is, near the cardinal points of the Atlantic. In addition, there were smaller centres at places such as St Thomas (West Indies), Para, Pernambuco and Bahia in Brazil, at Montevideo in Uruguay and as far south as Punta Arenas in the Magellan Straits. There was, therefore, a chain of supply centres up the east coast of the Americas from Cape Horn to New York. There were supply centres nearer home on the east side of the Atlantic at Tenerife and Togoland. A mid-Atlantic rendezvous was specified at Horta in the Azores.

The responsibility of each Supply Officer was to do his best to ensure that the required colliers were in his appointed area. Theoretically, the officers in a raider only needed to consult the 'Cruiser Handbook', and select one of the designated rendezvous where they could expect to begin the task of bunkering soon after their arrival. Another advantage of this arrangement was that there was no need for the raider to use her wireless equipment to state that she needed 'x' hundred tons of coal on, or by, a specific date. The fuel should already be available as and when required.

The Controller of all the supply centres was a well-known German naval officer, one Fragatten-Kapitän (Lieutenant Commander) Boy-Ed, who had been appointed to the German Embassy in Washington DC.

Boy-Ed had gained a reputation for being a very shrewd, able, subtle and dangerous operator. This Machiavellian organiser did his ample share of the work until late into the First World War when he was recalled from the United States and returned to Europe.

Ironically, during the first week to ten days of the war, German colliers carrying coal from Barry or Cardiff were able to get to Las Palmas and be available to supply the raider *Kronprinz Wilhelm*. The industrious Hamburg-Amerika Line chartered several neutral steamers to carry coal and other provisions for other German raiders. Newport News was a favourite supply base. German raiders were more than a little captivated by this Virginian port. The broad entrance to Chesapeake Bay was more than attractive, when British warships were hovering out to sea in the darkness. Other charms were provided by the ship repair yards, docking facilities, the means of embarking coal and other attractions to raise drooping spirits after long periods at sea.

The instruction to German liners to head for the nearest neutral port was not invariably the most sagacious move. It would have been better if the directive had been drafted along the lines of: 'Make for the nearest port of a neutral country which is most likely to remain neutral', even if this type of forward thinking was probably beyond the capacity of the most clever and well-balanced politicians. This thought is aired because at the beginning of August 1914, two of the Hamburg-Amerika liners were in the Western Approaches of the English Channel. They were informed by radio that war had broken out between France and Germany. These two ships obeyed instructions and, blamelessly, chose the first neutral harbour. British cruisers were soon to be seen off the harbour entrance and, within a short time, both liners were detained. German passengers and crew were taken ashore and within a month these two liners sailed towards the open sea; but with the White Ensign flying above their German colours and prize crews on board. The first of these ships was the *Kronprinzessin Cecile* and the second the slightly smaller *Prinz Adalbert*.

In like manner German ships which basically interned themselves in Portuguese and United States waters were to suffer similar indignities at later dates.

The first German merchant cruiser to pass through the Narrow Seas into the Atlantic was the *Kaiser Wilhelm der Grosse* and it is of interest to learn a little more about her cruise. This particular four-funnel passenger ship had been the fastest ship afloat in her younger days and was still in the possession of North German Lloyd. She was something over 14,000 tons in weight and at her best was capable of attaining a mean speed of over twenty-two knots.

At the start of August 1914 she was lying at Bremerhaven, but on the 3rd of that month her well-known yellow funnels and white upper works were all painted black. She received her outfit of guns, a naval crew repaired on board and Captain Reymann assumed command. On 4 August she departed from the Weser, stood up the North Sea and adopted a route which was to be followed by later raiders which were to leave Germany for deployment in the Atlantic. The British blockading cruisers created a marked sense of nervousness in the minds of the commanding officers of raiders. The wish to reach the open ocean without delay, and without being spotted by patrolling hostile warships, resulted in the evolution of a route which became in the nature of a standing dish and was only modified to cater for current weather conditions, or the hours of daylight at particular seasons. The aim of a raider's captain would be to make best use of fog, severe gales and the long, moonless wintry nights for transiting sections of the British-dominated waters where the chances of encountering unfriendly warships was at its highest. Daylight hours should, therefore, be as few as was practicable and ideally spent in a high latitude as far as possible from close patrols. In the final result, it became a question of selecting a ship with the correct speed of advance to bring her to her patrol area at the desired time. It also implied, and became the practice, that outward bound raiders did their best to leave Germany between late November and early December and not to return later than March.

Kaiser Wihelm der Grosse was the first of the pioneers and she had greater speed and higher tonnage than most. She was also, like the other fliers, very extravagant in coal consumption which could be about two hundred and fifty tons per day at half-speed. The disadvantages of this can easily be appreciated. Her shyness took her via such a circuituous route that she had consumed most of her fuel by the time she had arrived in her patrol area.

She would never have risked trying to rush the Straits of Dover or dashing through the short English Channel route. She had to skirt the Norwegian coast, proceed to Icelandic waters, next steam well to the west of the British Isles and then down to intercept the busy trade routes, working its way to and from south of Tenerife. On 7 August *Kaiser Wilhelm der Grosse* had travelled to a position no farther than fifty miles west-north-west of Stalberg, Iceland where she squandered time and effort sinking the British trawler *Tubal Cain* and taking the crew prisoner.

The ocean had to be ploughed for another eight days before she encountered her second ship. This was the Union Castle liner *Galician* which was passing through the Canaries area bound from the Cape to England. Captain Reymann had indubitably reached the correct area and his wireless began to intercept signals made in the clear, for example ordering coal at Tenerife. Names were given and it was a simple matter for Reymann to open Lloyd's Register and flip the pages of that invaluable publication until the place was reached where particulars of a ship such as her tonnage, ownership and so on could be promptly noted.

This particular incident was not without its lighter side. *Galician* was heard to ask whether the track was clear on her radio. Reymann replied to Captain E M Day of the *Galician* with a reassuring message so the two liners met at 2.45pm. 'If you communicate by wireless, I will sink you,' was the welcoming message sent by the German.

At five o'clock the following morning, another signal was made releasing the British ship. What made the German raider do this? The answer is that the *Galician* would have been nothing but an embarrassment to the raider. There were over two hundred passengers from South Africa, of whom some were women and children who would soon make inroads into the *Kaiser*'s stock of provisions.

Two hours after she had dismissed *Galician* the SS *Kaipara* of over seven thousand tons on passage from New Zealand and Montevideo with four thousand tons of meat and absolutely no passengers was encountered. This was ideal. She was promptly sent to the bottom and her crew taken prisoner.

The same day the Royal Mail liner *Arlanza*, out from Buenos Aires, was stopped and then released as she was a passenger ship with women and children embarked. On the same day, 16 August, the SS *Nyanga* came in view. She was a cargo vessel loaded with African produce. No problems here. The ship's crew was removed and she was sunk.

The raider herself was rapidly running out of fuel and proceeded eastward to reach the lonely, unfrequented anchorage of Rio de Oro, which was in Spanish territory on the north-west shoulder of the African continent. The area was administered by a sub-Governor who was responsible to the Governor of the Canary Islands. 'Might was right', and a German raider could not be expected to show any more respect for authorities in European settlements than might have been shown to a senior eskimo.

The raider waited for supply ships to reach this rendezvous which would bring fuel as well as other provisions. The raider's requirements were fully met in a comparatively short space of time; and captives from *Kaipara* and *Nyanga* transferred to the supply vessels.

The *Kaiser Wilhelm der Grosse* was still embarking coal when a three-funnelled British cruiser unexpectedly appeared. This warship was the 5,600-ton *Highflyer* armed with eleven 6-inch guns as opposed to the *Kaiser*'s six 4-inch weapons. The latter refused to surrender, was engaged and in due course sunk.

Germany's first raider had not achieved great success. To summarise, she had destroyed about £400,000 sterling's worth of shipping, but had lost her own more precious life. It is interesting to have given some attention to this ship's career as it brings out a number of lessons, beginning with the need to give the British Isles a wide berth in her break-out from Germany to the Atlantic.

It has to be admitted that the *Kaiser Wilhelm der Grosse* was not particularly well suited to the job to which she had been assigned. The characteristic German gap between the second and third funnel made it difficult to alter her profile with the mere application of a lot of paint. Her vast appetite for coal was both a negative point for herself and a terrible strain on the supporting supply organisation. The fact that she needed to spend so much time waiting for colliers and bunkering at Rio de Oro was a decisive factor in enabling *Highflyer* sufficient time for the cruiser to intercept and engage the raider.

Similar lessons were learned by the British who found that, with the exception of special 'rush' incursions, high-performance Atlantic liners were not the useful auxiliaries which the authorities had hoped that they might become. To use them to the greatest advantage was to turn them into minelayers or hospital ships. The same considerations were applicable to the ferries of the cross-Channel type.

In the first months of World War I, Britain made the same errors as did the Germans. Fast Cunard liners with famous names such as *Lusitania*, *Mauritania* and *Aquitania* were found to be too greedy with fuel and of too high a tonnage for cruiser work, which required a moderate consumption of fuel, either coal or oil, and reasonable mobility, as they had to be manoeuvered or stopped when apprehending or engaging another ship. A speed of, say, between fourteen and eighteen knots was considered to be efficacious. For the above reasons, *Lusitania* and *Mauritania* were returned to their owners as also was *Aquitania* after she had been involved in a collision.

Lusitania carried out excellent work in helping to maintain rapid sea communication between America and Britain until she was torpedoed. *Mauritania* was priceless in her role of hospital ship when large numbers of wounded and sick had to be rushed home from the Dardanelles in the Gallipoli campaign. *Aquitania* rendered distinguished service as a transport. Rapid, manoeuverable albeit short-range cross-Channel packets as personified by such vessels as *Empress*, *Engadine* and *Riviera* could be usefully converted to rapidly lay minefields and then dash back home.

CHAPTER VIII
Minelaying by Surface Raider

Minelaying can be an effective operation designed to sink or damage both surface merchant vessels and warships. As with the torpedo, a mine can damage a surface vessel where it is extremely vulnerable, that is below the waterline. Minefields may also be laid to bottle up enemy ships in their own harbours or anchorages and to defend friendly coastal waters from visits by unfriendly men-of-war.

Captains of ships must be wary of entering waters where it is suspected that mines have been laid. Considerable effort is needed to carry out large-scale minesweeping operations and a side-effect can be the diversion of men and materials which could be employed on other tasks.

During the First World War the 'moored mine' was the principal type to be widely used. The 'moored mine' is dropped, attached to a sinker, which sinks to the bottom of the sea, then releases a fine-wire moving cable which the mine's buoyancy takes to a pre-set depth below the surface. Moored mines can be connected to a neighbour or several neighbours, so that if a surface vessel strikes the connecting cable it will drag over one or more mines onto itself. The job of minesweepers was to sever the mooring wires of these mines so that they would pop up to the surface and could be punctured or detonated by small arms fire, a task which sounds easier than it often was, or they would lose their buoyancy and sink to the bottom or blow up.

During the evening of 4 August 1914, a smallish, two-funnelled steamer, owned by the Hamburg-Amerika Line received wireless instructions to proceed towards the River Thames at her best speed and to lay her cargo of mines. The vessel was the *Königin Luise* which had been an excursion vessel which had at times come as far west as the Solent in the days of peace. As soon as her yellow funnels and white hull had been decorated with a coat black paint, she looked similar to the Great Eastern Railway ferries which plied their trade between Harwich and the Hook of Holland. It was therefore believed that no undue suspicion should be aroused if she had been sighted along a fanciful line joining Orford Ness with the Maas Lightship. Another plus feature was that her after-deck was very appropriate to the task of minelaying as it was spacious and had ample room for handling mines and for fitting the small railway track which was needed for dropping mines over the stern.

At 2200 on 4 August the *Königin Luise*, armed with two guns and her highly explosive charge, put to sea under the cover of darkness, steamed westwards along the Dutch coast and was off the Maas Lightship at about 0800 (local German time). Course was then altered to pick up the East Anglia coast and the decision had been taken to mine the East Swin Channel, which was one of the busiest routes for merchant vessels trading between London and the North Sea and Baltic ports. In the event, *Königin Luise* was destined never to reach her goal. The reason for this was that at 1040 on 5 August she was proceeding at a fair speed, some thirty miles east of Orford Ness, when she had the ill luck to be sighted by HMS *Amphion* which had her flotilla of destroyers in company. Commander Biermann, in command of *Königin Luise*, became dismayed as the last thing he wanted was to be involved in any sort of engagement while his ship was loaded with mines. The Commander quickly decided to drop his lethal cargo into the sea, altering course to the south and the south-east with the aim of running back to home. This was not possible.

At 1115 (GMT) the flotilla began firing at her, but not before Biermann had transmitted a signal to warn the High Sea Fleet that the mines had been laid. Within the space of forty-five minutes *Königin Luise* had been sunk, and her survivors had been taken on board *Amphion* as prisoners. The tactical mistake made in this raid lay with the time taken for the German minelayer to set out. Had the schedule been planned so that the mines could have been laid during the hours of darkness, she would probably never have been detected; but the minefield would have spectacularly revealed itself later as an undefined danger area causing severe losses. This is what occurred some three weeks later during the night of 25/26 August, when extensive minefields were laid off the Tyne and Humber rivers. In this case, the minelayers were unobserved and returned safely to Germany.

It is, perhaps, thought-provoking to reflect that *Königin Luise* owed her sinking to a British trawler which just happened to be in the vicinity and noticed her 'throwing things' overboard as soon as the destroyer flotilla had been sighted. The trawler informed *Amphion*, and the action followed shortly afterwards.

Ironically, *Amphion* struck one of the mines the following morning and was damaged to such an extent that she foundered. The loss of *Amphion* was an unfortunate incident; but a huge 'plus point' was that a German minefield had been uncovered pretty well as soon as it had been laid. Admiralty charts covering the area off Orford Ness could be corrected to give a pink patch, indicating a danger zone, and minesweepers were informed exactly where to begin their work.

The next incident chosen for consideration involved the use of a much larger ship which the German Navy converted for use as a minelayer. To set the scene, it should be remembered that on 28 August 1914 the Battle of Heligoland Bight had been fought. The result of this engagement, which was more in the nature of a turbulent skirmish, had dismayed the Kaiser, who, it is understood, insisted on a future naval policy which was to be marked by proceeding with great caution. Military history tends to show that enforced inactivity can have a disastrous effect upon the morale of fighting men. As Nelson aptly put it, 'ships and sailors rot in harbour'. By the month of September 1914, this defensive attitude towards her British naval enemy was already adversely affecting the morale of German ships' companies. A raid beyond the Heligoland Bight, without risking the High Sea Fleet, was judged likely to improve the maritime ambience. The great potential of mines had been established off Orford Ness, the Humber and the Tyne and it was believed that a more ambitious minelaying raid might be highly effective. The question was: should the mines be laid with the aim of entrapping merchant ships, or should the target be the Grand Fleet?

There was a snag when it came to the problem of targeting the British Grand Fleet. In September 1914 German intelligence had yet to discover where the Grand Fleet was based. The British Navy had been using the Cromarty Firth in the year preceding the First World War, so the use of that area could be the basis of a logical guess; and it was in fact being used by two cruiser squadrons. The Battle Fleet and the battle-cruisers were, however, based on Scapa Flow from whose sheltered waters periodic sweeps were made into the North Sea in the general direction of the Heligoland Bight.

It is at this stage that attention should be shifted to the North German liner *Berlin*, which was another fine twin-screw, twin-funnel ship. *Berlin* had been completed at Bremen in 1909, weighed over 17,000 gross tons, was 590 feet long and had been constructed with lofty upper-works of typically teutonic style; and had been designed for the Mediterranean–New York service. She had been acquired by the German Navy, repainted and fitted out to be a minelayer. The duty to which she was assigned was the mining of areas in the north-west approaches to the British Isles.

The intention was well thought out. A large number of ships sailed in and out of the Clyde; and the potential minefield would strike a blow outside Glasgow. There was another very sound reason for laying mines across the Clyde channels; this lay in the fact that a large convoy of thirty-three ships had been planned to leave Canada bound for the British Isles with troops embarked who were finally destined to reach France. Germany came to know about the existence of the convoy; and that the sailing date was to be 23 September 1914. What had not been discovered was the actual port for which the convoy was routed. A fair assumption was that the nearest and most direct terminus via the north of Ireland would be Glasgow. The laying of a minefield at the entrance to the Clyde would be a menace to the Canadian convoy and all other sorts and condition of shipping.

The choice of a suitable date and time was the next item on the planning agenda. Ideally, the mines should be laid in darkness. This meant on a date not very far distant from the new moon when darkness could be relied upon; however, it should not be too far ahead of the convoy's estimated time of arrival in the Clyde. It so happened that a new moon was on 19 September and preparations were made for *Berlin* to sail from German waters on 21 September 1914. The ship was entrusted to the command of Captain Pfundheller, was loaded with two hundred mines, could achieve a speed of seventeen knots and was fitted with six 4.1-inch guns which meant that she could act in the dual role of a, far from insignificant, armed merchant cruiser.

The German Admiralty was not only aware of the existence of the Canadian convoy, but had gained possession of the names of individual convoy units. This meant that *Berlin* could be disguised to bear resemblance to some of the units sailing in the convoy; the aim being that if she were discovered anywhere between Ireland and Scotland, there was a fair chance she would be mistaken for a British liner.

Berlin's sailing instructions were dated 11 September, which indicated the leisurely manner in which this minelaying raid had been planned. Mines were to be laid athwart the Glasgow approach between Garroch Head and Fairland Head; or, failing that, the principal channel on the line Garroch Head to Cumbrae Lighthouse; or else between Pladda and Turnberry Head. The moored mines were to be set so that they floated six feet below the surface at low-water springs or tides. Once she had got rid of her dangerous cargo, *Berlin* was to begin her return journey, passing via Icelandic waters far north of British patrols and to make attacks on British fishing vessels plying their trade off Iceland. Next, she was to proceed north-eastward to raid mercantile traffic sailing between England and Archangel. This being achieved, she was at liberty to find her way down the North Sea to Germany if the customary autumn weather conditions of rain, fog and heavy seas should come to her aid. Otherwise, she might seek refuge in some convenient Scandinavian harbour and preferably one where a railhead was in the vicinity.

Should *Berlin* find herself boxed-in in the north and be unable to evade the hostile patrols in high latitudes, and should she be compelled to escape south down the Atlantic, after completion of her minelaying operations, she was directed to undertake cruiser warfare in the manner of *Kaiser Wilhelm der Grosse*. *Berlin*'s commanding officer was reminded of the great advantage a liner possessed over more conventional naval cruisers. A passenger liner exceeding 17,000 tons was designed to be comfortable in even the worst Atlantic gales; and would have little difficulty in displaying her seaworthiness over men-of-war of considerably lower tonnage. Bad weather and high seas would produce a most favourable condition for *Berlin* as the ship, built as a liner, would be able to hold her own while the British light forces and the old cruisers employed on the Northern Patrol would have their speeds markedly impaired.

Berlin sailed out of the Weser at 2300 on 21 September in conditions of high security. However, it so happened that the following morning broke with a clearness which was most unusual for a day in September. *Berlin* became edgy as she would, in the prevailing conditions, be an eminently conspicuous object at great range before nightfall descended. At 0800, therefore, her helm was put over and she headed back for home.

On the same day, 22 September, another German merchantman, converted to minelayer, and *Kaiser* departed from the Jade and made off in the direction of the Moray Firth. Her aim was to trap the ships of the Grand Fleet in their base. *Kaiser* held on across the North Sea with commendable determination and was favoured by running into misty weather at about noon the day after she had sailed. At 1325 she was approximately a hundred and fifty miles east of Aberdeen when she was surprised to receive loud British wireless transmissions. Shortly afterwards, a British naval vessel appeared out of the mist heading towards the Moray Firth. This was one of the railway-owned ferries, of about two thousand tons, which had been acquired by the Royal Navy and transformed into Armed Boarding Steamers. Their duty was to patrol such waters as the Moray Firth, Pentland Firth and Hebrides to keep a look out for suspicious craft, in particular, potential minelayers.

The Boarding Steamer promptly closed *Kaiser* which altered course and began running at her best speed of thirteen knots. The German managed to win clear of the patrol; but the encounter had spoiled *Kaiser*'s plans. The raiding minelayer's appearance would have been reported promptly. If she stuck to her original plan, she might reach the target area at, say, 0330; but this would be cutting the operation extremely fine as the time of darkness would end an hour later. If *Kaiser* were detected in clear daylight she would be running very grave risks. In the final event her captain decided to abort the operation and head for home. His nervous system was frayed and, on the morning of 24 September, another shock was in store. When she had reached a position about forty miles off Heligoland a British submarine appeared. *Kaiser* made haste to steer eastward to reach the shallows off Schleswig-Holstein. The minelayer got back safely; but the strain must have stimulated her captain's imagination. He was convinced that the submarine had fired a couple of torpedoes. This was not the case, no attack had been made, but a single torpedo could have detonated the cargo of lethal mines and made *Kaiser* explode with a monumental bang.

Perhaps, *Kaiser* was not the luckiest of ships. She made another effort to carry out her instruction on 28 September, but got caught in such dirty weather that at 1400 she once again turned back and soon afterwards was put into dockyard hands for a refit.

Berlin and *Kaiser* had both failed in their minelaying operations; but they had both been close to danger. The Grand Fleet was at sea, and at dawn on 22 September units were covering a line that reached for more than a hundred miles west from the Norwegian coast off Stavanger. It is true that at 1000 the British Fleet proceeded to the north-west; but two battle squadrons were detached to support cruisers which were searching North Sea areas for German cruisers, destroyers and submarines which had been reported to be tracking north. The receipt of a wireless message from the Admiralty, or some patrol vessel, would soon trigger such dispositions as would have made escape virtually impossible. In addition, it should be remembered that Lieutenant Commander Weddingen of U9 had been able to achieve the extraordinary feat of sinking the three British cruisers *Aboukir*, *Crecy* and *Hogue*, off the Dutch coast, between 0730 and 0835.

The above incident saw one light cruiser and seventeen destroyers being despatched from Harwich towards the Heligoland Bight in the hope of intercepting any enemy submarines which might be on their way home. This meant that only a slight extension of the search would bring the minelayers and eighteen hunters into the same picture frame. *Berlin* and *Kaiser* would have been overwhelmed.

A further unsuspected risk awaited *Berlin* which would have gone north past the Norwegian coast and thence to the Faroes–Iceland area. The two British armed merchant cruisers *Mantua* and *Alsation*, part of the cruiser squadron which was employed in the task of intercepting vessels bound through the northern entrance of the North Sea, had been despatched at 1030 on 22 September to reach a position off the Norwegian port of Trondheim and to patrol in that area until the 28th. The German liner *Brandenberg* lay in Trondheim, had been heard using her wireless equipment and was thought likely to emerge. However, it was soon established that she had been interned.

The few days under consideration are interesting as they illustrate what a narrow margin existed to separate either side from disaster. The more the individual episodes are considered and pieced together, the less there is to distinguish them in terms of cause and effect. For example, the Second Cruiser Squadron was employed in sweeping up the Norwegian coast on 23 and 24 September, and it would have been very strange if they had not encountered *Berlin*. However, on the evening of 25 September this squadron, based on Cromarty, arrived back there, transiting the Moray Firth with the purpose of fuelling. Had not the *Kaiser* accidentally been sighted by the Armed Boarding Steamer some one hundred and fifty miles offshore, the Moray Firth minefield would have been sown and some hours later the cruiser squadron would have stumbled into it. Such are the fortunes of war; but others were to follow in the comparatively near future.

It appeared as though *Berlin* had lost all opportunities for entrapping the Canadian Convoy; but the latter's departure was delayed. The actual date of sailing was altered from 23 September to 3 October 1914. However, to add to the problem, a new moon was due on 19 October and the dark autumn nights would provide ideal conditions for a more ambitious minelaying exercise. The amended plan would include *Berlin*'s original project and another aimed at disrupting the Grand Fleet off its Scottish bases. The second part of the scheme was to be implemented by the specially designed pre-war minelayer *Nautilus,* a two-funelled vessel with a clipper bow and bowsprit which gave her the appearance of a very expensive steam yacht. It was, in fact, this craft which had successfully laid the Humber minefield on the night of 25–26 August.

The date selected for the renewed effort was 16 October; and to try to make certain that the North Sea was temporarily safe, the German battle-cruisers made a short excursion as far as the Dogger Bank. They were followed by *Nautilus* which was escorted by the small cruiser, *Kolberg*. All went according to plan until 1640 on 17 October when they were about a hundred miles off May Island at the entrance to the Firth of Forth. At this time wireless signalling was picked up and clouds of smoke sighted of sufficient size to cause alarm. It all added up to the presence of units of the Grand Fleet. Another case of nerves attacked the German raiders who turned tail and made off in the direction of Heligoland. In the event, there was nothing to have caused dismay except coastal patrols of negligible fighting potential. There was no warship of significant combat strength within about two hundred miles. At the time in question, part of the Grand Fleet was carrying out firing practices to the westward of Scapa Flow until more secure defences against submarine attack could be arranged. From this decision a singular sequel was soon to follow.

After spending some time at sea, Admiral Jellicoe took part of his force into Lough Swilly in the north of Ireland where he arrived on 22 October. Eight days before this the Canadian convoy had reached Plymouth Sound safely, and had, therefore, arrived in England, rather than Scotland, as originally thought. Germany was not yet aware that the Grand Fleet had withdrawn from the North Sea, now that the convoy coming from Canada was already in harbour. On 16 October, a few hours after *Nautilus* and *Kolberg* had set out, *Berlin* sailed from the Jade and made her way up the North Sea. Shortly after dark, she crossed the line between Stavanger and Kinnaird Head; but there were no patrols operating between Norway and Scotland. The reason for this was that the cruiser blockade and lookout line had been withdrawn due to the perceived threat from submarines.

Cruiser squadrons and armed merchant cruisers were now north of the Shetlands and north-west of the Hebrides. Had she known it, *Berlin* was incurring no great risk at this juncture.

After proceeding north, *Berlin* passed between the Faeroes and Iceland on 19 October, then stood several hundred miles into the Atlantic until she reached longitude 20 west, and on 21 October, having given the British Isles a comfortably wide berth, headed east along the sixth parallel with the object of arriving off the coast of northern Ireland at dusk and after a further three-hundred-mile run. The adrenalin must have been flowing as the ship drew closer to the land and she began to intercept wireless messages which indicated that British naval units were patrolling off the Hebrides.

Berlin drew closer and closer to the bottle-neck which divides south-west Scotland from northern Ireland. To the north on her port side were the battleships *Albemarle* and *Exmouth*, while on her starboard side, to the south-west, other warships were operating. Between the Irish mainland and Scotland the armed boarding steamer *Tara* (one of the London & North Western Railway vessels) was keeping watch for any strange ships. The tenseness of the situation should be noted as it was only a short time before *Berlin* entered the area through which Admiral Jellicoe with units of the Grand Fleet had passed to reach Lough Swilly. Neither British nor Germans suspected each other's presence, yet they were only separated by a matter of miles.

The short daylight of the autumn afternoon disappeared all too quickly; wind clawed through the liner's rigging; the heavy Atlantic swell thumped against *Berlin*'s black hull; her engines vibrated steadily as they worked to maintain her seventeen-knot speed. Uneasy eyes were scanning the attenuated view of the inky black wilderness ahead as the officer-of-the-watch kept his charge on a south-east course. Captain Pfundheller was not a little surprised that the neighbourhood seemed to be patrolled in such strength. The immediate future might find him in a sudden action with, perhaps, a British cruiser. The prospect of such an engagement while *Berlin* was still carrying two hundred mines was not enticing. Would he be able to work his ship through the North Channel to the Clyde? Could she expect to be brought back again with so many vessels hovering around?

From now on, navigation would become more of a headache. The space of the Atlantic was being left astern and areas speckled with islands, rocks and confined channels were being entered. There was also the hazard of coming across unlit shipping and, perhaps, being involved in a collision. Mingling with the freshness of the ocean air was the soft scent of the land which would add to the unease of a deep-sea sailor commanding a heavy draught ship in these circumstances.

Mines and armament were being brought to short notice. At 2200 on 22

October soundings were taken which indicated that the coast of Ireland was not far away. To starboard the dark silhouettes of land loomed up. The Isle of Arran! *Berlin* altered course a few degrees to port and edged away from the shore. At 2300 Pfundheller, according to his reckoning, believed himself to be off Tory Island; but the navigation lights of Tory Island and Fanad Head were not operating due to wartime restrictions and it was not possible for *Berlin*'s position to be fixed, in the normal way, by using cross-bearings and flashing lights burning ashore; the raider's captain decided that the risk of attempting to negotiate the North Channel was too great, particularly as his ship was at the end of a six-day passage.

The original plan of mining the Firth of Clyde was discarded and it was decided that the cargo of mines should be laid to the north of Tory Island. The operation began at 2330 and was carried out without interruption. This enabled *Berlin* to move off to the north-west without being discovered, although at 0100 on 23 October she must have passed within about fifteen miles of HMS *Albemarle*. There must have been a general feeling of relief as the ship regained the spacious waters of the Atlantic. Further good luck came in the morning when the weather turned misty with squalls of rain. This provided ideal conditions for concealment. The aim was to gain the remote north-west regions where, it was hoped, no man-of-war was likely to be cruising. At the end of a week she had the cold shores of Greenland to port and Iceland to starboard. On 27 October *Berlin*'s wireless operators had intercepted the British warning to all ships that the Tory Island minefield had been laid.

The days when *Berlin* was busy making her getaway enabled her ship's company to attempt to get rid of any obvious characteristics which might have suggested that she had been converted to be a minelayer. However, much steaming at high speed tended to result in unwelcome defects. The ship had not been constructed to act out stunt raids lasting over fourteen days, during part of which she had been driven at forced pressure through high seas. Her engines had been designed to jog along at a steady scheduled speed. She developed boiler problems, and in the high latitudes it was not really unexpected that she should come across such gales and atrocious sea conditions from which self-respecting fishing fleets would be snugly sheltering in harbour. It was not much use hoping to make targets of these. The beginning of November 1914 saw *Berlin* proceeding to the east towards the Arctic limits of Norway in the expectation of raiding the route to Arkangel for food ships and colliers which were still trading between Great Britain and Russia.

On the night of 7–8 November the raider closed the bleak Murman coast; but the apprehensions of her commanding officer had not, in any way, been lessened. A couple of ships were sighted, one of which was (erroneously) deemed to be a British warship. Advantage was taken of a sudden snowstorm in which to escape back to the open sea. *Berlin* next proceeded into the Atlantic and aimed to the south towards the Lofoten Islands; here, at least she could be well placed to jump Anglo–Russian traffic. However, the weather was so appalling that it would have been out of the question to lower boats and send away boarding parties. No ships could be examined; but the raider's presence would have been truly compromised. Cruiser warfare could not be considered. Her boilers were now worse than ever, after continuous steaming for more than a full month, and her bunkers were nigh on empty. Pfundheller was at the end of his tether. If he proceeded much farther south, the probability of being caught by the British would be markedly increased.

The commanding officer decided to avail himself of a let-out clause in his original instructions and to take refuge in a neutral harbour. *Berlin* was brought out of the ocean during a snowstorm and she entered a land-locked fjord. She came to anchor off Trondheim at 0900 on 17 November. Twenty-four hours later she was finally interned with only coal-dust remaining in her bunkers. Her raiding days were over.

The time has come to ask, what had *Berlin* accomplished? She had not endangered what we have been pleased to call the Canadian convoy, nor had she laid a deadly ambush in the Clyde. As an armed merchant cruiser, she had not captured a single prize. She had not dropped her cargo of mines in any of the optional channels which had been specifically assigned to her. This said, *Berlin* had been favoured with the luck of a lifetime and had achieved more than might ever have been imagined for her. The mines had been laid in two legs, and a mean position gives this area as approximately nineteen miles north-east of Tory Island where their presence was not suspected until at 1415, just three and a half days later on 26 October, SS *Manchester Commerce*, outward bound from Manchester to Quebec, struck one of the large metal eggs and sank with the loss of her master and thirteen members of her crew. The basic intention of spoiling the Canadian track may have been partially achieved.

A far more serious tragedy was to follow. There was an understandable, if not happy, delay in transmitting the news about *Manchester Commerce* which did not reach Admiral Jellicoe in Lough Swilly until 1400 on 27 October. The Second Battle Squadron came out of Lough Swilly for gunnery practice under Admiral Warrender in HMS *Centurion*, who led the battleships *Ajax*, *Audacious* and *King George V* straight over the Tory Island minefield. The astonishing fact is that only one ship struck any of those mines.

The battleship which came to grief was HMS *Audacious*, a new capital ship which was completed in 1913. *Audacious* had been built at Cammell Laird, Birkenhead, and had a displacement of 23,000 tons. She had an armament of ten 13.5-inch guns, sixteen 4-inch guns and four three pounders. She was also equipped with three torpedo tubes and could achieve a speed of twenty-two knots. She had cost the best part of

£2,000,000 to build, which was no mean sum of money in 1913. Her complement was about nine hundred officers and men.

The time was 0845 when *Audacious* was a mile south of where *Manchester Commerce* had been sunk the previous afternoon. At this moment *Audacious* was struck on the port side aft at a considerable distance below the waterline. It is interesting to note that it is very rare for a ship moving at any speed to hit a moored mine bow-on. In most cases, though (as always) there were exceptions,a ship's bow wave had the effect of throwing the mine aside. Very shortly afterwards, the mine would be drawn, by suction, in towards the propellers. *Audacious* heeled over to port, the engine room became flooded and the port engines stopped. An unpleasant Atlantic sea was running, but with her starboard engines enabling her to steam at about nine knots, although she was steering badly, the ship started to limp towards Lough Swilly. As so often happens on these occasions, the situation quickly deteriorated, the water level inside the ship was rising and at about 1100, when about ten miles from shore, *Audacious* came to a grinding halt. The cruiser HMS *Liverpool* was standing by and the White Star liner *Olympic* arrived on the scene, having been alerted by distress messages. Boats from these two ships recovered *Audacious*'s ship's company with the exception of two hundred and fifty men.

Olympic, commanded by Commodore H J Haddock, took *Audacious* in tow, despite the impressive swell, the line being passed by the destroyer *Fury.* During this operation some very elegant seamanship was displayed.

It must have been an impressive sight – such a huge liner, *Olympic* being one of *Titanic's* sisters, acting in the role of tug to try to salvage an up-to-date battleship. Regrettably these efforts were of no avail and *Audacious* became as intractable as a demented bull. Other ships tried to tow her without success, and by 1800 she had to be abandoned for fear of capsizing. Some three hours later she did, in fact, capsize. A sad little incident now occurred when, in the act of sinking, the battleship blew up and dropped debris over HMS *Liverpool's* decks, killing one of her petty officers.

The war was not going too well for the Allies at the time *Audacious* went down. The Battle of Ypres was at a critical juncture and Britain's superiority in battleships over the Germans was down to about three. The British were, therefore, in no position to bear the loss of such a valuable capital ship and efforts were made to 'hush up' the incident; the press was kept from mentioning the calamity, but it is always difficult for such an important event to be kept secret indefinitely. The *Olympic* entered Lough Swilly and was detained there for three days, all communication with the shore being forbidden. Germany did not learn that *Audacious* had gone, and the loss was never acknowledged by the Admiralty until after the war.

Minesweepers were then set the task of clearing up *Berlin*'s minefield; the units of the Grand Fleet sailed from Lough Swilly on 3 November 1914 to return to Scapa Flow. A Norwegian grain ship foundered on the Tory Island minefield in April 1915 and the minefield itself was not a hundred per cent clear even in the year 1917.

Time has been spent on German minelaying activities during the First World War as this provides a fairly typical picture of the employment of surface vessels in the role of minelayers. The British also laid mines with the aim of preventing submarines exiting from enemy ports. Mines were laid in considerable numbers in the Heligoland Bight. The minefields laid made it necessary for the Germans to indulge in extensive sweeping operations before any parts of the High Sea Fleet could contemplate putting to sea. Such mine counter-measure exercises were useful in giving an indication to the British that some movement was intended. In view of the comparatively short distance of the Grand Fleet from German bases, which meant limited time available in which the units of the High Sea Fleet could be intercepted if they came out to carry out a raid on the British coasts or an attack on a convoy, early information could be of considerable value.

However, as Admiral Jellicoe pointed out in *The Crisis of the Naval War*, certain facts needed to be taken into consideration when mining operations in the Heligoland Bight were taking place. The first was the knowledge that the Germans themselves had laid minefields in some portions of the Bight, and it was necessary for British minelayers to give suspected areas a wide berth. Secondly, it was obvious that we could not lay minefields in areas very near those which we ourselves had already mined, since we should run the risk of blowing up our own ships with our own mines.

As has been mentioned previously, mining operations had to be carried out at night, and as there were no navigational aids in the way of lights, etc. in the Heligoland Bight, the position in which British mines were laid was never known with absolute accuracy. Consequently, an area in which British mines had been laid and to which a minelayer had been sent, could not safely be approached within a distance of some miles on a subsequent occasion. The use, in mining operations, of the device known as 'taut wire' gear, introduced by Vice-Admiral Sir Henry Oliver, was of great help in ensuring accuracy in laying minefields and consequently in reducing the danger distance surrounding our own minefields.

The British were driven farther out from the ports as their own mining operations increased in scope. The implication of this increased the area to be mined as the Heligoland Bight is bell-mouthed in shape; but this did have the advantage that it made the tasks of the German mine counter-measures vessels more difficult, and dangerous, as they had to work farther out, which gave the British forces a better chance of catching them at their labours and engaging them.

The British did not lay mines in Danish or Dutch territorial waters, and these provided an exit for German vessels as the British minefields grew more distant from the German bases. The policy was to lay mines in such a concentrated manner in the Heligoland Bight in order to compel German submarines and other vessels to make their exits along the Danish or Dutch coasts. At the end of these exits, submarines were positioned to report enemy movements and to attack hostile vessels. It was known that the Germans would sweep other channels for their ships, but as soon as the British identified the position of such safe routes, not an unduly difficult exercise, more mines would be laid at the end of the newly swept channels.

It was intended that, as mines became available, more deep minefields should be laid nearer the British coast in positions in which it was known that enemy submarines operated. The idea was that such minefields would be safe for surface ships; but that British patrol craft would force unfriendly submarines to submerge into them.

Mining and mine counter-measures in the First World War is a captivating and vast subject in its own right, and it is hoped that the examples given may stimulate the desire to learn more and to appreciate that offensive minelaying by surface ships can be an effective form of commerce raiding.

CHAPTER IX

Commerce Raiding by
Surface Warships in World War I

Germany's units for waging war along the commercial sea-routes during the first months of hostilities were made up of, firstly, those of her regular cruisers which happened to be on the Far East or West Indies stations and secondly, any of her ocean liners with the potential to become armed merchant cruisers and chanced to be in foreign waters.

The Germans were to gain their most resounding naval victory thousands of miles from the North Sea and any European waters. The engagement took place not far from the Chilean coast between a squadron commanded by Vice-Admiral Graf von Spee and a division of British cruisers under Rear-Admiral Sir Christopher Cradock. Shortly before the outbreak of war in August 1914, Admiral Tirpitz who had been appointed German Minister of Marine in 1897 and continued in that important post until March 1916, had reluctantly permitted the two modern armoured-cruisers *Scharnhorst* and *Gneisenau* to be transferred to the Pacific squadron. *Scharnhorst*, of 11,420 tons displacement, was built at Blohm & Voss of Hamburg in 1908, armed with eight 8.2-inch guns and six 5.9-inch guns and was capable of a top speed of 22.5 knots. *Gneisenau* (of the same weight and armament as *Scharnhorst*) was built by Weser of Bremen, was launched in 1908 and was designed to be capable of a top speed of 23.8 knots. In August 1914 they and a few light cruisers were in the Carolinas under von Spee's command. Von Spee, apprehensive that he might soon be outnumbered by an Allied force, detached one of his light cruisers, the *Emden*, to prey upon Allied merchant vessels, and then steered for the coast of Chile with the remainder of his ships. The presence of a potent German colony in Chile and the assurance of a friendly welcome, is probably one of the reasons for that decision.

Von Spee bombarded the French port of Papeete, on the island of Tahiti, and several of the Allied bases en route. He was reinforced by the two cruisers *Dresden* and *Leipzig* when off Easter Island in the middle of October. The strength of the German squadron was now brought up to two formidable armoured-cruisers and three light cruisers as von Spee continued his journey in the direction of Valparaiso.

Coronel

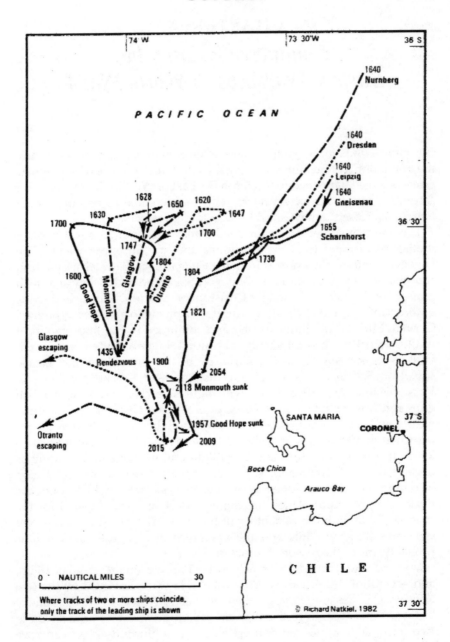

Falklands

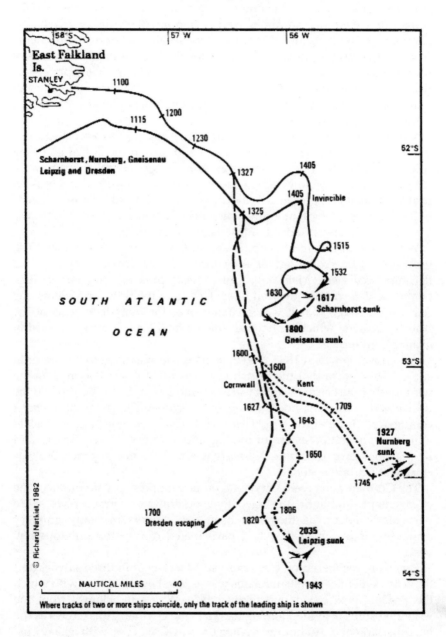

While the above events were unfolding, Admiral Cradock was hastening to intercept the Germans with a motley squadron of cruisers which were verging on obsolescence and which had had a long spell of sea-time in the Atlantic. One thing was certain and that was that both the British and German Admirals were determined on fighting a battle. Cradock, in the Nelsonian tradition, was seeking to destroy an enemy who was within his grasp. In addition, the mishaps of the early weeks of the war had roused the Royal Navy to seek action at almost any price. This had engendered a state of mind which might have been praiseworthy, but which was not exactly conducive to acting under the influence of thought-fully considered judgement.

Von Spee was eager for action because, if he could effectively dispose of the British force, he would have a free hand to raid the Allied shipping routes in the South Atlantic. Communications were not reliable and were subject to considerable delays. Cradock had scurried off as soon as he heard of von Spee's presence in those waters; but he had little intelligence of his enemy's strength at a time when his sole battleship, HMS *Canopus*, was still some three hundred miles distant from him.

When he encountered his opponent off Coronel on 1 November 1914, the British force consisted of only three elderly cruisers, namely the flagship *Good Hope, Monmouth* and *Glasgow* plus the auxiliary cruiser *Otranto* which was a converted liner. To add to the British problems, the sea was so rough that it was breaking over the maindeck guns of the British cruisers which enhanced the German superiority in readily available fire-power.

Action was joined at 1830. Von Spee had, with intent, held his fire until sunset. This meant that the British were steaming towards him from the west, so that the German ships were half-hidden in the twilight while the British were clearly silhouetted against a glowing horizon. *Scharnhorst* commenced firing at the *Good Hope*, while *Gneisenau* engaged *Monmouth* which was in station astern of the flagship. *Leipzig* took on *Glasgow* and *Dresden* took care of *Otranto*. *Nurnberg* was still at some distance, but was closing at her best speed.

The German guns were very soon on target and many accounts of the engagement highlight the fact that *Scharnhorst*'s gun crews were particularly adept, as they had been the winners in many gunnery competitions in which they had participated during the previous few years.

Hits were registered on *Good Hope* and *Monmouth* in three salvoes and the achievement of excellent results was assisted by the clarity with which the British ships stood out against the setting sun. Flames from the wounded ships provided aiming marks to the German guns' crews as the horizon darkened. An hour of savage fire saw *Good Hope* with a heavy list and her engines stopped. She went down soon afterwards. One of

Monmouth's turrets had blown up; the ship was still afloat, but only had one gun in action. When *Nurnberg* arrived on the scene, she finished *Monmouth* off in a short time.

Glasgow and *Otranto* vanished into the gloom. Von Spee decided not to give chase. He was aware that *Canopus* was in the area; and he had to husband his stocks of ammunition as there was no chance of obtaining further supplies before returning to home waters. He put in to Valparaiso where the ships' companies were given an enthusiastic welcome by the large German colony.

Coronel was a disastrous episode as far as the British were concerned. The land war was not going at all well. Belgium had been occupied, and the Allied armies were in retreat. It was not only at far-distant Coronel that the Germans were scoring naval successes. On 3 November three battle-cruisers under the command of Admiral Hipper had bombarded Yarmouth a couple of days after von Spee's victory. What is more, the three German battle-cruisers involved had slipped away without any intervention by the Royal Navy. There was an immediate outcry in Britain and questions were asked along the lines of: 'What was the Navy doing?' 'How was it that British warships were caught on the wrong foot at Coronel?' and so on: the usual queries which fly about on this sort of occasion, when people are worried or frightened, and human nature tends to seek a witch hunt.

The Admiralty seemed to keep its counsel, but reacted quickly. Winston Churchill, the First Lord of the Admiralty, with some prompting by the First Sea Lord, Admiral Lord Fisher, directed Admiral Jellicoe commanding the Home Fleet to detach two of his latest battle-cruisers for a 'secret mission of the highest importance'. The two ships selected were the *Inflexible* and the *Invincible,* command being given to Vice-Admiral Sir Frederick Doveton Sturdee who, as Chief of Naval Operations, could be deemed to have had a portion of the responsibility for the Coronel debacle and who would have been keen to rescue an unfortunate situation. In addition, *Princess Royal* was despatched to cover the West Indies.

Inflexible and *Invincible,* with their bunkers replenished to capacity, proceeded at speed to their distant destination. They refuelled at the Cape Verde Islands on 19 November; and by 28 November they were off the Brazilian coast, where they were joined by the South Atlantic squadron commanded by Rear-Admiral Archibald Stoddart. Some colliers carrying supplies were in waiting at the Falkland Islands in case the search for the enemy should develop into a long hunt.

The inhabitants of the British colony in the Falklands were expecting von Spee's approach at any moment. Watchers had been placed at every useful point of vantage, each linked by line to HMS *Canopus,* which had been launched in 1897 and was being treated more like a fort than a warship. Apparently, two old ladies were working watch and watch as lookouts on the roof of a farmhouse at Port Darwin and telephoning news to *Canopus* at Port Stanley on the other side of the island.

The anxiety of the colonists was more than justified as the Falkland Islands were von Spee's next objective. At the time Sturdee was scrutinising the South Atlantic with his ships stationed at intervals along a fifty-mile scouting line, the Germans were negotiating Cape Horn and encountering the customary vile weather conditions. On 6 December they rendezvoused with a supply vessel off Pitcairn Island. At 1200 the following day the elderly lady, who was on watch on the roof of the farmhouse, spotted smoke on the horizon and, shortly after, picked out eight ships steaming as a formed body.

Enter von Spee; but the Germans only had six ships. It was Admiral Sturdee's force which had caught the watcher's attention. Sturdee's ships included the two battle-cruisers, the armoured-cruisers *Carnarvon*, *Cornwall* and *Kent*, plus the light cruisers *Glasgow*, *Bristol* and *Orama*. The Falkland Islanders must have been intensely relieved. The Germans were not far astern and at 0800 the following forenoon, 8 December, the smoke from the funnels of two of their ships appeared above the horizon. The Germans might easily have been the first to reach the Falklands if *Inflexible* and *Invincible* had been delayed in the English Channel at the very beginning of their voyage. This potential mishap gives rise to a fascinating incident which does not seem to be widely known; the two battle-cruisers could have been late in sailing.

There was thick fog in the Solent when *Inflexible* and *Invincible* were due to sail. The battle-cruisers could not rely upon their magnetic compasses as these had not been checked after recent work on the ships' armour-plating had been completed. This dockyard work could have altered the permanent magnetism of the ships and hence the deviation corrections which needed to be applied when specific courses were ordered. In brief, the vessels had not been 'swung'. It appeared that the ships would be unable to sail on the required day. Happily, someone at the Admiralty remembered that Elmer Sperry, a young American engineer who had developed a gyro-compass, might be reachable at the hotel where he had been staying. Sperry had offered his compass to the Admiralty where, in the all too familiar way, it had been politely refused, which only goes to show that the NIH (not invented here) syndrome is far from being a new phenomenon when new items of equipment are offered to government departments. Sperry was quickly found, put onto a train for Southampton with his 'Yankee device', and a few hours later this was fitted to the compass platform of *Invincible* under the disapproving gaze of her commanding officer. Followed by *Inflexible*, she made her way down the Solent in thick fog until the two ships reached clear weather and open water without untoward incident. A euphoric Sperry returned in the pilot boat, certain that his invention would be adopted by the Royal

Navy. It was, and it became accepted generally by the world's navies.

The two German ships, whose smoke had been seen by the watchers in the Falklands were *Nurnberg* and *Gneisenau,* which von Spee had sent to attack the islands, in the belief that they were undefended. One of *Gneisenau's* lookouts reported smoke over Port Stanley. This was, in the first instance, believed to come from the destruction of stocks of coal prior to the evacuation of the island. Later, the mastheads of warships were recognised, and a cruiser was spotted feeling her way out of the harbour. The *Nurnberg* and *Gneisenau* broke their ensigns and hurried to attack.

Scharnhorst, farther out at sea, had marked the distinctive topmasts of British battle-cruisers, uncovered by the light of the rising sun. This put the ball into a different court. Here were ships which were capable of attaining speeds of up to twenty-six knots and were armed with eight 12-inch guns apiece. Von Spee hastily recalled his ships and, not unreasonably, made off to the south-east. However, his slowest ships kept the speed of advance down to about fifteen knots.

The British were completing the exercise of replenishing with coal when the alert was given. In the event, they raised steam in record time and proceeded to sea. *Glasgow* was the first away, and joined *Kent* which had been on patrol outside the harbour. An hour later, at half past ten, the two British battle-cruisers and HMS *Cornwall* had left harbour. The enemy was no longer in sight; but *Glasgow,* which was farther out, signalled that she had their mastheads in view twelve miles to the south-east. This was fortuitous as the wind was blowing the battle-cruisers' smoke in the direction taken by the Germans and an opaque cloud of it was shrouding the horizon.

The hunt was now on, and Admiral Sturdee was in possession of the major advantage for, with his greater speed capability, the enemy could not escape. *Inflexible* had drawn sufficiently close to open fire on the rear German ship, the *Leipzig,* which was outranged and had very little chance.

Admiral von Spee directed his three light cruisers to scatter while he attempted to hold off the enemy with *Scharnhorst* and *Gneisenau*. However, Sturdee's two battle-cruisers were quite capable of dealing with them, and he despatched his other ships in pursuit of the fugitives. *Inflexible* was in action with *Scharnhorst* at 1330. *Scharnhorst* succeeded in achieving a hit on the English battle-cruiser, although firing at extreme range. Sturdee turned away to open the range and to enable full advantage to be taken of his heavier guns. The German's shells fell short while *Inflexible's* main armament continued to be effective.

While these events were in progress, *Invincible* had engaged *Gneisenau* and damaged the German ship badly. The German vessel was obliged to flood one of her magazines. Matters were not going at all well for von Spee at this stage and he tried to slip away under cover of smoke; but Sturdee rapidly closed the range to finish him off. *Scharnhorst's* armour was of scant protection against *Inflexible*'s 12-inch shells and smoke and flames were soon pouring from the German ship. *Gneisenau* could probably have escaped behind this dense black cloud, but she bravely remained by her sister, firing her remaining armament.

Shortly after 1600 the blazing *Scharnhorst* swung round and headed towards *Inflexible*. For a brief time, questions remained in the air. Was she going to try to ram, or to discharge a torpedo? Had the ship's steering jammed? The questions will never be answered as her guns suddenly ceased firing and she sank rapidly by the bows. The last seen of her was the ensign of the Imperial German Navy. There were no survivors.

Gneisenau remained in action for about a further hour before she also started to founder. In this case, twenty officers and sixty-seven ratings were picked from the water. In the meantime, Stoddart's cruisers had ended the careers of the other German ships with the exception of *Dresden* which contrived to achieve a clean escape. Later, the German supply vessels *Baden* and *St Isabel* were caught and sunk. The defeat at Coronel had been avenged and the British squadron was intact.

Time has been spent on the engagements off Coronel and the Falklands because the defeat of von Spee's squadron saw an end of the raiding of Allied merchant shipping by large surface ships, in which exercise the Germans had great hopes. These warlike activities in the South Atlantic also spawned the raiding careers of the two cruisers *Dresden* and *Emden* which will be covered in more detail.

The cruiser *Dresden* had had a far from uneventful life between late July 1914 and her rendezvous with Admiral von Spee off Easter Island in the middle of October 1914. However, the aim here is to cover what can be thought of as the second phase of *Dresden*'s odyssey in which she was to transfer her operations from the Atlantic to the Pacific Ocean. The Atlantic could be described as becoming somewhat unhealthy for German warships as British cruisers were steaming many miles carrying out surveillance sweeps along the coast of Brazil. Having said this, a raider with access to adequate supplies of fuel could probably play blind-man's-bluff in the wastes of the Atlantic for many weeks or months unless she were to be extremely unlucky. The German cruiser had managed to keep her whereabouts covered in mystery, and made intelligent use of her supply vessel to act as a link between herself and Germany – perhaps an example of the valuable co-operation which the German Navy had built up with auxiliary support ships.

It was after this that *Dresden* conformed with Admiral von Spee's aim to effect a concentration of cruisers off Easter Island, with its huge stone idols, in mid-October 1914. *Dresden* had been able to survive the Battle of the Falklands by getting away in the thick afternoon weather. At first, Captain Ludecke intended to aim for Picton Island, where von Spee was to have rendezvoused. However, Ludecke's calls on the radar could obtain no response from a supply ship. *Dresden* needed coal and she needed it very urgently. The problem was how could she obtain it and from what source? Punta Arenas, inside the Magellan Straits, seemed to be the only answer. It was highly probable that British cruisers would be patrolling off the eastern entrance to the Straits. A solution was found by choosing the difficult Cockburn Channel which Captain Ludecke entered on 10 December. He anchored his ship at 1600 in Sholl Bay, which is about sixty miles south of Punta Arenas.

The situation had become so desperate that Ludecke had to send men ashore to cut down trees and at the same time to bring off fresh water. Forests abound in the neighbourhood of Magellan, indeed Darwin had recorded the density of the forest when he visited the area in the *Beagle* during 1834.

Only a hundred and sixty tons of the cruiser's maximum capacity of eight hundred and fifty tons of coal remained, which meant that *Dresden* could not carry on for much longer. During the night a Chilean torpedo gunboat called on *Dresden*. She was lightly armed and a quarter of a century old; but she represented the law in those parts. Ludecke was informed that he could not extend his stay beyond twenty-four hours.

Dresden weighed anchor at 1000 on 12 December and arrived at the modest town of Punta Arenas which seemed to be noteworthy mainly for the driving storms which inflict themselves on the locality. The Captain knew that the United States collier *Minnesotan,* chartered by the German Government, was lying there, but this vessel's master flatly refused to let *Dresden* have so much as a shovelful of coal. He was not prepared to supply a warship.

The situation was awkward and time was precious as British cruisers could not be very far away. Fortunately, the German Roland Line *Turpin* had been there since the beginning of the war, and *Dresden* was able to obtain some seven hundred and fifty tons of briquettes from her and load them on board by the evening of 13 December. At 2200 the German cruiser headed south down the Straits. About five hours later the British cruiser HMS *Bristol* appeared. It had been a close call.

From this time onwards *Dresden* was to exist from hand to mouth, playing a large-scale game of hide-and-seek with some of the world's most stirring scenery as a backdrop. A simple description of the background would be to ask that a twin of Norway should be imagined with valleys, gorges, snow-covered mountains, peaks and precipices and nature itself in a state of primitive isolation. In brief, the severe, forbidding, barren region at the extremity of South America provided an ideal, if unusual, sanctuary for a cruiser which was hiding after escaping alone.

Dresden was relentlessly hunted by British cruisers. She was finally trapped, engaged and shelled into submission by HM Ships *Kent, Glasgow* and the armed merchant cruiser *Orama* at Mas Afuera Island, Chile on 14 March 1915.

The last month's of *Dresden*'s life show something of the career and adventures of a World War I German raider cruiser. However, *Dresden* should probably be remembered for the achievement of retaining a halo of mystery for three months rather than for her share in battles or successful raids upon her enemy's shipping. A lesson to be learned is that courage and determination can achieve much. On the reverse side of the coin is the inference that without some suitably placed dockyard facilities, fuelling arrangements and general logistic support, a lone raider's operations, however brilliant, cannot be enduring. It is very much part of the theory that a *guerre de course* should not have a decisive strategic effect upon a superior navy.

CHAPTER X
The Adventures of Emden and Compatri

I first heard the cruiser *Emden*'s story when I was still a child. I also saw the remains of this famous ship in early 1956 at the end of a short visit to the Cocos Islands at the start of the journey to Perth in Western Australia. Visits to the Cocos Islands tend to be rare so I was lucky to have seen what little still existed of, arguably, the most celebrated warship of the First World War.

Emden was launched in Danzig in 1908, she displaced 3,544 tons, was 364 feet in length and had a beam of 44.5 feet. Her armament consisted of ten 4.1-inch guns, four 2.1-inch guns and four machine guns. She could achieve a speed of twenty-five knots. *Emden*'s range of operation was extremely good for her day. When cruising at economical speed, around twelve knots, she could cover six thousand miles when fully fuelled. She was the last German cruiser to be built with reciprocating steam power plant.

It is tempting to spend time on *Emden*'s pre-World War I service with the German Pacific squadron based on Tsingtao and its excellent harbour, which the Germans had gained in 1890, and where it was thought that Germany was creating its version of Hong Kong. At that time, Europeans based on the east China coast led very pleasant lives. When painted white for service in the tropics, *Emden* became known as the swan of the east, and her ship's company were able to take advantage of the pleasures which their Far Eastern base had to offer.

Kapitän Karl von Muller was appointed to take command of *Emden* towards the end of 1912. This officer was destined to become as famous as the ship he commanded. *Emden* had been to Tsingtao to have marine growth scraped from her bottom and was in the Yellow Sea when news was received that Germany was at war with France and Russia. Muller cleared the lower deck, gave his ship's company a pep talk and indicated that he intended to proceed towards Vladivostok to raid shipping even though there might be a chance of encountering French or Russian warships. *Emden* did not have to travel very far before she made her first seizure in the form of the Russian mail ship *Ryaezan*, which was carrying eighty passengers and scant cargo en route from Nagasaki to Vladivostok.

She was a modern merchantman, built in Danzig, with a fair turn of speed. Muller decided that *Ryaezan* was too good to sink and he escorted her to Tsingtao for conversion into an armed merchant cruiser. She was then re-named *Kormoran*.

Emden left Tsingtao in time to avoid Rear-Admiral Jerram's cruisers on 6 August and in company with her supply ship, the collier *Markomannia*, sailed for the Marianas where a rendezvous was made with von Spee's group on 12 August 1914.

Muller had been thinking for some time of the best use which might be made of *Emden* and during a meeting which von Spee held with his commanding officers in his flagship *Scharnhorst* on 13 August, Muller voiced his ideas. These were that it would be potentially valuable to send at least one light cruiser to the Indian Ocean where the conditions for cruiser warfare might be particularly favourable. Also, that the appearance of a German unit off the coast of India might have a telling effect on the minds of the local populace. Von Spee concurred and when the German ships put to sea the following day, a signal was made from *Scharnhorst* detaching *Emden*. Muller could therefore act as a free agent from the time of his detachment.

The German raider took four weeks to reach the Indian Ocean which had been allocated to Muller as his specific operational area. The voyage took *Emden* through the Flores Sea and waters bordering the Dutch East Indies. During this time a dummy funnel was added to the ship's outfit of three real ones. This was at the suggestion of Muller's First Lieutenant, von Mucke. The fourth funnel gave the raider a silhouette remarkably similar to that of Royal Navy cruisers of the *Yarmouth* class. At the end of the first week in September 1914, *Emden*, still in company with *Markomannia*, was in transit across the Bay of Bengal to work the shipping lanes into Calcutta.

It might be possible to claim that the fitting of a dummy fourth funnel worked a treat, because the coming weeks saw *Emden* at the peak of her raiding career. On the night of 9/10 September, a Greek freighter called *Pontoporros* was captured. Examination showed that she was carrying over six thousand tons of Bengal coal for the UK Government. Muller thought that this cargo was too good to miss and the fact that the Greek merchantman was working for the British Government made the cargo legitimate contraband so he put a prize crew on board.

The following day a British ship called *Indus*, en route to Colombo to transport troops was stopped, her crew transferred to *Pontoporros*, and the transport herself sent to the bottom. It was noted that *Indus* would be unlikely to be registered as missing until she had failed to make her estimated time of arrival in Bombay on 15 September. This should give the German raider some time to play with, or in which to leave the area if so desired.

1. Q-ship *Penshurst* under attack. A dress rehearsal showing the panic party rowing away in one of the ship's boats and the guns about to fire. The mizzen mast is raised. Compare next picture.

2. *Penshurst* at sea. In contrast to the previous picture, the mizzen mast is lowered, the funnel is painted a different colour with a white band near the top and, as if she were a tramp steamer, the crew's washing is drying. Behind the white screen on the lower bridge is a six-pounder gun on each side, with a range from ahead in an arc to astern.

3. Q-ship *Penshurst* at anchor. This picture shows the bridge-screen lowered on the port side and the bridge gun ready for action. The mizzen mast is raised.

4. Q-sailing ship *Mitchell* at sea. One of the most famous of the sailing ships drafted as a Q-ship. *Mitchell's* armament is concealed by the dummy deckhouse on the poop.

5. Q-ship *Baralong* at Malta. The former three island tramp steamer, *Baralong,* is at anchor in Malta's Grand Harbour after being transferred to the Mediterranean. She was victorious in two actions against submarines. Note the hospital ship in the distance.

6. Q-ship *Redbreast.* A rare photograph of *Redbreast* which had only six month's service as a Q ship from March to September 1916.

7. Q-ship *Antwerp* looking astern, showing the collapsible dummy life-raft which concealed the two twelve-pounder guns. A far cry from her former life as a Great Eastern Railway passenger ship.

8. Gun's crew of Q-ship *Antwerp*. The crew prepares to fire on a submarine. The sides of the dummy life-raft have been collapsed to permit the gun's use.

9. The dummy deckhouse of a Q-ship. A photograph looking astern showing the guns and collapsed sides of the deckhouse which concealed them when not in action.

10. Q-ship *Farnborough*.
With her White Ensign still flying, *Farnborough* is seen listing heavily after her arrival at Berehaven.

11. The hunt for *Dresden*.
H.M.S. *Kent*, in company with battlecruiser *Invincible* and merchant cruiser *Orama*, prepares to leave the Falkland Islands to search for *Dresden*, December 1914.

12. *Dresden* discovered.
Dresden at Juan Fernandez in a photograph taken from one of the British cruisers on 14 March 1915. Her guns are trained on the British.

13. *Dresden's* end.
14 March 1915. The raider *Dresden* finally sinking in the bay at Juan Fernandez.

14. The raider *Karlsruhe*.
Karlsruhe was a successful raider until 4 November 1914 when she exploded for no apparent reason about 300 miles from Barbados.

15. The sinking of the raider *Cap Trafalgar*.
Carmania sinking the raider *Cap Trafalgar*. This merchant cruiser was also involved in the hunt for *Moewe*. (From the painting by C.E. Turner).

16. Minelayer *Konigin Luise*.
On 3 August, 1914 *Konigin Luise* completes provisioning at Ems before heading into the
North Sea to lay mines off the Thames estuary.

17. Minelayer *Meteor*.
In August 1915 German minelayer *Meteor* is pictured on fire after officers had ignited a
time-bomb just before the approach of British cruisers.

18. H.M.S *Audacious* sinking.
After striking one of the mines laid by *Berlin*, H.M.S. *Audacious* foundered. This picture was taken from the White Star liner *Olympic* and shows a destroyer standing by *Audacious* to rescue her crew.

19. H.M.S *Orion*. Two pen and ink sketches made by the author when a midshipman in H.M.S *Orion* after the events described, in which *Orion* served as part of Admiral Pridham-Wippell's force in the eastern Mediterranean in 1941.

20. H.M.S *Warspite*.
In 1941 *Warspite* was part of Admiral Cunningham's contingent in the eastern Mediterranean. The author served on the 'Old Lady', a veteran of World War I, at D Day in 1944 – her last active engagement.

The meeting with the packet boat *Lovat* took place on 11 September 1914. She was flying the Blue Ensign of the Indian Government and could be looked upon as a bigger edition of *Indus* having been converted for the transport of troops and horses. Like *Indus, Lovat* was en route to Bombay to embark soldiers. Muller kindly allowed the crew to take personal effects with them and transferred the new captives to *Markomannia*. *Emden's* sinking party did their work and when they had been re-embarked, fire was opened at short range. Generous quantities of stores and luxury items had been transferred from *Indus,* so *Emden* took practically nothing from *Lovat.*

On 12 September the British ship *Kabinga* was taken after *Emden* had sailed closer to the Calcutta Lightship off the north of the Hooghly river. Muller had considered eradicating the light vessel and, perhaps, apprehending the pilot boat for the Hooghly. This difficult waterway is hardly passable without the aid of an experienced pilot. These actions would have played merry hell with seaborne trade in the area. The raider was snooping about south of Calcutta as the two captured masters divulged that at least three other ships had been astern of them. One of these was the *Kabinga* which was loaded with goods from Calcutta-based British companies destined for North American ports. They were technically neutral property and therefore untouchable, which implied that the vessel carrying this cargo should not be harmed. Muller decided that there was another role for *Kabinga* to play. He transferred the crews of the previous victims and directed that they should be transported to Calcutta.

The next day, 13 September, yielded two more offerings, namely the *Killin* and *Diplomat* the latter being an elegant ship of 7,600 tons loaded with a valuable cargo of tea. Muller ordained that she should be sunk without delay.

The *Clan Matheson*, with an enticing cargo of motor cars, locomotives, typewriters and other expensive items including a splendid racehorse was sunk on 14 September. Animal lovers will be relieved to know that the horse was given the '*coup de grâce*' with a pistol shot to the head before the ship was left to her doom. *Clan Matheson* had been en route between Britain and Calcutta until she had her encounter with *Emden*. Her ship's company were transferred to *Markomannia* before their ship was scuttled. They were permitted to take the usual liberal allowance of personal belongings with them. The *Trabbock,* another British freighter, was sunk later on the same day.

By this time, a state verging on panic had begun to spread among shipping using the Indian Ocean. The Australian authorities delayed the departure of troop transports destined for Britain and the *Emden* legend began to spread.

Those released by Captain von Muller told their stories when they were back on shore; and even though many of them had never met Muller himself, the myth was indelibly fixed. The ship and the captain whose leadership decided her code of conduct and built her fine reputation became known as the 'Gentleman-of-War' to his main antagonists at sea, the British Navy, its Allies and a vast number of admirers on a global basis.

Muller, in the meantime, having stopped a scruffy Italian ship, *Loredano*, and allowed her to continue, came to the conclusion that it might be prudent to proceed into other waters. *Emden* therefore appeared off Madras during the evening of 22 September 1914, and shelled the storage tanks of the Burma Oil Company from a range of a mile and a half. One hundred and thirty rounds were discharged and of the order of a thousand tons of fuel were set ablaze. A shore battery opened fire on *Emden,* but completely without effect. The German raider withdrew, displaying her port navigation lights to give the illusion that she was proceeding to the north. The ship was soon completely darkened and headed south.

The effects of the German bombardment in material terms were minimal, but the psychological leverage caused by the gun strike was great. For some days after the short bombardment, trains going inland were crowded with people who were anxious to transfer themselves out of the range of shells fired by the mystery ship lying offshore. This fear not only took root in the Madras area, but it spread quite widely along the coast. The local economy was affected for weeks, largely due to the fact that money-lenders were amongst the most zealous of the fugitives and took their wealth from as far away as the city of Calcutta comfortably inland.

Emden was off Colombo on the night of 25 September, and Muller had the presumption to use the ambient glow of the searchlights being operated from sites ashore to take the crew off a large merchant ship with a cargo of sugar and incarcerate them in *Markomannia's* hold. He then sank the merchantman.

Four more names were added to *Emden*'s growing list of victims during the next two days. On 28 September a collier by the name of *Buresk*, loaded with seven thousand tons of Welsh steam coal, was captured. The prize could not have appeared at a more opportune moment. The supplies of fuel on board *Markomannia* had all been consumed and the coal in *Pontoporros* had proved to be of indifferent quality. In addition, the time was nigh for the raider to carry out another disappearing trick. There were sixteen Allied warships, from Britain, France, Russia and Japan, searching for Muller although it must be admitted that at this time they were also seeking von Spee, whose position was not known until he bombarded Papeete.

The Allies were well-equipped with bases in the Far East, namely Colombo, Singapore, George Town (at the head of the Malacca Straits),

Hong Kong and others. German ships did not have the luxury of this type of support.

It might be appropriate at this stage to consider the great importance of coal in this conflict. King Coal provided the lifeblood of raiders, in the days when the majority of ships propelled by steam used coal to produce steam by heating water to the appropriate temperature in their boilers.

A raider basically needed to have her own colliers with her, or to arrange rendezvous points where she could meet a friendly collier when its services were necessary; and to be able to rely upon meeting a supply vessel where and at the time required was a risky business. Another, not so satisfactory option, was to capture enemy colliers. However, it should not be forgotten that from the turn of the century into the years of World War I coal was one of Britain's major exports and could be transported in either sailing or steam-powered colliers. Perhaps as much as seventy per cent of world trade was connected with coal. Britain was fortunate in having vast quantities of good quality coal in its mining areas. Welsh steam coal, for example, had a worldwide reputation for excellence. As late as the early 1930s, British naval officers were arguing against the bondage to oil. To quote from *The Times*, dated 29 April 1926:

> It is an open secret that during the Great War there were occasions on which the ships of our fleet with their boilers burning oil were in serious straits for the fuel necessary to enable them to put to sea; if all, or even a majority of our merchant ships had been dependent on oil, the importation of essential supplies of food and material must have been more gravely jeopardised than it was, because of the absence of oil the vessels on which we relied would have been unable to move.

The arguments went on to explain that if such were the case in the 1914–18 war when the great majority of British ships, both naval and mercantile, were coal-burners, and when America was neutral or an ally, what would the situation be when the Navy had expelled coal from its ships and the Merchant Marine was feverishly engaged in the same pursuit?

Do not forget that British offshore oil sources were not thought of in the years under discussion and conventional wisdom had it that a mere two per cent of the world's oil was to be found within the British Empire and some eighty per cent was possessed by America. The oil which England controlled was for the most part managed financially by international organisations. Financial control in times of peace may be perfectly acceptable; but in war it is physical possession which really matters. Great Britain might have financial control of pretty well everything in the world; but when a war becomes hot the nation might find that it has remarkably little control of anything at all. The argument continued that the substitution of foreign oil for British coal as the lifeblood of the nation's seapower, and progressively of industrial enterprises, had added enormously to the responsibilities of the Royal Navy and thus to the size of the fleet that it was necessary to maintain. The complete dependence of the British Isles upon oil and therefore upon foreign nations and more especially America, could be an even greater source of weakness than the tragic, and growing, deficiency of Britain's home-grown food supply. It can be debated whether Britain could have defended its seaborne food if the propulsion plants of its ships could not be operated. However, Britain could not carry or defend its food or its small remaining fuel supplies if, say, the USA were to place an embargo on oil supplies.

More arguments and debating points on the oil versus steam theme could be deployed and many people still believe that Britain is wasting its potential asset of very large coal reserves. Nevertheless, colliers were a very common sight on the world's oceans at the time when the cruiser *Emden's* exploits were at their peak.

It was time for *Emden* to carry out another vanishing move, as mentioned earlier. Muller was able to deduce from the increase in radio traffic that a significant number of hostile warships were carrying out surveillance activities in his operational area. Perhaps fortunately for the Allies, *Emden* was not fitted with direction-finding equipment which would have assisted the raider to estimate the positions of the hunting men-of-war. Muller decided to track south, aiming for the attractive island of Diego Garcia in the Chagos Archipelago. Diego Garcia was a remote British possession centrally placed in the Indian Ocean, about ten degrees south of the Equator. *Emden* arrived on 10 October 1914.

At that time the island's only connection with the world at large was a quarterly, or less frequent, visit by sea from Mauritius. The vessel's last call had been made before the outbreak of the First World War. *Emden's* ship's company was hospitably welcomed by their British cousins and were, naturally, extremely careful not to disturb this amicable relationship. Advantage was taken of the cordial situation to tilt the ship and to scrape as much of the ship's bottom as possible, rather as sailing ships were careened and submarine growth removed from below the waterline in the days of sail.

While the *Emden's* ship's company were occupied in attending to some of their raider's needs, the Royal Navy took some restitution for recently received injuries. On 15 October the British cruiser *Yarmouth* discovered and sank *Markomannia* and also recaptured *Pontoporros* and routed her to Singapore.

Emden soon made her presence felt again; on this occasion she was active in shipping routes to the west of the southern tip of India, Cape Comorin. On 15 October, in a matter of hours, the raider made short work of four British merchantmen and a dredger, then stopped another ship and transferred prisoners from the first five to her, then she captured a seventh victim. This chanced to be the British collier *Exford*, which was then co-opted as a successor to the lamented *Markomannia*, to act as *Emden*'s supply vessel.

The British media and public were now becoming distinctly upset. Previously people had seen the racy side of *Emden*'s exploits and the crews of her prizes had spoken of the excellent and fair treatment which they had received at the hands of Muller and his subordinates. However, enough was becoming enough. The value of ships lost, to say nothing of their cargoes, was being counted in terms of millions of pounds, marine insurance rates were climbing sky high, and merchant shipping in the Indian Ocean was grinding to a virtual halt.

There was not very much that the British Admiralty could do, except to issue the odd soothing statement pointing out that several commerce raiders were plying their trade in the Atlantic, Indian and Pacific Oceans, that a large number of Allied warships were hunting them, and requesting that the great British public should exercise the virtue of patience.

On 28 October *Emden* eclipsed her previous achievements. This time the target was Penang which is an island lying just off the north-west coast of the then British colony of Malaya and a popular stopping point for liners to give their passengers a run ashore.

The harbour of George Town is situated on a tongue of land which cuts about halfway across the narrow strait, which separates the island from the mainland and gives natural shelter, with approaches from north and south. The southern approach is shallow and only suitable for smaller vessels. Muller's plan seems to have been to enter the harbour at speed, select one or more targets, engage the same and to rush out again. It was a daring concept which depended for its success largely upon the element of surprise. As always on these occasions, there were a number of unknowns, for example, Muller could not know how many and what size warships there might be in harbour. He did not know that Royal Navy ships used George Town and that the cruiser *Yarmouth* was a not unknown visitor. The moon was not due to be up until 0200 on the day of the attack and the German cruiser ought not to be visible from a raised observation post which overlooked George Town at that time.

Emden duly entered the roadstead before daybreak and proceeded into the sheltered bay. The ship was meticulously darkened and the dummy funnel had been rigged so that she resembled a British light cruiser. The raider was also flying a White Ensign which was shifted just before she opened fire.

A Russian light cruiser of somewhat ancient design, of about three thousand tons and completed in 1903, became the target for a torpedo as *Emden* passed. *Zhemchug*, the Russian cruiser, was also swept by German gunfire. Incidentally, other spellings of the Russian ship's name have been encountered, but the sound is much the same.

Muller turned and discharged another torpedo which triggered off a very large explosion on board the Russian cruiser which broke in two and sank within seconds rather than minutes. The time was then approximately 0530.

The captain of the Russian cruiser, Baron Cherkassov, a captain second grade, equivalent to a commander in the Royal Navy, seems to have been a very laid back officer and was ashore when his ship was attacked. In the film I saw in my early youth, the gallant Russian Commanding Officer was enjoying a romantic dalliance with a voluptuous girlfriend ashore. This is believed to have been based on what actually happened.

Cherkassov had been warned that Penang was undefended and that there was a need to take special precautions in case *Zhemchug* were to be subjected to an attack from the sea. Before he went ashore, *Zhemchug*'s captain had directed that torpedoes should be disarmed and ready use ammunition be secured, with the exception of twelve rounds. In addition, the fires were let out in all but one of *Zhemchug*'s boilers. No attempt was made to detail extra watchkeepers for duty and no directions were given that the cruiser should be darkened. It seems that *Zhemchug* could only be described as a 'slap happy', negligent ship.

After shifting his attention from the Russian, Muller was about to deal in like manner with the large French gunboat, *D'Iberville* which was moored farther into the harbour. At this moment, one of the German lookouts reported what he thought to be a sizeable British destroyer standing off the entrance to the bay. Muller immediately headed for the open sea, where he could fight to better advantage, but discovered that he had become a victim of a trick of the light. The ship in question was the British cruiser *Glenturret,* which was awaiting the arrival of a pilot. *Emden* sent a boarding party, but this was hastily recalled, and their boat hoisted, as a dense cloud of smoke had been seen bearing down from the north. This was the small French destroyer, *Mousquet,* which was returning at the end of a patrol in the Malacca Straits. She had been at too great a distance to have heard gunfire or the explosion which had heralded the end of the Russian cruiser. *Mousquet*'s commanding officer took the four-funnelled cruiser to be a British warship and duly hoisted his recognition signal.

No one could deny that the roadstead was anything but poorly guarded. *D'Iberville*'s captain had raised the problem with the British authorities on a number of occasions, but to no avail. At this time his ship was incapable of putting to sea as her engines were being refitted. As a matter of interest, he and members of his ship's company had also mistaken *Emden* for an Allied cruiser. During the previous night some of *Zhemchug*'s liberty men had returned from their shore leave in a very obstreporous state, having shown little self-control in doing justice to the local liquor. It would not have been surprising if some of the more inebrated had let off a few rounds in the relaxed state of discipline which seemed to be the mark of this ship. This could have provided an explanation of the firing which had been heard earlier.

Two other small French destroyers, the *Fronde* and *Pistolet*, were secured alongside a jetty. Their crew members had rapidly realised what was really afoot. *Pistolet* had trained her torpedo tubes on *Emden* but the raider had not passed closer than seventeen hundred yards while the maximum range of *Pistolet's* torpedoes was a mere six hundred yards. Her captain raised steam but *Fronde* like *D'Iberville* was immobilised because of work being carried out on machinery.

Pistolet sighted *Emden* in the distance as soon as she cleared the bay. Strenuous efforts were made to raise the steam pressure, but *Pistolet* was not able to reach the scene of action in time to assist *Mousquet* in engaging the raider. This was probably just as well as she could only have suffered the same fate as *Mousquet*, which had not yet been sunk, but soon would be after a gallant yet hopeless action.

The time had been shortly before 0700 when *Emden* first opened fire. By 0715 *Mousquet* had gone down, firing to the last and taking forty-three members of her company with her. *Emden* rescued thirty-six survivors, but five of these died later.

The German raider retired at speed, heading north-west with the aim of clearing the Straits as soon as practicable. *Pistolet* attempted to keep *Emden* in sight, but without success due to the cruiser's superior performance and the effects upon the smaller ship of a swell.

Muller stopped the British cargo ship *Newburn* on 29 October 1914. The survivors from *Mousquet* were transferred and *Newburn* was instructed to go to Sabang. By this time *Emden* had sunk or captured some seventy thousand tons of Allied shipping to say nothing of the ships she had set free after capture or the *Pontoporros* which had been recovered by British naval action. Allied warships were now at Muller's heels and spirited efforts were being made to hunt him. The fact that about thirty thousand Australian and New Zealand troops were then embarked in a convoy which was tracking across the Indian Ocean on their way to help the 'Mother Country' in her hour of danger made it all the more necessary to deal with threats such as that posed by Muller and his ship. The Admiralty was doing its best to send reinforcements to Admiral Jerram's squadron. However, an unforeseen chance was soon to allay worries connected with *Emden's* operations.

The presence of the German raider in the vicinity of the shipping routes between Ceylon and Sumatra was becoming too well known and this was the area in which *Newburn* had been accosted. Muller, therefore, decided that it was time to move to the south once again. As part of this exercise, the two supply vessels, the prizes *Buresk* and *Exford*, were ordered to rendezvous with *Emden* at the Cocos Islands.

The small specks of land, which *Emden* was closing from the north-east and the troop convoy was approaching from the south-east in the early days of November 1914, are approximately 840 miles south of the equator and 2,300 miles to the west of Darwin in northern Australia. The land area of the islets only amounts to some five and a half square miles; and there are two atolls about sixteen miles apart. The northerly atoll features a small island called North Keeling, while the southerly comprises twenty-six small islands and islets which are grouped around a shallow lagoon about ten miles wide at its widest point, with an entrance at its northern end.

I vividly remember the clear, unpolluted water when the ship in which I was serving anchored in the lagoon. The anchor could be clearly seen on the bottom and the sailors were asking if hands could be piped to bathe. That is until the sharks arrived and began to nose around the visitor, as clearly visible as though they were moving about in a beautifully kept aquarium.

The islands were discovered in the year 1609 by one William Keeling who was a mariner in the employ of the British East India Company and who gave them his own name. Time passed until the 1820s when the islands were settled, in a manner of speaking, by an adventurer called Alexander Hare, who appeared with a personal harem and a suite of slaves which he had recruited from the Malay Archipelego. Hare, possibly worn out by his seemingly golden life, made way for John Clunies Ross, a descendant of Shetland Islanders, who settled on Direction Island with his family in 1827. John Clunies Ross employed the now resident Malays in the development of coconut plantations. His heirs stayed on. In 1857 the islands came under the British Crown and were administered from Ceylon, now Sri Lanka, from 1878. George Clunies Ross regularised his family's possession of the islands by obtaining a grant in perpetuity from Queen Victoria. In 1903 the islands were transferred to the Straits Settlements for bureacratic purposes. 'Perpetuity' is rather an elastic word when applied to possessions such as colonies, and in this instance it lasted until 1978 when another John Clunies Ross gave up his family's title and sold off the islands to Australia, whose flag had flown there since 1955.

The name Cocos used as a title for the island group stems from the great number of coconut trees which grow in graceful abundance. There must be 300,000 growing in the limited acreage of the Cocos–Keeling group.

Cable & Wireless run a communication station on Direction Island. In 1914 the owners went by the name of the Eastern Extension Telegraph Company Limited. The station has furnished an important junction of three cables, to Fremantle and the Australia–New Zealand network, to Batavia and the British and Dutch networks in south-east Asia and to Rodriguez Island and nearby Mauritius which was linked in turn to South Africa and, via the Seychelles, to East Africa. In 1914 the station was a vital point in one of only two cable connections between Britain and Australia passing through solely British Empire territories. It is, perhaps, worth recording that the other cable was that which passed across the Atlantic, to Vancouver in Canada, then across the Pacific via Fanning Island, Fiji, Norfolk Island and New Zealand.

The German light cruiser *Nurnberg,* belonging to von Spee's squadron, raided Fanning Island on 7 September 1914. *Nurnberg's* landing party made such an effective job of their cable-cutting operation that it took practically two months to achieve repairs. The cable service was reported as having been restored on 1 November 1914.

To return to the cruiser *Emden,* Muller's aim was to destroy the radio station and cut the cables at Direction Island as an overture to raiding shipping using the Sunda Strait. This strait separates Sumatra from Java and is the area in which Captain Ahab at last ran down Moby Dick, the great white whale, in Herman Melville's stirring story. *Emden* appeared off Port Refuge, a bay on the north coast of Direction Island, at first light on 9 November. The raider was disguising herself as a four-funnel cruiser, but the dummy was so sorely battered by frequent use that it was unlikely to deceive anyone. The shore radio operator reacted quickly and began to transmit distress calls. *Emden* tried to jam the signals but she was too late.

The previously mentioned convoy of Australian troops was passing about fifty miles north of the Cocos Keeling Islands when the distress messages were intercepted by the cruiser *Melbourne.* Two other cruisers were stationed among the escort force, namely the Australian *Sydney* and the Japanese *Ibuki.* Captain Silver, the escort force commander, detached *Sydney* and at 0700 Captain Glossop, commanding *Sydney,* was ordered to proceed to the Cocos Islands at his best speed.

Muller, at this point in time, did not seem to be aware of any danger. He had sent his executive officer, von Mucke, ashore with fifty men to blow up the wireless station and to cut cables. The latter exercise was proving to be lengthy and laborious due to a lack of suitable tools. Only one cable had been cut when Muller gave signs of impatience and signalled for the landing party's work to be expedited. The signalling was soon followed by short blasts on the ship's siren. *Emden* was next seen standing out to sea, leaving von Mucke and his party on shore. The reason for the sudden departure became clear when the cruiser's guns commenced firing.

In the forenoon of 9 November 1914 Muller signalled his landing party to return; and at 0915 Muller precipitately took his ship to sea as *Sydney* had been sighted approaching from the north-east at high speed. At about 0940 *Sydney* was on *Emden's* port beam. Captain Glossop turned *Sydney* on to a parallel course and opened fire at a range of about 10,500 yards, say, five and a quarter miles. The engagement began at the extreme range of *Emden's* 4-inch guns, but comfortably within the range of *Sydney's* 6-inch armament. Another factor which should be taken into account is that *Sydney* had not been very long at sea since her last spell in dock, and had a comparatively clean bottom. As six weeks had elapsed since *Emden's* somewhat makeshift and incomplete scraping off Diego Garcia, taking everything into consideration, *Sydney* had a four- to five-knot speed advantage over her adversary, on the occasion of *Emden's* last battle. This would have given Captain Glossop the advantage of being able to adjust the range, more or less, as he thought fit.

Despite any disadvantages under which they might be working, *Emden's* guns' crews were the first to find their target. The Australians were about a thousand yards over, due to a range-finding error. This caused a few men to suffer wounds and resulted in the destruction of the after control position; but that was the final damage which *Emden* succeeded in inflicting. The German cruiser started to suffer severely as soon as the necessary corrections had been applied to *Sydney's* gunnery control system. Captain Glossop basically kept his distance and was able to steadily shoot his victim to pieces.

Among other things, a hit damaged the *Emden's* steering mechanism which meant that Muller was obliged to steer using his main engines and this resulted in a further reduction in his speed of advance. The forward funnel and mainmast were brought down, several guns were put out of action and fires were started in a number of sections of the ship.

Sydney closed the range to 5,500 yards and discharged a torpedo which ran wide of its target. Captain Glossop then increased the range once again and the unequal contest continued with the two ships on nearly parallel courses. When this phase of the engagement had continued for about forty minutes, all *Emden's* funnels had collapsed, gun control facilities had been knocked out and large clouds of smoke were being given off by the fires on board. So much so that, at one moment, observers in *Sydney* could no longer see their antagonist and thought that she might have gone down. However, *Emden* reappeared, steering towards the east and still firing. The German ship then turned in a wide circle and *Sydney* conformed with her movements so that both ships were steering towards North Keeling Island. Before *Sydney* could take any useful action to intercept her, *Emden*, which was subsiding lower in the water, was driven ashore by her captain. At 1115 engines were stopped and the German cruiser took to the ground between two reefs, gliding under her own momentum. For the last time, Muller ordered full steam ahead with the aim that the wreck should be driven as high as possible on to the reef.

Sydney fired two more salvoes at the helpless ship. Certain that his prey could not get off the reef, Captain Glossop turned away to cope with the supply ship *Buresk* which had been hovering some miles to the south-east of North Keeling Island to await the result of the engagement between the two cruisers. When it became obvious that *Sydney* had started to pursue her, the German crew of *Buresk* scuttled their ship.

At 1600 *Sydney* returned to *Emden* where colours were still flying.

Captain Glossop made a signal to enquire whether the German cruiser wished to surrender. Muller replied that the message was not understood. Two salvoes were discharged which added to the chaos on the decks of the wounded German raider. Muller, whose position was hopeless, hauled down his flag.

The use of conventional warships of the cruiser type in World War I has been given some attention, with particular emphasis on the cruiser *Emden* which illustrates what one well-commanded vessel can achieve; and the effect it can have upon a superior navy's efforts to hunt it down. German raiders have been chosen against the background of the First World War. There is also good reason for this choice as the Royal Navy held the exclusive position of being the superior naval force and this position was enhanced when the US Navy joined in the struggle on the same side as its British equivalent. It is also fascinating to see some of the techniques used by British decoy ships being applied to disguise surface raiders. In the later months of the year 1915, Germany had dusted off plans to revive the war against her opponent's maritime commerce and to try out some fresh techniques. A number of the new ideas were displayed when the German authorities picked an unremarkable ship which had been launched at Geestemunde in May 1914. The specially selected vessel was a single-screw steamship of 4,500 tons, fitted with two masts and with a designed speed of fourteen knots. Another characteristic was a length of 385 feet. The original intention was that the completed ship should be employed in transporting loads of bananas from Germany's colonies in Africa to the port of Hamburg. She was accordingly fitted to produce adequate supplies of electricity and the appropriate refrigerating plant. The banana boat was originally given the name *Pugno*, but this was changed to *Moewe* ('seagull' in English) when the ship was acquired by the German Government.

Moewe was painted black, with poop, forecastle and superstructure coloured white. She was fitted with a number of cunning devices; but, despite this, the objective was maintained of ensuring that she should present the appearance of being a very ordinary deep-sea steamship.

Bulwarks were erected between the bridge and the forecastle to screen the ship's guns and torpedo tubes. She was also capable of disguising herself within a very short space of time by such subterfuges as raising or lowering fake sections of superstructure, and even extending the upper part of her stern. Many of the tricks were used by British Q ships; and it is astonishing how simply the individuality of a ship can be disguised by the employment of some ingenuity and a generous application of paint. As a matter of interest, the use of a fake funnel was a far from new idea and had been indulged in by British warships during periodic exercises held by British naval vessels long before the outbreak of the First World War. The underlying doctrine of disguising men-of-war goes back to the days when sail and rigging provided the motive power of naval vessels.

A slow-moving, eighteenth-century warship could entice an enemy merchant vessel or warship by acting the part of a merchantman, then suddenly opening fire when the latter was within comfortable range. Pests, such as pirates, could also be trapped in like manner. Among the French, such mystery ships were known as *vaisseaux-trompeurs*. The old-time commanding officers of men-of-war could convincingly deceive victims by painting out gun-ports or giving a slovenly impression to the set of sails or the positioning of yards; this apart from the use of false colours. Even in the seventeenth century British commanding officers were able to deceive such competent mariners as the Dutch by housing guns, showing no colours and working their warships in an awkward fashion. In the reign of King Charles II a naval vessel, called *Kingfisher*, was specially built by the British to resemble a most common type of substantial merchantman. This ship was fitted with collapsible bulwarks and a detachable head. She was then despatched to the Mediterranean to give the Barbary pirates something to think about. Somewhat later, Lord Cochrane disguised his brig *Speedy* to impersonate a Danish brig which was familiar to the Spaniards. He went so far as to employ a Danish quartermaster to add the necessary realism when hails were being made.

When the Germans decided to rely upon subterfuge rather than speed for the prosperity of their surface raiding operations, they were employing a well-tried and sound method.

Moewe was equipped with two 4.1-inch guns mounted under the forecastle, two more guns of the same calibre which were mounted abaft the break of the forecastle, and a 22-pounder mounted on the poop and disguised as manual-steering gear (another popular Q ship artifice). Two torpedo tubes were sited between the bridge and the foremast. *Moewe* was also designed to carry a few hundred mines and to have the appropriate facilities for the laying of them.

In *Moewe* there was a very different type of raider. She was, in no way, an exceptional ship like an ex-liner or an elegant high performance military cruiser, which had been detailed to carry out commerce-raiding duties, but a quite run of the mill steamship of moderate size and speed. The advantage of that concept was that she was just the type of vessel which could be expected on pretty well any trade route and would be unlikely to excite suspicion. This new-style raider required carefully selected personnel to man her, the personal attributes being very similar to those which the British found to be needed when choosing the ship's company of a decoy ship.

In the event, the German Admiralty selected Korvettan-Kapitän (Commander) Graf Nikolaus zu Dohn-Schlodien who was a very able officer well-suited to *Moewe's* special service as a raider.

Moewe's commanding officer received instructions before setting out from Germany, which essentially directed that the raider should lay mines in various places along the enemy's coast, then carry out cruiser warfare.

Shortly before Christmas 1915, everything seemed to be in order and, in thick weather, the ostensibly innocent cargo ship set forth into the North Sea. Her route took her close enough to the Norwegian coast for the snow-clad mountains to be visible. Advantage was taken of the long hours of darkness, associated with the weeks adjacent to the shortest day, to avoid the British blockade and to arrive without incident at the area where the first minefield was due to be laid. This was off the north coast of Scotland, east of Cape Wrath, and useful assistance in fixing her position was given to *Moewe* by the beams emanating from Sule Skerry Lighthouse, west of Orkney. On New Year's Day the raider disgorged her horrible mines.

For the technically minded, the mines had been stowed in long rows in the parent ship's hold and were run on rails to a lift which raised them to the upper deck where they were arranged in rows, on rails. This was a conventional method of operation in largeish vessels which had been converted to minelayers. The upper deck rails projected about three feet outboard to ensure that individual mines would be dropped clear of the ship's side. It could be a little awkward if this sensible precaution was not taken.

The minelaying exercise was carried out between about 1800 and 2330. The prescribed gaps between the release of individual mines were regulated by the simple, but effective, control of an officer who was armed with a stop-watch. In spite of the all too customary gale, often up to force 10 to 12 on the Beaufort Scale, which blows in mid-winter in the northern extremities of the British Isles, the German visitor was able to lay two hundred and fifty mines in eleven different lines. The aim of this nautical feat was to catch deeper-draught vessels in sea areas where British warships were known to carry out exercises and firings of various sorts, or to pass when going to more southerly ports for, say, refits.

Thanks to *Moewe*, the western approach to the Pentland Firth had been contaminated and it could only be a matter of time before some sort of maritime mishap occurred. It did on 6 January when the battleship *King Edward VII*, of 16,350 tons, which had been completed in 1905, was en route to Belfast from Scapa Flow to refit. As ill-luck would have it, it chanced to be low water when this capital ship unsuspectingly steamed over the south-eastern corner of the minefield. At 0700 a severe explosion erupted below her starboard engine room which caused water to pour in and the ship to heel over to starboard. A heavy sea was still running; but she was taken in tow until she finally needed to be abandoned. Fortunately there were no lives lost; but the warship turned over and sank that evening.

King Edward VII was not the only ship to suffer. The following day, the Norwegian SS *Bonheur* foundered; and HMS *Africa,* another battleship on transit between Belfast and Scapa Flow, had the almost unbelievably good fortune to pass through the mined area untouched only a few hours before *King Edward VII* met its fate.

The minesweepers soon started their work and large ships were routed well north of Orkney. The mined area was partially cleared, but it tended to be avoided until shortly after the First World War had ended. By that time the lousy weather of three winters in these unfriendly waters was deemed to have cleared all remaining mines.

From the German viewpoint, *Moewe*'s minefield had been a splendid success. However, it was more harmful to the Allies than could be measured by the sinking of a ten-year-old battleship. The weather was too boisterous for the minesweepers to carry on with their task for weeks on end, so extra time and fuel was taken by British warships having to make lengthy detours to avoid the area.

From the point of view of the British Grand Fleet, two serious dangers were shown up. The first highlighted the fact that there was a significant risk that the Grand Fleet could be 'mined in' at its own base. The second pointed to the Admiralty's need to order more minesweepers and for the shipyards to deliver them as soon as was humanly possible. A ray of light glimmered in the form of a paravane which could be launched and streamed from a ship's bows, one operating from either side. As a protective device, the paravane had the great advantage that it was attached to the parent ship itself.

The position of *Moewe*'s first minefield had been selected well, and before its existence had been discovered by the Allies, the raider was miles away in the Atlantic having made its way west of Ireland and into the Bay of Biscay until the French coast was closed. On about 9 January the remainder of the German ship's mines were laid off La Rochelle, not far distant from the area in which it had been suggested, in the eighteenth century, that French decoy ships should loiter in the hope of intercepting British privateers. Two Spanish merchantmen fell victim to the German mines during the first half of January.

When she had laid her dangerous cargo, *Moewe* was at liberty to carry out the second part of the directions which had been given to her commanding officer, namely, to open hostilities against the commercial activities which Britain had been continuing with great regularity with overseas powers and, incidentally, to the chagrin of Germany.

It would be tempting to launch into a blow by blow account of most, if not all, of *Moewe*'s encounters with merchant ships belonging to Britain and her Allies. However, that is not the purpose of the present study which seeks to look at the broader picture and the lessons learned from the activities of this particular raider.

There is an exception to the above, which needs to be covered for reasons which should later become obvious. On 15 January 1915 two

British merchant ships fell into the hands of *Moewe's* commanding officer. The first was the *Ariadne*, a vessel of some three thousand tons, which was loaded with a cargo of maize and which was intercepted about a hundred and forty miles east of Madeira where the German raider was well placed to ambush shipping tracking to the northwards from West Africa or from south-east America. *Ariadne* was disposed of by gunfire and the, perhaps, extravagant expenditure of a single torpedo. Soon after *Ariadne's* demise, an impressive-looking passenger liner was spotted on a northerly heading. *Moewe's* course was established to cross her bows and to verify her identity with reference to that invaluable publication, *Lloyd's Register*.

The elegant new arrival turned out to be the Elder-Dempster liner *Appam* which initially refused to stop and began to signal for help on her wireless transmitter. A shell across her bow soon brought *Appam* to, because defensively armed though she might be, there were the lives of the passengers to be taken into consideration. It was one thing to discharge shells from aft at a submarine; but it would be a very one-sided duel with women and children on board, to engage a much more heavily armed surface raider. *Moewe* jammed the radio signals so that they would not have meant very much had they been intercepted by any of Sir Archibald Moore's naval units.

The British flag officer controlling the Madeira–Canaries area had under his control HM Ships *King Alfred* and *Essex,* which were both cruisers, and the two armed merchant cruisers *Carmania* and *Ophir*. Farther south, off the Cape Verde Islands, was the cruiser *Highflyer* together with the armed merchant cruiser *Marmara*. *Moewe* had been taking a considerable risk in visiting this area and her only hope of safety really lay in her masterly skill at changing her outward appearance while maintaining a keen lookout for any vessel that might remotely resemble a hostile warship. In this instance, when a fairly fast and substantial ship needed to be approached, nervous tension must have built up in the raider whose company could not be certain whether this was to turn out to be a potential victim or an armed merchant cruiser like herself.

Appam, due to her high masts, wireless aerials and absence of ensign, must have initially stirred up uneasiness; but this rapidly passed when *Moewe's* naval ensign revealed her true identity. Strangely, the sight of the German Ensign triggered an unexpected welcome from a section of *Appam's* passengers, about twenty of them: this was a party of German subjects who were being transported from West Africa for internment in the United Kingdom, but, to their intense surprise, suddenly found rescue close at hand.

Appam was approximately a hundred and thirty-five miles to the east of Madeira when she was captured; and she made a distinguished prize. She was carrying a valuable cargo, which included some gold, and among her passengers were high-ranking colonial officials, such as the retiring

119

Governor of Sierra Leone, the Administrator of Lagos and the Chief Commissioner of Ashanti. *Appam* was a recently built ship and valuable to the Germans as a means of sending off their accumulation of captives. However, *Moewe's* commanding officer placed a German prize crew and one of his junior officers on board *Appam* and directed her to remain with him for the time being.

On the following night (16 January) *Moewe* came in contact with the British *Clan Mactavish* which was sunk after putting up a spirited, but unequal resistance. *Moewe* steamed farther towards the south-west and, on 17 January, parted company with *Appam* which was told to make for a United States port. The distance was such that some days would elapse before news of the raider could be publicised. In due course *Appam* had crossed the Atlantic and on 16 February landed her human cargo at Newport News. *Moewe* learned of *Appam's* arrival via her wireless equipment, of which she always seemed to make intelligent use. It was only after *Appam* had reached the United States that the British Admiralty even became aware of *Moewe's* existence; but, of course, by that time the Count had taken his command to another area. The German raider's captain exploited the technique of keeping moving from one sphere of operations to another which meant that there was an element of surprise in his ship's appearances. The Count did not merely zig-zag across a lucrative region; but would travel from one trade route to another. To put it another way, he became a sort of ghostly pirate using his ship as a wraith-like bird of prey which would pounce out of nowhere, disappear for weeks on end and then make its presence felt in a completely different part of the ocean. Employing this form of tactic, he left few helpful traces in his wake.

Having released *Appam,* the Count realised that a comparatively recent position of *Moewe* might have fallen into British hands in, for example, the form of a cruiser. He, therefore, shifted position to the south-west with the aim of having a look at that happy hunting ground where some months previously *Kronprinz Wilhelm, Karlsruhe* and other raiders had been able to reap a handsome crop of prizes travelling up and down the north-east trade route. So rewarding had the Cape Verdes–Pernambuco section proved itself to be to his predecessors that the Count could not afford to skip a visit or waste an opportunity of dealing British commerce another blow in one of its more sensitive regions.

However, before that laudable, to the Germans, objective could be achieved, it would be essential to replenish with coal. The prize, *Corbridge,* had been despatched to a clandestine rendezvous and was awaiting *Moewe* with her valuable cargo of solid fuel. At this point, it is worth remarking how comfortably the German raider had managed to cope, independently of any supply vessels, or captured colliers, due to her economical power plant.

With the advantage of hindsight, it is known that the anchorage to which *Corbridge* made her way was Maraca Island, at the mouth of the Amazon river. *Karlsruhe* and *Patagonia* had met at this spot, for a similar replenishment exercise during August 1914, meant that the Count could take advantage of a valuable item of information which had been brought back by *Karlsruhe*'s survivors.

On passage to Maraca, and when about seven hundred miles west by south of St Vincent, in the Cape Verdes, *Moewe* met the British three-masted barque *Edinburgh* which was bound for Liverpool. The captain and ship's company of this lovely sailing ship were taken off and she was destroyed on 20 January by explosives. Flames rapidly engulfed hull and rigging, making a spectacular effect in the brilliant tropical moonlight. *Moewe's* captain was prompted to say of *Edinburgh* that 'she was beautiful even in death'.

A week later, *Moewe* reached Maraca, having collected *Corbridge* on 27 January. Vigorous coaling occupied the next three days and nights amid a background of constant heat and dust. The raider having filled her bunkers to their utmost capacity, she then towed *Corbridge* to sea and sank her. At the risk of repetition, it is worth highlighting the fact that *Moewe* had cruised between Germany and South America for over a month without taking fresh supplies of coal on board. She had not been supplied by any shore organisation nor had she been in company with any tenders. This was no mean feat.

Moewe suffered disappointment during the second part of her cruise. The north-east approaches to Pernambuco seemed to have been emptied of shipping. Ships had become cautious and evasive. British arrangements for warning shipping appeared to have been extremely effective. The raider resorted to frequent changes of appearance using much paint and other more ingenious mechanical devices. On one particular occasion, *Moewe* was sighted in the distance by HMS *Glasgow*, who immediately set off in hot pursuit; but just as it seemed that the raider's capture was only a matter of time, a sudden heavy rain storm covered both ships so that contact was lost. *Glasgow* soon passed another merchant ship which had three, instead of two masts. Quite excusably, it was assumed that this was *Moewe* which must have indulged in one of her quick-change acts. Unfortunately, *Glasgow* wasted time examining an innocent merchant-man. *Moewe* was quick to take advantage of the delay caused by *Glasgow*'s error and she used it to make her escape.

On 4 February *Moewe* found a victim when she captured the Belgian SS *Luxembourg* which was loaded with about 6,000 tons of coal for the railway authorities in Buenos Aires. The *Luxembourg* was sunk. Two days later, when three hundred miles north-east by north of Pernambuco, *Moewe* apprehended and sank the British SS *Flamenco*, a vessel of about 4,500 tons.

The Rocas Reef area was, at last, beginning to prove rewarding to the German raider; but she also clearly understood that she was running great risks and should think very seriously of leaving the area. The British light cruiser *Amethyst* was searching for *Moewe* as was *Glasgow*. At the same time, the British armed merchant cruisers *Orama*, *Macedonia* and *Edinburgh Castle* were all operating on the south-east American station.

During the hours of darkness on 5 February *Glasgow* must have passed extraordinarily close to *Moewe*; and SS *Flamenco* tried to seek cruiser assistance, using her wireless equipment. One of the neutral personnel, brought from *Flamenco,* informed the raider that on 5 February *Glasgow* had stopped *Flamenco* and warned her of *Moewe's* proximity.

The Count was smart enough to break away while the going was good and he travelled up the old north-east trade route until 8 February when he was about 530 miles north north-east of Pernambuco. *Moewe* had found the Norwegian SS *Estrella;* but noticing that she had wireless aerials the Count yet again altered his ship's appearance. In the evening of the same day a steamship of 3,300 tons was successfully pursued. She was old, slow and laden with a cargo of coal. She became an easy prize and turned out to be the British SS *Westburn*. At 0500 the following morning, the British SS *Horace*, of similar tonnage to *Westburn*, was captured eighty miles farther up *Moewe's* route. This vessel was destroyed by explosive charges.

Westburn was kept intact; but was used to take on board a hundred and eighty prisoners of war. Under the command of an officer and prize crew of eight ratings, *Westburn* was detached and reached Santa Cruz in Tenerife on the evening of 22 February. Here the captain and crew regained their liberty. The next day *Westburn* put to sea again to avoid being interned; but the cruiser HMS *Subtles* was awaiting her just outside the three-mile limit. The German prize crew, therefore, blew her up.

Moewe had another narrow escape from the cruiser HMS *Highflyer,* which had sunk *Kaiser Wilhelm der Grosse*. *Highflyer* was on passage between St Vincent and St Paul Rocks.

The German raider knew that the trade routes could no longer be looked upon as happy hunting areas; and the Count confessed that the British system of warning and reporting seemed to work admirably. A further consideration which weighed heavily upon him was how to reach Germany through the dreaded British blockade.

When outward bound, the blockade was evaded by taking every advantage of the long, dark nights and heavy weather associated with the depths of winter. However, it was now well into February, and by the time *Moewe* reached northern Europe, the days would be longer, the nights correspondingly shorter and the gales less frequent. It would be foolhardy to linger in the hot latitudes.

The Count took his ship straight up mid-Atlantic, proceeding north-ward so that he crossed the numerous lanes which led between the Old

World and the New. *Moewe* was in radio communication with Berlin so the Count was able to inform the German Admiralty of the ship's successes, to recommend members of the ship's company for awards and to learn that fifty of them had been awarded the Iron Cross, which seemed to be a generous allocation. However, with much of the High Sea Fleet in harbour, opportunities for giving naval awards were no doubt to be welcomed.

Moewe made no captures between 9 and 23 February, which was hardly surprising as the ship was following no conventional traffic route. On 23 February, when well into the Atlantic to the north-west of Finisterre, the French SS *Maroni* was met. This merchantman weighed three thousand odd tons and was carrying general cargo from New York to Bordeaux. Her crew was transferred and *Moewe* sent her to the bottom.

The German raider continued to proceed to the north, cutting across the lateral North American tracks and aiming to pass several hundred miles west of the British Isles which would provide the optimum chance of avoiding likely hostile patrols. On 25 February, when some six hundred miles west of Fastnet, the British SS *Saxon Prince,* of about three and a half thousand tons, was confronted and sunk en route from the USA with a cargo of such useful items as explosives, grain and cotton. Her ship's company were taken prisoner.

At this point it is worth noting that the masters of merchant vessels are usually indoctrinated in the need to destroy, or place in weighted bags, such items as secret sailing instructions, charts and confidential documents which might indicate the positions of minefields and any other classified information. However, less obvious items of paper can easily be overlooked, for example, newspapers picked up during visits to Allied or neutral ports.

This source of information has been used over the centuries. In the case of *Moewe,* the raider had been at sea for a couple of months; but *Maroni* and *Saxon Prince* were comparatively fresh out of harbour and carrying newspapers up to the day of departure. These newsheets gave the Count welcome facts covering the effects of *Moewe*'s operations on the shipping world in general, including insurance rates, news of the arrival of *Appam* at Newport News and so forth. Other details included estimated values of ships and cargoes destroyed by *Moewe,* speculation on the raider's future activities, the possibility of her being sunk, etc. – all useful intelligence and food for the imagination.

The raider tracked northwards, giving a wide berth to the coasts of Ireland and Scotland. The apprehensiveness of the crew must have inevitably increased at this stage as the vigilance of the British patrols, which were enforcing the blockade south of Iceland, must have been kept at a high level.

They say that fortune favours the brave. In this instance, a combination

123

of courage, resourcefulness and, possibly, above all, good luck worked miracles for *Moewe*. Nor were some of the basic requirements forgotten. By day the raider kept an impeccable lookout and avoided any hint of another ship extremely carefully. On 28 February *Moewe* had travelled well to the north where she had the good fortune to run into thick squalls of snow and a severe gale. The Count had chosen his dates well. The following night was devoid of moonlight and very dark. The time had come to turn south, which was done, and the ship proceeded in this general direction until the snow-clad Norwegian coast was sighted again.

The last twenty-four hours of a memorable cruise were exciting for both *Moewe* and the German naval authorities. Wireless communication was maintained, but there was always the possibility of a British warship appearing, for example, anything from an armed merchant cruiser, armed boarding vessel, destroyer or even units of the Grand Fleet making one of their periodic sweeps down the North Sea. The raider could be rounded up and sunk within a matter of a few minutes. For this reason, the Commander-in-Chief of the High Sea Fleet sent out as escort and covering party three cruisers and four battleships in addition to the inevitable destroyers. Nature provided the most valuable protection in the form of a thick fog.

Moewe finally steamed into Wilhelmshaven displaying the house-flags of her captured victims, accompanied by hovering seaplanes and to the cheers of fellow-German seamen who were being confined to harbour by the British Grand Fleet.

The brilliance of *Moewe*'s cruise could not be denied. Planning was good, the selected period and duration of the same were admirable. The time spent in each area was never overdone and the ship and those who manned her appeared to be very well-suited. With only one coaling, though more than one collier had been captured, the entire voyage had been accomplished and no demands had been placed upon any overseas organisation. Casualties had been minimal; and yet this raider had inflicted the loss of fifteen ships upon the Allied nations.

It is difficult not to admire Count zu Dohn-Schlodien's unquestionable bravery and effective techniques. His humanity and courtesy to captives should also be respected. He had originated a new type of military campaign which it would be hard to stop. The flaw in this method of waging war was the need to land or transfer the majority of the prisoners taken before the raider was able to reach Germany again. Had it not been for this defect, the Count would probably have been able to maintain the enigmas of his cruise for months. The news about *Moewe* which was flashed from America to Britain after *Appam*'s survivors had been released caused both anxiety and the formulation of new measures on the part of the British Admiralty and the Commander-in-Chief of the Grand Fleet. The grave danger to seaborne trade through raiders, such as the one under discussion, gave rise to two preventative measures. First, the employment of a suitably armed form of decoy ship to operate along the trade routes. The old principle of setting a detective, disguised as a felon, to catch a professional thief. Second, and this subject is dealt with in greater depth later, the re-vitalisation of the convoy system which had proved so effective in former wars. This was, probably, the first occasion when the idea of convoys was seriously considered during the First World War. The convoy system was not initiated for some time, but it received a boost when Admiral Jellicoe left the Grand Fleet and was appointed to the highest echelons of the Admiralty.

The activation of the convoy system was the wisest of all moves; but, in the first instance, a considerable effort was made by taking up ten colliers, fitting them up with wireless equipment and setting them to work in the twin roles of bait and scout in conjunction with cruisers. Incidentally, as well as increasing the cruisers' range of vision, the colliers could also carry the cruisers' fuel supply. A nice thought was that a hostile raider might apprehend one of the colliers, begin transferring the coal and be caught 'in flagrante delicto' by a British cruiser. It is good to be optimistic.

CHAPTER XI
The Exploits of Wolf

The aim of this part of the book is to look at a cross-section of German surface raiders which operated during World War I. There must be many notable omissions; but a ship which sailed from Germany during the autumn of 1917 deserves a close look as considerable thought and imagination has been expended on her.

The ship in question was one of the Hansa liners. She was driven by a single screw, weighed about 5,800 tons gross and was launched as the *Wachtfels.* Her length was 419 feet, with a beam of just over 56 feet and a draught of about 29.5 feet. She was built at Flensburg in 1913 and was driven by a triple-expansion power plant. Her speed was very moderate, namely ten and a half knots; but she could maintain this speed by burning sixty tons of coal per day. At eight knots she consumed a modest thirty-five tons of coal a day. *Wachtfels* was an economical vessel to run and well suited for her naval mission. Her holds and bunkers could carry some 6,000 tons of coal which assured over three months of fuel independence.

Her general aspect was just right for a raider. She looked like an ordinary cargo ship, with one medium-size black funnel, and two slightly raked masts with exceptionally tall topmasts which could be raised and lowered as part of the exercise of altering her current disguise. She was equipped with wireless with the aerial running down to the bridge, which with her upper bridge was painted very dark grey; but everything else was coloured black. The main armament was more appropriate to a light cruiser and consisted of two 5.9-inch, two 4.1-inch guns, two 4-pounders and two machine guns at the fore end of the bridge deck. A field gun was stowed below in case assistance needed to be extended to the army which was engaged in the East African campaign. Two pairs of above-water torpedo-tubes were fitted. One pair was placed forward and one aft which had dropping doors. Immediately abaft the funnel a searchlight was mounted on a collapsible platform, while a smaller mobile equivalent was situated at the after end of the boat deck which also gave house-room to the range-finder. A cask could be hoisted up the foretopmast head to permit a good lookout to be maintained.

The ship's own armament was cunningly hidden by dummy fittings, canvas screens, collapsible boxes and other devices very reminiscent of subterfuges used by British Q ships. Eleven boats were carried, one of these being a power-boat which could be used by boarding-parties.

Wachtfel's ship's company numbered about 380 officers and men and she was commanded by Commander Karl August Nerger, who spoke no English; however, the First Lieutenant was a fluent English speaker.

This raider, like *Moewe* on her first trip, carried an outfit of mines; but, unlike any previous raider, she carried a seaplane which enabled her to survey miles ahead. In 1916/17 the addition of this small aircraft was a notable innovation. The seaplane was normally to be found resting, at short notice, on a staging erected over number three hold; but it could be stowed safely out of harm's way in bad weather conditions. Two derricks on the mainmast were used for hoisting out both the aircraft and, as required, the mines.

During the first parts of her cruise *Wachtfels* gave all shipping a wide berth. This was a sensible precaution as she had five hundred mines embarked which was nothing but a lethal cargo. It says much for the technical efficiency of the German wireless equipment that even when operating in the Indian Ocean messages from Berlin were readily received by the raider.

The original name *Wachtfels* was changed to *Wolf* before the ship sailed from Germany; and the seaplane was given the name *Wölfchen* ('wolf cub'). Commander Nerger's instructions directed him to interfere with enemy shipping in distant waters and especially in the Indian Ocean, where the cruiser *Emden* had formerly so distinguished herself, to campaign against commerce and to lay mines.

Wolf eventually departed on the last day of November 1916, steamed up the North Sea at her best speed and disguised herself as a neutral. Despite bad weather, the raider had run the blockade and was in the vicinity of Rockall by 2 December.

Proceeding south down the Atlantic, *Wolf* made no attempt to molest anyone, and on 16 January 1917 she was off South Africa. She sighted a British convoy in the distance, with an armoured cruiser as escort; and the same night laid her first batch of mines off the Cape of Good Hope. From the Cape, *Wolf* sailed to the Indian Ocean to lay mines off Bombay and Colombo and she reached the Ceylon area by mid-February. Thanks to *Wolf*'s minelaying activities, the British SS *Worcestershire* fell victim to a mine ten miles south-west of Colombo on 17 February. Two lives were lost. Four days later, another British vessel, SS *Perseus* met her fate with the loss of three lives.

Wolf next opened her distance well away from land between South Africa and Bombay and between Aden and the Sunda Strait. On 27 February, when she was approximately six hundred miles west of Minikoi, the raider captured SS *Turitella*, then British, but originally the

German *Gutenfels.* This was a ship of five and a half thousand tons. A prize crew was embarked and twenty-five mines were provided from *Wolf*'s supply. *Turitella* was then despatched to the north-west to lay the mines off Aden; but at first light on 5 March she scuttled herself, the prize crew being taken captive by HMS *Odin.* It was only when *Wolf* intercepted a wireless message which gave a detailed description that Commander Nerger appreciated that *Turitella* had been accounted for.

Wolf next left a position north-east of the Seychelles and started a long ocean voyage steaming in the general direction of south-west Australia. During the early stages of the trip she was still where traffic routes crossed and she might be expected to achieve captures. On 1 March, not far from the position which had given her *Turitella, Wolf* made a prize of the British SS *Jumna* of a little over four thousand tons. Some nervous excitement was apparent during this operation. Nerger thought that *Jumna* was going to ram his ship and in the resulting confusion *Wolf*'s port after gun was fired before it was trained outboard. The result of this mishap was that five Germans were accidentally killed and twenty-three were injured. If this was not enough, one of the torpedoes was damaged.

Jumna was made to follow astern for three days; but having been cleared of her coal and useful stores she was destroyed by explosives. *Wolf* continued tracking to the south-east until 11 March when she was about 680 miles east of the Seychelles where she captured the British SS *Wordsworth,* of about three and a half thousand tons and loaded with rice. *Wolf* helped herself to what she wanted and sank her victim about a week later. The track between Somaliland and southern Australia is a lonely one. The result of this is that potential prizes were few and far between, and patrols were conspicuous by their absence. Nothing happened until the last day of March when *Wolf* overhauled the British barque *Dee* of 1,160 tons which was en route to Western Australia. Captain John Rugg had been skipper of his ship for over twenty years and never expected that the innocent-looking steamship which had overtaken him could conceivably be a German warship. Captain Rugg hoisted a British ensign and number and signalled 'report me all well'. Then came the horrid surprise. The barque was taken and sunk by explosives about 410 miles west by south of Cape Leeuwin and Rugg found himself a prisoner. It must have been a rude shock for this to happen in such a remote area of the ocean.

Wolf's voyage had not the concentrated activity of *Moewe*'s exercise; but its very differences created such a sense of mystery and uncertainty that it sometimes seemed impossible to cope with her. The only clue had come from *Turitella;* but the raider had long since vanished from her last reported operational area and disappeared into the widest of seas. The time spent at sea and the distances travelled might have seemed out of all proportion to the results achieved; but there is a genuine fascination in the long sea roving undertaken in a century when that type of activity was not often indulged in.

Weeks passed completely devoid of any success. *Wolf* passed south of the Australian land mass where she had reckoned on trapping grain ships and colliers; but not a vessel was sighted. In early June the raider was at Sunday Island, in the Kermadec group. These uninhabited islands are about six hundred miles to the north-north-east of New Zealand and strategically placed for attacking the trade route from New Zealand to San Francisco. *Wolf* was anchored under the shelter of this volcanic spot and was able to send up her aircraft. On 2 June the latter overflew the British SS *Wairana*, of the best part of 4,000 tons, bound from Australia to San Francisco with a cargo of 1,200 tons of coal and items of foodstuffs.

Wölfchen swooped low over the astonished merchant vessel, dropped a canvas bag on to her deck and hovered about in the general vicinity. The canvas bag contained a message the purport of which was: 'Stop immediately. Take orders from German cruiser. Do not wireless or I will bomb you.'

Wairana eased her engines, but refrained from stopping until the seaplane released a bomb which dropped a short distance ahead of her and indicated that the German clearly meant business. By this time *Wolf* had weighed and proceeded to head *Wairana* off. The capture was complete when a prize crew brought the merchantman under the lee of the island, anchored her and sent all officers, except the master, on board the raider.

The following day, because of a shift in the wind direction, *Wolf* was moved round to the other side of the island to occupy a more sheltered anchorage. *Wairana* followed and was secured alongside. The next few days were occupied in transferring fuel, water, stores and anything else *Wolf* felt would be useful. On 7 June bad weather dictated a shift in billet back to the other side of the island again.

Work went on until 12 June when the two ships put to sea, but they returned two days later to continue transferring cargo. On 16 June preparations were made to sink *Wairana* and, as part of this exercise, hatches were battened down, cabin doors nailed up, lifeboats smashed and tanks holed. At 1800 both ships were got under way, but they had proceeded no more than about three miles from the island when a sailing vessel was sighted. *Wairana* was sent back to her anchorage. The seaplane was despatched to investigate the alien which was identified as the United States schooner *Winslow* which had sailed from Sydney to deliver 500 tons of coal to Samoa.

It is interesting to note that the German raider was making intelligent use of passive electronic warfare. *Wolf* had intercepted a message to accept instructions for loading at Sydney. Later, *Wolf* intercepted another message stating that Winslow had left with her cargo: this particular message being transmitted from Sydney to Samoa. It was, therefore, scarcely a surprise when the US vessel happened along. She was, of course, taken captive. It was at 0745 on 17 June that *Wairana* was eventually sunk after the expenditure of a quantity of explosives and shells by the German raider.

During the next three days *Wolf,* with *Winslow* in company, remained at sea; but on 20 May *Wolf* towed the schooner under the lee of Sunday Island and spent a couple of days stripping her. On 22 June *Winslow* was towed out to sea and set on fire. She was left burning when *Wolf* moved off that evening in the direction of the setting sun.

Wolf's next enterprise occurred on 25 June when she laid twenty-five mines between Three Kings Island and the New Zealand mainland. This exercise took place under cover of darkness between 2200 on 25 June and 0230 the following morning. She then proceeded to the Cook Strait where fifty more mines were laid between 2230 on 27 June and 0200 on the subsequent morning. From the Cook Strait area, the raider made her way to the south-east coast of Australia to lay seventeen more mines off Gabo Island on 3 July. Proceedings were interrupted when *Wolf* sighted a number of ships without lights; and it was thought that these vessels were made up of HMS *Enterprise* escorting a convoy. On 6 July the British SS *Cumberland* sank when she detonated a mine about sixteen miles south-west of Gabo Island. The same day, the alert German raider intercepted this news by monitoring the appropriate frequency.

Wolf passed Lord Howe Island, making a considerable detour to get well away from the coast of Australia. On 9 July she was between Samoa and New Zealand when she captured the American barque *Beluga* with a cargo of case oil. *Beluga* had at one time been a whaler, but was now transporting benzene and gasolene. The benzene was welcome to *Wolf* and the gasolene was useful to help setting *Beluga* on fire. At dawn the next morning, *Wölfchen* was sent into the air on a scouting mission as smoke had been sighted. Nothing transpired and on 11 July *Beluga* was finished off by shellfire. Two more days elapsed and on 13 July the raider encountered the four-masted sailing ship *Encore*, which was bound from the Columbia river to Sydney, carrying timber. Oil was, in due course, poured over her and she was set alight. This incident took place in the vicinity of New Caledonia.

Wolf continued her journey to the north-west, past Fiji and the Solomon Islands and what had once been German New Guinea. The seaplane earned its keep by being sent on daily scouting missions between 25 July and 6 August for the raider which was loitering to find a victim. On 27 July she was close to the former German possession which had passed into British hands in September 1914 when Rabaul in Neu Pommern had been occupied by British forces. It was, obviously, now impossible for *Wolf* to avail itself of the facilities which had been available in what had been a German colony; but on 28 July Nerger's wireless operators picked up an interesting message:

> Burns Philp Rabaul. Donaldson left Sydney on the 27th via Newcastle-Brisbane with 340 tons piece goods, 500 Westport coal for Rabaul, and 236 tons piece goods for Madang. Signal Burns.

This was good news for *Wolf*. Messrs Burns, Philp were well-known Pacific shipowners signalling from Sydney to their Rabaul agent, where a British Governor had been appointed instead of a German equivalent. For a time Commander Nerger wondered who on earth Donaldson could be; but another wireless message was intercepted which read:

> 29th July, 8pm. Steamer *Matunga* at Brisbane. Next Monday we are off Cape Moreton.

Further encouraged by this intelligence, gratuitously received from intercepts, Nerger kept the seaplane airborne at frequent intervals scouting over the sea. On 5 August yet another message was intercepted which told the Rabaul agents that *Donaldson* would arrive the next day at 0700. This arrival never took place. On 6 August, when 300 miles to the east of Riche Island, New Guinea, the SS *Matunga* was spotted by the German seaplane at 0745; and *Wolf* made the British ship stop. The prize officer, on boarding, greeted the master with a salutation which caused more than a little surprise:

'Hello, Captain Donaldson, where are your five hundred tons of Westport coal?'

Coal was not the only important item on board. *Matunga* also happened to be carrying the Acting-Governor to his place of appointment at Rabaul, provisions aimed at the British garrison at Rabaul and a number of bicycles, all of which were put on board *Wolf*. In the first instance, the two ships proceeded to the north-west and west, past the north New Guinea coast, and eventually, on 14 August, arrived at a landlocked harbour which had previously been reconnoitred by the seaplane.

In this lonely spot the Germans erected a wireless station, placed lookouts and tried to scare their prisoners by telling them that it was fruitless for them to attempt to escape as the natives were cannibals and the water nurtured a vigorous crocodile population. Ten days were passed in this isolated area trans-shipping coal and cargo. A diver was sent down to try to scrub as much a possible of the ship's bottom which had become foul with marine growth.

On 26 August both ships proceeded to sea until they were about twelve miles from the shore. *Matunga* was then sunk by the use of explosives, and

Wolf resumed her voyage westward, passing Celebes on 29 August, and arriving in the Java Sea the following day. With dauntless courage the raider carried on until she was off Singapore on 2 September; and, under cover of darkness, laid a 108 mines between 2200 and 0400 the following morning. All mines had been disposed of and *Wolf* was free to return home.

Wolf was in the vicinity of the Maldive Islands on 26 September when she sighted the Japanese SS *Hitachi Maru* among the atolls of the group. The raider closed the Japanese vessel and hoisted the signal whose text was: 'Stop and do not use your wireless.' Initially, the Japanese continued on their way; but two rounds were fired across their bow followed by fourteen more shells which killed sixteen members of the Japanese ship's company. *Hitachi Maru* began calling on her wireless, but *Wolf* jammed those transmissions. Soon another victim was added to Commander Nerger's list. The passengers, among whom a number of females were counted, were taken on board *Wolf*.

Hitachi Maru was not disposed of at this stage, but followed *Wolf* as directed by a prize crew which had been put on board. The two ships tracked to the westward until they secured alongside one another on 27 September off an atoll situated north of the Equator. This was Dewadu Island in the middle of the Suvadiva Atoll (south of the Maldives), and until 29 September the captured coal was transferred, plus cargo and stores, etc. Every day the seaplane was airborne for a couple of hours or so, engaged in scouting activities. *Wolf* left the atoll on 3 October and three days later the Japanese ship was ordered (by seaplane) to follow. The two ships then proceeded to the west and south-west. They reached Coco Island, to the west of the Cargados Carajos group and secured alongside one another, at anchor, for another exercise in transferring coal and cargo though, after a time, bad weather conditions dictated that they cast off. On 1 November it was deemed desirable that everyone should be inoculated against typhoid. The voyage was resumed six days later and began with the *Hitachi Maru* being sunk in deep water sixteen miles offshore. *Wolf* was once again a 'loner'.

An interesting sidelight is that it was possible to patch up the wings of the seaplane using some of the raw silk and white satin which had formed a part of *Hitachi Maru*'s cargo. The aircraft had made a large number of flights during *Wolf*'s cruise and some of the fabric was showing significant signs of 'wear and tear'.

The raider was working its way between Mauritius and Madagascar when the Spanish SS *Igotz Mendi* was sighted under way with all lights burning brightly. The Spanish vessel had departed from Lourenço Marques (now Ihaputo) on 4 November and was laden with 5,500 tons of coal destined for Colombo. In view of the precious fuel, she was taken captive. A prize crew brought the prisoner to Coco Island where the two ships were secured alongside one another, and by working through the night, *Wolf* was 'topped up' with coal.

Igotz Mendi was not sunk, as had happened to a large number of her predecessors. The two vessels, having been painted grey, operated together for a period of time. *Wolf* then acted alone, sinking the US sailing ship *John H Kirby* which was bound for Natal from New York.

Igotz Mendi was still on her own on 2 December when she was about 150 miles south of the Cape. Three days later, the raider and the Spanish ship met and proceeded across the South Atlantic in the direction of the Brazilian island of Trinidada. During this leg of their odyssey, *Wolf* sank the French sailing vessel, *Maréchal Soult*, which was bound from Melbourne to Dakar with a cargo of wheat.

Wolf, still monitoring wireless transmissions, picked up messages from a Japanese cruiser on 14 November and sent off the seaplane for an hour's scouting activity. On 19 December wireless transmissions from British cruisers were intercepted which made the raider and her Spanish prize rapidly alter course and leave the area at their best speed.

On Boxing Day both ships were approximately seven hundred miles east of Montevideo when they secured alongside one another so that the raider could again top up with coal. The Atlantic swell made them bump severely which resulted in *Wolf* being somewhat seriously damaged and taking in uncomfortable quantities of salt water. On 30 December, with the raider keeping eight miles ahead, both ships continued their progress northward up the Atlantic. On 4 January 1918 the Norwegian barque, *Storfbror*, sailing from Beira to Montevideo in ballast, was sunk by *Wolf*. The pretext for this unfriendly action was that the Norwegian vessel had been owned by the British County Shipping Company prior to the outbreak of war. This imaginative excuse seemed to be a specious justification for sinking a neutral vessel. This was the last prize to be dealt with by *Wolf*.

It is interesting to note that this one German raider had denied to the Allies seven British ships, three American, one Japanese, one Spanish, one French and one Norwegian. It must also be remembered that the following vessels had been sunk or seriously damaged by *Wolf*'s mines: five off the Cape of Good Hope, two off Colombo, five off Bombay, one off Gabo Island, and one in Cook Strait. This was really a most impressive score, from the German point of view.

The *Igotz Mendi* had been the recipient of a number of prisoners, of various categories, who had been wished upon her by the raider. The *Wolf*'s commanding officer had no intention of putting captives ashore and thus letting loose the secret of his ship's rovings. The Spanish prize was to be taken to Germany. During early February, which was an ideal time of year for returning raiders, *Igotz Mendi* slipped through the blockade and, after overcoming a number of navigational problems caused by unfriendly weather conditions such as fog, ran aground in Danish waters with her complement of prisoners. So near to Germany, yet so far. In due course, the prisoners were landed and taken care of by the local British Consul.

Wolf's saga had a more propitious ending than the termination of her Spanish prize's voyage. Commander Nerger brought his ship safely back to Germany on 19 February 1918. However, a fair share of fog and ice floes had been experienced. The raider had been given up for lost; but after 450 days' cruising and the covering of 64,000 miles, in practically every sea in the world, *Wolf* had been returned to her homeland. This was no mean achievement on the part of the ship, her commanding officer and her company.

Time has been spent on *Wolf*'s exploits because they illustrate how much can be achieved by a disguised merchant ship of a very average speed capability which selects the correct tactics and is able to maintain her aura of mystery.

A valid criticism of Germany's employment of raiders during the First World War is that they were deployed in 'penny packets'. Had a significant number, say twenty plus, been unleashed upon the world's trade routes and focal-points at the beginning of hostilities, the problem posed might have been difficult for Britain and her Allies to solve. Germany seems to have nibbled at the task when big bites were called for. This is a typical failing in time of war. The first use of the tank was another example. The surprise factor of these larger, armoured fighting vehicles was lost when they were used in comparatively small numbers at Cambrai in 1917. Their first appearances 'shook' the German soldiery; and deployment in greater numbers might have resulted in a decisive breakthrough. Perhaps, being human, people tend to 'test the temperature of the water' before leaping into a swimming pool unless the ambient temperature has been hot for a number of consecutive days.

The experiences of World War I suggested the desirability of a seafaring nation having an adequate number of light cruisers and merchant-vessels which have the potential to be converted into armed merchant cruisers at short notice. Good seakeeping qualities are important, together with a long radius of operation at economical speed, and propulsion which can enable the ship to accelerate to a high speed in a reasonably short period of time. A fast ship of short endurance is probably the least suitable candidate for acting in the role of commerce raider.

There were, of course, other surface raiders than those mentioned above; but the object of relating activities of a few noteworthy examples has been to offer an over-view of typical commerce raiding.

CHAPTER XII

German Surface Raiding in World War II

U-boats were the main form of sea raider used by the Germans in World War II and they very nearly brought the United Kingdom to its knees. However, Nazi Germany had a number of very effective surface warships and armed merchant vessels which Winston Churchill is said to have thought, at one time, to be more of a menace to Britain's naval pre-eminence than even the hostile submarines. This is borne out by the great efforts which were made, and casualties incurred, in trying to sink Germany's major surface vessels.

One of the tasks allocated to Allied capital warships at the Normandy Landings in June 1944 was to provide flank protection in the event of a German attempt to use their remaining surface fleet to disrupt the assault and the work of the covering warships. I was a teenage Midshipman on board the battleship HMS *Warspite*, and I found the attention of shore batteries frightening enough and was thankful that no major German warships appeared to add their armament to the opposition.

The German capital ships won a number of tactical victories during the course of the Second World War. They also had a great strategic utility in that they tied down large numbers of Allied warships and aircraft for much of the war. The German Nazi leadership were very land oriented and seemed to fail to understand the role of a 'fleet in being'. At one crucial stage in the struggle between Germany and the Allies, Hitler ordered that the capital ships should be demilitarised, the guns transferred elsewhere and the remaining parts of the vessels be scrapped. Admiral Raeder, the Chief of Naval Staff, had many contretemps with his fellow Chiefs of Staff, in particular the flamboyant Hermann Goering. A case in point was that two aircraft carriers had been authorised for the German Navy. *Graf Zeppelin*, the first of its class was launched in late 1938; but was never completed as she became a sacrifice to the power struggle between Goering and Raeder for control of German naval aviation. Over the years, the Royal Navy and the Royal Air Force have not been strangers to differences of opinion on similar subjects, but have tended, perhaps, to resolve varying points of view in an outwardly more effective manner.

The German Navy was not helped by the fact that Hitler had, on a number of occasions, given assurances that overt hostilities with Britain were impossible before 1946. In the event, the timescales used by planners for the build-up of the German Fleet were markedly truncated. Major warships are not the type of article which can suddenly be constructed in a matter of days, or whose building programme can be drastically tampered with without causing a lot of pain. It seems that Hitler, in general, opposed Raeder's recommendations, but turned out to be 'way out' when he ordered that there was adequate time to build the necessary hardware in the form of ships. At least the Kaiser, in the run-up to World War I, was quite determined that the German Navy would be a direct challenge to the Royal Navy.

In September 1939 Admiral Doenitz stated that 'the decisive point in warfare against England lies in attacking her merchant shipping in the Atlantic'. Submarines played a major part in trying to achieve that objective; but it is difficult to refrain from speculating on the possible results if the major German surface warships had been operated with more dash and imagination. In a number of cases, the large German ships were sailed in the role of raiders when the potential of the damage which might have been inflicted if two or three, or more, had been gathered together to act as squadrons provides a comfortable feeling of gratitude on the part of the Allies that Adolf Hitler was not a student of naval history. Like Napoleon before him, the German Supremo believed that it was possible to win the sea-battle on terra firma, aided, in this era, by land-based military aircraft whenever their distance from airfields ashore permitted their effective use against shipping.

The aim of the pages that follow is to give a few details of the use of Nazi surface raiders during the Second World War.

To 'reverse course' a little, it is interesting to go back to the 1919 Treaty of Versailles which prohibited the defeated Germans from building warships exceeding 10,000 tons displacement. Skilled German naval architects responded to these limitations by developing an imaginative type of naval ship. The staff target was to design a fighting ship, within the specified displacement tonnage, which would be fitted with guns with greater potential power than those mounted in a British heavy cruiser and to incorporate protective armour which would be of sufficient thickness to withstand the British heavy cruisers' 8-inch projectiles. Two rather unusual techniques, for warship construction at that time, were adopted. These were, firstly, the use of welding techniques which saved the weight of large numbers of rivets and, secondly, the fitting of diesel engines rather than the more customary steam-turbines. In addition, steps were taken to cut thick armoured protection to an absolute minimum. A radius of operation of some 12,500 miles at economical cruising speed, was achieved by the employment of the above methods. The three new German warships were provided with a main armament of six 11-inch guns mounted in two triple turrets and a secondary armament of eight 5.9-inch guns. To summarise, the pocket-battleships could outgun every British cruiser and outpace any British battleship. There were only three ships in the Royal Navy which had the speed to overtake the new German warships and the calibre of gun to sink them. These were *Hood, Renown* and *Repulse,* and this trio of battle-cruisers were all First World War veterans.

Command of the *Admiral Graf Spee* was given to Captain Hans Langsdorff who was in his mid-40s. It has been said that both the ship and its commanding officer were well-suited; but, in the final test of action, it was the man who did not 'come up to scratch', rather than the ship which failed.

Graf Spee departed from Wilhelmshaven on 21 August 1939, which was ten days prior to the outbreak of hostilities and her area of operations was the mid-Atlantic. *Deutschland, Graf Spee*'s sister, departed for a similar operational waiting zone, this time in the North Atlantic. Each of the military raiders had a supply vessel loosely in company. The *Altmark,* which was later to gain fame of a rather notorious nature, had been detailed with *Graf Spee.* The pocket-battleships had been assigned the unmistakable aims of the 'disruption and destruction of enemy merchant shipping by all possible means'. At all costs, engagement with hostile naval forces was to be studiously avoided unless it should be absolutely necessary to achieve the principal aim.

Graf Spee duly made her way into the sometimes heavy, tepid warmth of the South Atlantic and fell in with her first quarry on 30 September 1939 off Brazil. This was the five-thousand odd ton SS *Clement.* The tramp steamer reported the pocket-battleship as being the *Admiral Sheer.* This report had the effect of confusing the British Admiralty and its opposite number, the French Ministry of Marine as well as the Raider Hunting Units deployed by these authorities.

Graf Spee's second victim was the SS *Newton Beech* which was one of three merchant vessels apprehended and sunk during the period 5–10 October. The raider rendezvoused with the *Altmark* in the middle of the Atlantic to replenish. Opportunity was taken of this evolution to transfer the captives taken from *Graf Spee*'s recent victims. Thus began *Altmark*'s saga in the role of prison ship.

Roughly a week later, SS *Trevanion* was sent to the bottom the day after Trafalgar Day (22 October). Kapitän Langsdorff next took his ship round the Cape of Good Hope where she sank the small 700-ton tanker *Africa Shell* on 15 November. *Graf Spee* then altered course, retraced her steps back round the Cape, replenished from *Altmark* on 27 November north-east of the volcanic island of Tristan da Cunha and, several days later, despatched the 10,000-ton cargo liner *Doric Star*. Before she went down, the liner was able to clear the prescribed distress message which included the letters 'R-R-R', to indicate surface raider.

The day following the sinking of *Doric Star*, SS *Tairoa* was sunk; and on 7 December *Graf Spee* put paid to her last victim which was the 3,895-ton cargo ship *Streonshalh*. This operation brought the raider's serve to an aggregate of nine British merchant vessels with a total displacement of 50,089 tons. It should be noted that not one life had been lost during *Graf Spee*'s assaults on British shipping. This bloodless achievement was a source of considerable satisfaction to Kapitän Langsdorff. A number of his captives eventually bore witness to his courteous firmness and remarked upon his distinguished appearance, chivalry and sense of fair play.

The explanation for the lengthy and 'nail-biting' search for the slippery German pocket-battleship lay upon the Allied Forces G, H and K who were working to this end in the vast spaces of the South Atlantic. They knew that a considerable factor in their success, or failure, would depend upon the ability of merchant ships suffering attack to transmit their R-R-R message plus a position. The importance of getting off a position in this type of situation cannot be stressed too strongly.

Without a reasonably accurate and up-to-date position, hunting warships have nothing upon which to establish a 'datum' for their surveillance plans. In point of fact, Kapitän Langsdorff was pretty well 'in the picture' as regards the movements of British fighting ships. He knew, for example, that the cruisers *Ajax*, *Achilles*, *Cumberland* and *Exeter* were cruising off the coast of southern Argentina, that the heavily armed cruisers *Sussex* and *Shropshire* were in the vicinity of the Cape, and that the aircraft carrier *Ark Royal* and the battle-cruiser *Renown* were off the West African coast.

Commodore Harwood of the America and West Indies Squadron was flying his broad pendant in the six-inch gun cruiser *Ajax*, which was commanded by Captain Charles H L Woodhouse RN.

The Commodore had forecast that Kapitän Langsdorff would leave his mid-ocean patrol and head for the River Plate estuary in the hope of coming across succulent prizes. This Langsdorff duly did, so that the German raider and the British squadron were converging on the same general area.

Commodore Harwood's eight-inch gun cruisers *Exeter* and *Cumberland* were at Port Stanley, probably to act as cover in the event of a German attack to avenge the Battle of the Falkland Islands where Admiral von Spee's squadron had been decimated on 8 December 1914. The six-inch gun cruiser *Achilles*, generously manned by some 327 New Zealanders, was on patrol in the sea area off Rio de Janeiro. *Ajax* had recently departed from Port Stanley bound for the River Plate.

Commodore Harwood estimated that, based upon the information provided by the sinking of *Doric Star*, the German raider could well arrive at Rio by 12 December and be in the vicinity of the River Plate the following day. With this very much in mind, the Commodore ordered a concentration of his cruisers. *Exeter* was told to leave Port Stanley on 9 December; and *Achilles* was diverted to steam south to make contact with the senior officer on 10 December. Perhaps, sadly, *Cumberland* was obliged to remain in the Falklands to finish a very badly needed self-refit. This must have been a frustrating experience for her ship's company.

The three functional cruisers were in company by 0600 on 12 December in a position about 150 miles off the River Plate.

Commodore Harwood had for some time been studying the possible tactics which his squadron should employ if they needed to confront a large adversary with the 'punch' of, say, a pocket-battleship. Undismayed by the prospect of having to cope with the markedly superior firepower of such an antagonist, he made it clear to his commanding officers that, with three cruisers in company, the aim would be to attack at once, day or night if a single pocket-battleship were to be the enemy. This dictum was very much in accord with the traditions of the Royal Navy; and it must be part of the 'mystique' of the British Fleet that an opponent knows that the ingrained instinct of a British warship has been to fight, regardless of the odds.

At dawn on 13 December the three British cruisers were formed in column (line ahead) in the order of: *Ajax, Achilles, Exeter*. The distance between ships was 2,000 yards (one nautical mile) and the squadron was zig-zagging about a base course of 060 degrees at a speed of fourteen knots. At 0540 the ships' companies relaxed from the customary dawn action-stations. At the time in question the sea state was calm with a light swell. At 0520 the squadron's position was about 250 sea miles to the east of Punta del Este.

Soon after six o' clock, distinct smoke was sighted from *Ajax*'s bridge bearing 320 degrees. Commodore Harwood detached *Exeter* to investigate. The cruiser swung out of line, and at about 0615 signalled that she thought the contact could be a pocket-battleship. Soon afterwards, the signal for 'enemy in sight' was hoisted.

While all this was taking place in the British squadron, *Graf Spee* was on a course of 155 degrees and proceeding at fifteen knots. Langsdorff, it seemed, held every advantage. The Germans had sighted Harwood's ships some twenty minutes before *Ajax* spotted a trace of smoke. At 0552 more masts were seen fine on *Graf Spee*'s starboard bow which later transformed themselves into *Exeter*'s unmistakeable superstructure accompanied by what, at this stage to *Graf Spee*'s lookouts, appeared to be two fleet destroyers.

At this point, a bit of a mystery seemed to unfold on board the German pocket-battleship. This was the ideal time for Langsdorff to order a large alteration of course and to refuse an engagement. In retrospect, it appeared that Langsdorff made a grave error in that he maintained his present heading. The German commanding officer not only stuck to his ship's present track; but he resolved to 'throw his cap over the mill' and to attack. This decision flouted the instructions which had been given by the German Naval Operations Command. The *Graf Spee*'s navigating officer reminded his captain of the directive that he was to avoid even inferior hostile naval forces. Langsdorff indicated that he suspected a convoy and ordered a high speed to close the range. It is interesting to recall that the opening phase of the Battle of the River Plate had begun before the British cruisers had sighted their adversary.

Once the Battle of the River Plate had commenced in earnest, I remember that members of my school boarding house would seek every possible opportunity of turning on the communal radio to keep in contact with the far away drama which was beginning to unfold and which would have been difficult to top by most authors of nautical fiction.

The German pocket-battleship had a heavier main armament than any of the British cruisers. However, Harwood's previously thought-out tactic of engaging the *Graf Spee* simultaneously from two different angles proved its worth. The aim was, of course, to coerce Kapitän Langsdorff into dividing the fire of his big guns. When *Exeter* had identified the German pocket-battleship, her captain moved off to the west. Harwood, meanwhile, directed *Ajax* to close the range. *Achilles* conformed generally with the senior officer's movements during the action and this enabled the two smaller cruisers to concentrate their fire with commendable effort.

A running combat followed, during which *Graf Spee* disabled *Exeter* to such an extent that the pocket-battleship was presented with a good opportunity to finish her off. However, at this time, the concentrated fire from the 6-inch guns of *Ajax* and *Achilles* proved to be an adequate distraction.

Langsdorff, whose ship had sustained a considerable amount of damage, headed for the coast with the two British light cruisers harrying him like a pair of ocean-going terriers. At 0725 an 11-inch shell knocked out *Ajax*'s X and Y turrets which presented Langsdorff with a second opportunity to win the battle. Commodore Harwood altered course towards the east, making smoke; but when he discovered that the pocket-battleship was still withdrawing from the fray, he resumed the chase in the direction of Montevideo towards which *Graf Spee* was heading.

The Germans could not help but be impressed by the tenacity of *Ajax* and *Achilles*. Langsdorff must have believed that the two light cruisers would not have pressed home their attack with such dash if they had known that heavier warships were not coming up to support them.

Langsdorff managed to obtain a seventy-two-hour extension of stay in Uruguay, rather than the permissable twenty-four-hour stay of a belligerent warship in a neutral port. British complaints were more diplomatic than genuine. Ideally, there was no desire for the battle-cruiser to be forced to put to sea prior to 19 December. The ruse of arranging for a British merchant vessel to sail each day was implemented; this because International Law ordained that merchantmen leaving harbour had to be given a 'start' of twenty-four hours over a hostile warship.

The British also nurtured the idea that the aircraft carrier *Ark Royal* and the battle-cruiser *Renown* were, in point of fact, some thousands of miles distant. The only reinforcement which Commodore Harwood had received was the cruiser *Cumberland,* which arrived at 2200 on 14 December. The British had ordered *Ark Royal, Renown* and the cruisers *Devonshire, Shropshire* and *Neptune* to the River Plate area, but this overwhelming concentration could not have been achieved before 19 December.

Langsdorff had inconveniently reported to Berlin that he believed that a concentration of British warships was already in situ off the River Plate. Gross-Admiral Raeder discussed the dilemma with Hitler the same day. It was argued that an attempted breakout, which would involve heavy fighting, would be the correct and heroic action; but that to scuttle *Graf Spee* would be a preferable alternative to the internment of this major warship.

At 1815 on 17 December the German pocket-battleship sailed with a substantially reduced ship's company. Langsdorff had transferred 800 men to the German oil-tanker SS *Tacoma* which followed in the *Graf Spee*'s wake. The ship stopped and dropped anchor soon after the three-mile limit had been crossed. Tugs approached the warship and her ensign was lowered for the last time. Six fuses were activated. Boats, with the Commanding Officer in the last one, moved away from the doomed *Graf Spee* and steered across the River Plate in the direction of Buenos Aires in Argentina. Six violent explosions occurred. The pocket-battleship settled in the shallows and it is difficult to avoid thinking that such a fine fighting ship was worthy of a more graceful end.

A couple of days later, Langsdorff wrote a suicide letter in which he took upon himself the sole responsibility for scuttling the *Graf Spee*. The German Lieutenant H Dietrich discovered Langsdorff the following morning. The Captain had shot himself in the right temple. I remember at the time hearing that Langsdorff was stretched out on the flag of the Imperial German Navy and attired in his full dress German uniform.

The effect of the Battle of the River Plate in Britain was great, and probably out of proportion to its military significance. The people of the United Kingdom, at this time, were somewhat starved of victories. The assured manner in which Commodore Harwood's weak squadron had been handled, and harried its extremely powerful opponent to the death was reminiscent of past Royal Navy engagements. The battle seemed to be a harbinger of better days. Neutral countries started to speculate whether the British had really become as decrepit as the Nazi propaganda machine had tried to lead them to believe.

To revert to the battle, Langsdorff's tactics have been open to criticism. When *Exeter* was severely damaged, Langsdorff should have, perhaps, used the speed advantage of his pocket-battleship to try to keep out of range of the cruisers' guns and to use the greater reach of his main armament to despatch the British light cruisers in detail, one after the other. Later in the battle it would have been wise to have taken the badly damaged *Exeter* 'off the board' and to go hard for *Ajax* when the ship's after turrets were crippled. However, it is easy to float criticisms with the benefit of hindsight rather than to pick an optimum situation, operating in the heat and noise of battle when instantaneous decisions are frequently needed. The famous American Admiral Arlegh Burke, who distinguished himself in the Pacific during World War II, was once asked what the difference was between a good and an indifferent officer-of-the-watch ('officer-of-the-deck' in US parlance). The Admiral is alleged to have paused for a few moments and replied: 'I should think ten seconds.'

The activities of the German pocket-battleship came to a virtual end soon after the elapse of not much more than the first three months of the Second World War. The foray of *Graf Spee* had, as has been seen, come to a close not all that far from where the Admiral whose name the warship bore had been sunk in *Scharnhorst* some twenty-five years previously, and *Deutschland* had been obliged to return to her base. To shift focus, the commerce raiders were achieving no more noteworthy successes than had their forebears during the First World War, although a few words will be said about these vessels anon.

The evacuation of Dunkirk and the almost unbelievable saving of large numbers of British and Allied troops from neighbouring beaches in late May and early June 1940, together with the expansion of Nazi control over France presented the German Navy with favourable opportunities for renewing the activities of commerce raiders. Before the end of the summer of 1940 the Germans were in possession of the whole European coastline from northern Norway to the beginning of Spanish waters. This can be attributed to the increase in the number of bases which became available to the operators of the U-boat fleet; but similar considerations can be applied to the surface warships. The first raider to sail again was the pocket-battleship *Admiral Scheer*. The ship's cruise lasted for five months and resulted in the capturing, or sinking, of some sixteen ships totalling of the order of a hundred thousand tons.

Admiral Scheer departed from Stevanger on 23 October 1940, and slipped into the Atlantic, sailing round the north of Iceland in poor visibility. On 5 November the raider was lying in wait for a substantial convoy of thirty-seven ships (HX 84) which was known to have left Halifax on 27 October. The pocket-battleship's seaplane had been launched by catapult and her reports assisted *Admiral Scheer* to sight eight merchant vessels and to sink one, the *Mopan*, after taking off her ship's company. By that time, the main body of the convoy had been sighted. Luckily for the convoy, the day was well advanced and the onset of darkness near.

The convoy was escorted by the armed merchant cruiser *Jervis Bay* which was only armed with 6-inch guns; but her commanding officer, Captain Fegen, showed no hesitation and steered his ship directly at the *Admiral Scheer*. He also ordered the convoy to scatter. There could only be one result of the engagement, as Captain Fegen knew only too well. However, it took the pocket-battleship the best part of three hours to sink *Jervis Bay*. Thanks to this heroic resistance, only five of the ships in convoy were despatched when a capital fighting ship could have been expected to destroy, or nearly destroy, all the merchantmen being escorted. *Admiral Scheer* next tracked south, made a rendezvous with a supply vessel, and after destroying several merchant ships in the South Atlantic and Indian Oceans, finally arrived back in Kiel during early April 1941.

The next surface raider to arrive in the Atlantic was the heavy cruiser *Admiral Hipper* which sailed from the Elbe estuary on 30 November 1940. This ship was followed a month later by the battle-cruisers *Scharnhorst* and *Gneisenau*. However, these ships ran into extremely foul weather conditions which caused them to put back to harbour for repairs. It was not until 22 January 1941 that they returned to sea. The two vessels sighted Convoy HX108 which had left Halifax a week before, on 7 February; but unfortunately for the raiders the 15-inch battleship *Ramillies* was escorting the convoy. However, due to their superior speed the German battle-cruisers had an advantage. One could keep the *Ramillies* occupied while the other could have destroyed the practically defenceless convoy, but Admiral Lutjens, commanding the two battle-cruisers, had specific instructions not to engage a superior hostile force. *Scharnhorst* and *Gneisenau* therefore withdrew to search for other targets elsewhere. They found a goodly number, and by the time they reached Brest, on 22 March, they had disposed of twenty-two ships whose total weight was 116,000 tons.

The cruiser *Admiral Hipper*, which had made its sortie into the Atlantic at the end of November 1940, had attacked a troop convoy to the west of Cape Finisterre. The cruiser had inflicted little damage and reached Brest safely on 27 December.

In February 1941 the *Admiral Hipper* again left Brest and during the course of a short cruise in the capacity of raider managed to destroy thirteen merchant ships.

These events were the last successful operations conducted by German capital ships in the Atlantic Ocean. Three months later the spectacular hunt for, and end of, the battleship *Bismarck* saw this type of raiding operation virtually cease.

Bismarck was the latest big ship in the German Fleet, its pride; and when commissioned it was the most powerful warship in the world at that particular time. No other could claim to mount such an armament which boasted eight 15-inch guns, twelve 6-inch, sixteen 4-inch anti-aircraft guns and sixteen smaller weapons. Her maximum speed of thirty knots was something to be reckoned with for a warship of its size. On paper, only the British battle-cruisers *Hood, Renown* and *Repulse* had the speed and fire-power to take the German on; but these ships were of a late First World War vintage and were, in some respects, obsolete.

The search for and destruction of *Bismarck* has been written about on a number of occasions and many of the accounts make gripping reading. The aim of this brief account is to remind readers of the main events. Perhaps it is another case of 'tell me the old, old story'.

The magnificently constructed battleship *Bismarck* broke out into the Atlantic from a fjord in the vicinity of Bergen, Norway accompanied by the German heavy cruiser *Prinz Eugen*. These two ships were not sighted until they were intercepted by the battle-cruiser *Hood* and the battleship *Prince of Wales* on 24 May 1941, to the west of the Denmark Strait; a shell from a broadside fired from *Bismarck* at a range of about 19,500 yards scored a hit in one of *Hood*'s magazines which resulted in the battle-cruiser blowing up and sinking extremely rapidly. The *Prince of Wales* sustained some damage in the short action. In addition, Bismarck was hit twice and at one time sustained a fire and some damage to her fuel tanks.

The Germans had planned that *Scharnhorst* and *Gneisenau* would be able to make a sortie from Brest; but the Royal Air Force had effectively ensured that this part of the German exercise could not take place.

The pursuit and destruction of *Bismarck* was, as previously mentioned, one of the most celebrated dramas of the Second World War at sea. The story includes the fact that contact with the great warship was lost for twenty-four hours, until she was sighted by a Coastal Command Catalina flying-boat when only about six to seven hundred miles distant from Brest. The narrative continues by describing how she was courageously attacked by torpedo-carrying Swordfish aircraft ('string bags') launched from the British carrier *Ark Royal*. *Bismarck* was the next target of destroyers which attacked when night had fallen, under the command of Philip Vian.

The next morning the battleships *King George V* and *Rodney* engaged with broadsides fired from their main armaments. Hits were soon registered and *Bismarck*'s fire was shortly silenced.

The great battleship disappeared beneath the waves at 1036 on 27 May 1941. It is interesting to note that *Bismarck* had been hit by nine torpedoes and several tons of high explosive shells before she was sunk. Nearly all her ship's company of 2,000 men died with their ship.

To obtain some idea of the 'gearing' exercised on its opponents by a battleship of *Bismarck*'s calibre, it is worth recalling that the British

Admiralty deployed five battleships, two aircraft-carriers, three battle-cruisers, five cruisers and twenty-one destroyers to bring *Bismarck* to action and, finally, to destroy her.

I, when serving as Flag-Lieutenant to the Commander-in-Chief, South Atlantic, had the privilege of having breakfast with Admiral Sir Benjamin Martin when he stayed at Admiralty House, Simonstown. The Admiral had been commanding officer of the cruiser HMS *Dorsetshire* which administered the coup de grâce to *Bismarck* with an exercise in the well-aimed placing of torpedoes. The opportunity to listen to a senior participant in the *Bismarck* episode provided a never-to-be-forgotten experience to a young officer. Incidentally, Admiral Martin imparted some of the best tips on the art of ship-handling which his enthusiastic audience of one had ever received.

The battleship *Bismarck* might never have been the last German warship to have been employed in the role of commerce raider; but several 'disguised raiders' in the form of armed merchantmen operated in the Indian Ocean and the Western Pacific. These marauders were extremely successful.

Atlantis disposed of twenty-two Allied merchantmen totalling the best part of 146,000 tons and her cruise was the basis of at least one book which gave the raider fictional treatment. The raider *Thor* sank the same number of ships giving a total of approximately 150,000 tons, and the German *Michel* sank seventeen victims totalling about 122,000 tons. Top of the class, and record-holder, was the *Pinguin* which sank thirty-three Allied ships totalling between 165,000 and 166,000 tons. *Pinguin* was finally caught and sunk off the Seychelles by the cruiser HMS *Cornwall*, on 8 May 1941. The majority of these raiders were, in due course, destroyed by Allied ships.

PART THREE

Convoys

CHAPTER XIII

Protectors of Trade: Reminiscences of Convoys

My first practical experience of real life convoys occurred during the late spring/early summer of 1943 when a school friend and I, both working for the Special Entry Examination to obtain a cadetship in the Royal Navy, managed to obtain a billet in a merchantman.

At this time the Special Entry Examination was highly competitive. The standard of the examination papers was broadly that of the Higher School Certificate (today's 'A' Levels). Candidates had to score over fifty per cent in the written papers before they could be summoned to face 'ordeal by interview'. The interview was a 'make or break' exercise. However well a young hopeful had performed in the written examination, his hopes of becoming a cadet RN could be dashed by the members of the Interview Board. The chairman of this board was usually an experienced Head-master and his colleagues were a senior Royal Marine Officer and senior serving officers in various branches of the Royal Navy. The exercise was probably as fair as any which could have been devised in this imperfect world, and it would be reasonable to assume that experienced serving officers would have an eye for the type of young man who had the potential to join the ranks of the 'Officer Corps' in their own service.

I had given some thoughts as to how it might be possible to enhance the chances of obtaining good interview marks and lit on the brainwave of going to sea. As luck would have it, a Lieutenant Colonel Lance Wright OBE, RA was a near neighbour and happened to be working in the Movements Branch of the War Office. The Colonel's advice was sought, and school friend Robin Momber and I were interviewed at a shipping office in London and were taken on as apprentices in an elderly vessel called *Normandy Coast*, belonging to Coast Lines Limited.

A year later when serving as a midshipman in the famous battleship *Warspite*, during the invasion of Normandy, I saw the *Normandy Coast* beached on the French shore as part of a Mulberry Harbour: an appropriate and honourable end for a maritime 'old timer'.

To revert to my period of service on board the *Normandy Coast*, a significant slice of the time was occupied in sailing as one of the ships making up East Coast Convoys. These generally included a mixed bag of merchant vessels and could range from the low-profile colliers to ocean-going ships. The colliers sailed between, say, Newcastle and the major east coast ports such as Hull and, above all, London where they discharged their priceless loads at such vital places as Battersea Power Station to maintain the electricity needed to keep the wheels of industry turning and to provide lighting and heating to the population in general. The colliers' physical profiles were low to help them to negotiate the Thames bridges. The ocean-going ships also had cargoes to discharge in the east coast ports and the docks in London's East End.

The sea routes running down the east coast were regularly swept for enemy mines, and friendly preventive minefields also needed to be meticulously marked. A passage down the east coast of Britain involved a 'buoy hopping' exercise to keep the narrow fronted convoys of, say, two columns of ships within the confines of the swept channels.

I and my colleague took our 'tricks' at the wheel, learned not to 'chase the lubber's line' and to pay strict attention to the steering when following the next ahead lest the column should degenerate into an unacceptably sinuous line of advance.

Several transits of E-boat Alley were experienced. At night, trails of tracer, farther out to sea, marked where the British Coastal Forces were engaged with German E-boats. The E-boats were not averse to using crafty tricks such as nudging navigation buoys so that they might avoid detection by radar-fitted naval ships. They could reveal themselves when the time seemed right, for example when the convoy was very close to the buoy which the E-boat was using as a concealment aid. The altering of revolutions was probably an imprecise exercise. The officer who had the watch would blow down the mouth-piece of a narrow voice-pipe which produced a whistling note in the engine room; and the revised revolutions would be communicated to the engine room staff. Similar routines were, no doubt, commonplace in many older merchant vessels which were at sea in the first half of the 1940s. Accurate station-keeping was very important to warships operating in company and more sophisticated methods for adjusting revolutions had been evolved over the course of time. It should also be remembered that naval ships had more generous scales of personnel which, in wartime particularly, were based upon numbers needed to permit an armed ship to comply with requirements at the all-important 'Action State'.

During World War II, Merchant Navy personnel tended to operate on a 'pool' basis which implied that individuals might serve in a variety of ships and 'trades', that is be placed in a vessel which needed to fill a vacancy and not be tied to a specific trade or shipping company as might be the norm in times of peace. The same basic rules were applicable to merchant service officers, as well as to seamen and engine personnel.

Normandy Coast was armed with a single 4-inch gun in the stern and several verliken mountings whose purpose was to deter attacks by hostile aircraft. The weapons were manned by a small team of naval personnel known as DEMS (Defensively Equipped Merchant Ship) ratings. This team in a ship such as *Normandy Coast* was controlled by a Leading Seaman usually referred to as the 'gun lager'.

When I mentioned to one of the DEMS ratings that my aim was to join the Navy, the advice forthcoming was usually on the lines of: 'What do you want to join the Navy for? The Merchant Navy gets better paid; and they get most of the glory too.'

Joking apart, going to sea in Allied merchant ships during World War II could be a hazardous calling and ships' companies suffered distressing casualties. The Merchant Navy was officially a civilian job; but roughly a quarter perished during the wartime years. Specific sections of the armed services suffered greater casualty rates, but, taken overall, a higher proportion of merchant seamen died than was the case with the military forces. As with the 'fighting' services luck played its customary part. Many members of the Merchant Navy probably never came under attack, while others had to endure several sinkings and the associated sufferings of being adrift in open boats or on rafts in terrible weather or climatic extremes. Hunger, sunburn, lack of medical facilities and intense thirst were just some of the miseries which had to be endured, together with the mental agonies of not knowing what the chances of rescue might be; and being in the closest of quarters with shipmates who died of wounds, or were unable to cope with the extreme hardships with which they were not physically or psychologically equipped to contend. This could test the strongest of wills to the limit.

Taken all round, the Merchant Navy could count a very fair share of dauntless men among its company as was indicated by the fact that some 6,000 decorations for gallantry were awarded to members of the service.

Human nature being what it is, the Merchant Marine also included a number of poltroons and malingerers among the steady and loyal members of the profession. Every now and then ships were unable to put to sea because of the failure of crews who declined to appear despite the fact that they had signed the appropriate articles. The law prohibited merchant vessels from sailing if they were undermanned. Perhaps not surprisingly, firemen featured quite regularly. The expression 'not surprisingly' is used because firemen could work in particularly uncomfortable surroundings,and if a ship should be torpedoed, the exercise of evacuating machinery spaces could be physically testing to say nothing of being hard on the nervous system.

It is well worthy of note that a National Union of Seamen existed, certainly during the Second World War; but, to its great credit, it refrained from strike action or the threat of the same, when it could have been in a strong position to apply pressure for more money. This at a time when unions representing other important groups of workers did resort to strike action.

Sailors of the British Merchant Marine have not invariably been treated well in times of peace, but they have, in general, served their country faithfully during war. 'If blood be the price of Admiralty then I have paid it in full' could well be said to cover the merchant service as well as their naval counterparts.

I found that a considerable number of Merchant Navy officers and men were the first to say that they wished that they had not decided to 'follow the sea'. To take a few examples, the Master of *Normandy Coast* said, more than once, that he had been brought up in a vicarage. When he told his father of his desire to be a sailor, the response was: 'I will support your wishes; but if you come to me, after a few months whining that you don't like a nautical life, you will get no sympathy. I will not give you any encouragement to "swallow the anchor".' The Master would then add: 'When I had been to sea for a few months in a sailing ship, I would have swallowed the biggest bloody anchor in the British Merchant Marine.'

The Chief Engineer Officer would usually say that being a seagoing engineer was 'something attempted; but nothing achieved'. He would say that he bitterly regretted not having been a civil engineer as those men can 'build their own monuments'.

Other snippets may help to build up a picture of the type of person to be found in the ship's company of a merchant vessel. The boatswain of *Normandy Coast* was over 70 years of age. When asked if the time was not yet ripe to think of retiring and enjoying the prospect of a more leisurely existence, the reply would be: 'I have tried to retire and give up seagoing several times; but after three or four months I tend to become restive and, before I know it, I find myself on board a ship again.'

A slightly disconcerting habit of this worthy was his love of chewing tobacco. Any tobacco would do, at any time; and, if painting the superstructure, it was necessary to grow accustomed to the prospect of one's handiwork being embellished by a stream of unsavoury, yellowish spittle followed by an approving, or critical, comment.

Another character who sticks in the mind was a large Irish Able Seaman, not too surprisingly called Kelly. My colleague and I were very thirsty in the warm spring evening of our first day at sea and stumbled upon Kelly when searching for a source of drinkable fresh water. When we asked if Kelly knew where we could find something to drink, his response was: 'The only liquid you will find to drink in this ship is water. My God, it's terrible!'

As we grew to know him better, we found that Kelly had begun his nautical career in a Grand Banks schooner. He would give vivid descriptions of the artistry with which the mate of this sailing vessel could use his seaboot to keep any recalcitrant sailors on the move when it was necessary to alter the vessel's course.

Kelly also seemed to have a fund of knowledge, which he would willingly impart to the young, on the reasons why northern European females were attracted to males who hailed from the more torrid areas of the earth's surface; and other, perhaps, lesser known biological secrets which it might be difficult to unearth in the normal school text book.

Invitations to attend the Naval Interview Board of the Civil Service Commission in London followed, after which I and my school friend joined the MV *Southern Coast*. This was a small, but very new motor vessel. The greatest 'character' on board *Southern Coast* was, without doubt, the Master who was a portly gentleman with a well developed sense of humour and an insatiable appetite.

During the meals in the officers' saloon, the Master would be served extremely large helpings, but having made short work of these he would call for the steward and say: 'I enjoyed the sample; but would now like a decent helping.' Fair enough! He would also be fond of saying: 'When I go home I am the skipper, after a day or two I become the mate; but after I've been home for more than five days, I am the ruddy cabin boy!'

The first time we entered the Tyne in *Southern Coast*, the Master uttered a little gem: 'The last time I entered this harbour the ship ahead of me was mined, I took my ship in without mishap and the vessel following "sat on a mine". That's what you get for being good looking!'

By 1943, the year in which I had carried out my short stint in the Merchant Navy, it is highly unlikely that anyone could dispute that American and British merchant vessels made up the major part of any Allied convoy. At the same time it was commonplace to find ships of neutral countries and other Allies sailing in convoys.

In 1940 and 1941 the Germans inflicted themselves on something like half of Europe as a result of their 'Blitzkrieg' campaigns. During this period a significant slice of the merchant fleets of countries which had been occupied were 'pushing the oceans around' and thus avoided capture. It would be useful to spare a thought to what happened to the vessels in question when the head offices of their ships' companies were being controlled by Germans. The masters of these vessels found themselves placed on the horns of a daunting dilemma; and the earliest to have to face most unpleasant options were the Danes and Norwegians in April of 1940. The British Broadcasting Corporation, without delay, transmitted a series of broadcasts offering protection to these ships and payment for their services from their owners. At the same time the opposition put out rival broadcasts alleged to come from the owners, but in the real world of that time, emanating from the German authorities; and trying to entice the commanding officers to return to their home ports. This, of course, would have been good news for the occupying power. The

German transmissions customarily started with the words 'My Dear Master' – a form of 'lead in' which the shipowners would have been most unlikely to use.

Fortunately, the masters were finally allured into sailing for an Allied controlled port. I have for a considerable time understood that appeals transmitted by an esteemed Norwegian shipowner, Mr Hysing Olsen, who fortuitously happened to be in the United Kingdom at that time, played a major part in 'tipping the scales' in favour of the Allies.

An essentially similar exercise was implemented with success when Holland and Belgium were raped about a month later. It was a splendid success to think that not a single ship belonging to these countries went to the Germans.

A further injection of merchant shipping fell into British hands when Greece and Yugoslavia in their turn were invaded by the Germans. The large Greek Merchant Marine provided an especially precious contribution.

When I began my nautical career, through contacts made in seaport towns, I came to understand some of the feelings being experienced by members of the crews of those ships which accepted the challenge of working for Britain and her Allies. They were unable to see their native countries or families for the next five years. Instead of changing ship pretty well every voyage, they tended to remain with their ships on a permanent basis, with the result that their ships became the only home known to them.

Welfare organisations in ports did their best to look after the foreign ships' companies ashore; and families extended hospitality to them in countries such as America and Britain. However, this could never really make up for the lengthy, involuntary expatriation; and anxiety as to how their families might be faring when close relatives were known to be living in areas which were under the occupation of German authorities. Letters were always eagerly awaited by Commonwealth serving men; and mail to and from prisoners-of-war or relatives in occupied countries could be a rare commodity.

It was by no means uncommon to see ships from neutral countries sailing in convoy at times when their owners detailed them to work for, say, the British. This, when one thought about it, appeared strange, especially after 1940 when Hitler declared a state of total blockade of Great Britain and issued a warning that any ship of any nationality could be sunk on sight, and without warning. Sweden was the main neutral country to be affected. Some sixty per cent of the Swedish merchant fleet had been offered on charter to Britain outside the limits of the Baltic Sea. Neutral ships in the above category agreed to respect British security classifications and to conform with convoy rules.

The sagacious British actions resulted in an effective increase of approximately a quarter in the size of her disposable merchant shipping and the contribution of this increment can only be described as priceless.

Another personal experience of sailing in convoy during World War II occurred when I and several other midshipmen, joined the Norwegian liner *Bergensfjord* which had been converted to a troopship, to proceed to the Mediterranean to join our respective RN ships. Because of the need for evasive routing, it seemed to take a long time to reach the Straits of Gibraltar. The ship virtually crossed the Atlantic to the vicinity of Newfoundland before heading in the general direction of the Rock. The Master of *Bergensfjord* was a most experienced mariner who had made many Atlantic crossings in conditions of very poor visibility and in pre-radar days. He gave a never to be forgotten gem of advice: 'Never permit yourself to get ahead of your DR [Dead Reckoning]'. The voyage was basically uneventful although escorting destroyers did investigate a few submarine contacts and even dropped the odd depth charge.

CHAPTER XIV
Second World War Convoys

It is high time, after having had a general glance at some of the ships and men of the merchant marines of several countries which were involved during the Second World War, to turn attention to the steadfast naval vessels which escorted them back and forth across the Atlantic and to and from other parts of the globe.

It is easy to think predominantly of the submarine threat, particularly during the earlier phases of World War II. However, this had also been the potential and, from time to time, real menace of surface raiders. A large surface warship could probably make short work of a convoy if it were able to deal with such a juicy collection of merchantmen at comparatively short range. A convoy might have had pretty well anything from a battleship to an armed trawler as part of its escort during the earlier parts of the war until the Royal Navy had, to a great extent, put paid to the threat of interference by hostile naval ships. This left submarines as the main danger. Threat by surface warships, of course, reared its head again when the large Japanese Navy entered the war against the United States, Britain and their Allies; but that was not until the post Pearl Harbor days, that is after 7 December 1941.

Having said that the threat from surface warships had been largely eliminated during the early years of World War II, there can be no disguising the fact that the Allied Navies were pathetically short of the smaller types of warship. The growing, and to a great extent ubiquitous, web of convoy routes ideally needed vast numbers of escorts, running into the hundreds. It had been agreed with the United States of America that the Western Theatre of War was of paramount importance and that the North Atlantic was, consequently, the decisive area as far as the war at sea was concerned. Despite this, the maritime authorities had to 'make do' with whatever vessels they could get. Until, say, early 1943, this was never sufficient.

The work of protecting convoys had, in the main, alighted on the shoulders of two types of naval vessel: the destroyer and, in expanding numbers, the corvette. Assistance was given by a comparatively small number of other types such as sloops and, later, frigates. The main stream in the North Atlantic had been taken by the Royal Navy with growing aid from the Canadians and, until the United States entered the war, a smallish force of American vessels.

The Royal Navy could boast of more than one class of fine modern destroyers, for example the Tribals and Js and Ks; but with competing demands for these splendid vessels, the oldest and least effective destroyers tended to be assigned for work with convoys.

The thousand-ton V and W classes had been built in considerable numbers during the course of, and just after, the First World War and were a pleasure to watch as they bustled about their tasks; but they suffered from the great disadvantage that they were unable to cross the Atlantic without calling at Iceland to top up with fuel. Some twenty-two of the V and W Class had undergone extensive modification in that one of the three boilers which had been built into these destroyers had been removed in each ship. The space thus gained was used to house an additional fuel tank. This exercise, plus the removal of the forward funnel, meant the loss of some speed, but it increased the range of these vessels to the extent that they could cross the Atlantic without the need to replenish with furnace fuel oil en route.

The other principal destroyers employed in escort work were the Town Class, the elderly ex-American vessels given to the British in exchange for the use of bases such as Bermuda. I was only one of many who believed that the Americans had struck a one-sided bargain, but 'needs must when the devil drives'. Escort vessels were a very precious commodity and it is difficult to know what would have happened if these elderly 'cans', to borrow US parlance, had not been collected by British ships' companies and effort been given to try to make them useable for up-to-date anti-submarine warfare. The Town Class destroyers were widely known as 'four stackers' thanks to their very obvious four funnels and were arguably the most easily recognisable warships in the Atlantic Ocean.

I spent some time in Rosyth as a midshipman in the battleship *Warspite* which was being patched up after detonating a mine off Orford Ness following the landings in Normandy in 1944. The remaining ex-American destroyers were still quite common users of the Rosyth 'Timber Jetty' at this time and conversations with officers serving in them indicated that they were not exactly beloved by their ships' companies. The hulls were narrow and they rolled maliciously. The propeller shafts protruded several feet beyond the stern and they were extremely tricky to handle. The turning circles of these vessels were prodigious which was not of great assistance when attacking a submerged U-boat. They were not suited to Atlantic bad weather conditions and in at least two incidents their bridges were smashed by heavy seas.

Paradoxically, six modern destroyers which were permanently allocated to the North Atlantic were admirable ships. These were the vessels of the *Havant* Class which had been built in the United Kingdom for the Brazilians, but were commandeered by Britain on the outbreak of the Second World War. These destroyers were fast, fitted with 'state of the art' depth-charge equipment and could carry sufficient fuel to provide them with a good endurance. They also had the merit of being more stable in a seaway than either the Vs and Ws or the four-stackers. A pleasurable additional merit was the fact that the Brazilian Navy had specified a higher standard of living accommodation than was usual for ships of the Royal Navy.

Any study of convoy work in World War II would be sadly lacking if it omitted to give some mention to the corvettes which must be categorised as extraordinarily versatile little ships. Each weighed something, but not very much, over nine hundred tons; and they were based upon the design of a whale-catcher. This type of vessel had started to be ordered shortly before the war with the intention of being used as a coastal patrol craft. The corvettes, which were simple to construct, were produced in large numbers as the U-boat war spread into the Atlantic, to provide convoy escorts. This was in the nature of a stop-gap pending the discovery of a more suitable alternative. The Royal Navy corvettes were named after indigenous British flowers which seemed somewhat inappropriate when one takes into consideration the violent lifestyle they were destined to lead. The Canadian corvettes were named after towns in their homeland.

Corvettes functioned as useful anti-submarine vessels in a number of ways. They were definitely seaworthy and carried adequate fuel to make the Atlantic crossing. They could also make effective attacks upon a U-boat once the submarine had been 'put down'. A corvette's main drawback was lack of speed. Its sixteen knots was insufficient to catch a U-boat tracking along the surface. Also, if it remained for a longish period over a submerged submarine, or engaged in rescue activities, it could take hours to regain station in the convoy it was alleged to be escorting.

The winter months of 1942–43 saw of the order of seventy corvettes operational in the North Atlantic. They were becoming obsolete as far as anti-submarine specialists were concerned; but they were still sorely required despite the more effective, and sophisticated, frigates which were appearing on the scene.

No doubt, an inevitable question must be : 'How did escorts operate during the period under consideration and what was their theoretical organisation?'

The basic escort organisation was 'on paper' centred on the group. The group could best be described as a cluster of anti-submarine vessels which, in a perfect world, would remain together under an overall commanding officer who would be responsible for the protection of one convoy for all or some of its passage. The burden of guarding the North Atlantic convoys was essentially carried by twelve escort groups comprising seven British and five Canadian groups. The 'paper' strength of each of these escort groups was nine ships made up of three destroyers and six corvettes. The group commander's ship was normally one of the destroyers. As far as the British groups were concerned, this was generally one of the *Havants* which, as has been noted, were originally destined for the Brazilian Navy.

To take the story a bit further, the British groups all had main bases on their own side of the Atlantic. Liverpool and Londonderry were bases for three groups each; and the remaining group used Greenock. The Canadian escort vessels were based at St John's, Newfoundland. The usual drill for a British group was to shepherd one convoy across the Atlantic to a position off Newfoundland, proceed into St John's for a few days rest and recreation before bringing another convoy back to Britain and a longer spell of rest at its main base. The Canadian groups carried out a similar operation in reverse. It was possible to calculate the timetable of convoys and escort groups for some months ahead. However, this said, with twelve habitual groups and up to eight convoys at sea at any one time, there could be little fat to spare on occasions when things went awry, as they inevitably did.

Merchant ships sailing in convoy might see escorts other than those comprising mid-ocean groups. U-boats had made aggressive inroads on the shipping routes off the east coast of America in early 1942. A result of this unfriendly behaviour had been the creation of the Western Local Escort Force which sought to protect North Atlantic convoys between the 'Western Ocean Meeting Point', colourfully abbreviated to WOMP, and the terminal ports such as Halifax, the Cape, Breton Island, Sydney and New York. The Royal Canadian Navy took care of this exercise. The Canadians used small, generally freshly commissioned vessels as this normally quiet coast enabled them to work-up pending allocation to the more potentially dangerous deep-sea routes.

There were a small number of escort vessels which were operating in the undoubtedly active section of the Atlantic in the earlier months of 1943 which were not components of regular groups. These ships were, for the most part, based in Iceland. They constituted a handy reserve for escorting merchantmen aiming for Iceland or could be deployed to 'beef up' escorts which had their hands full trying to deal with high levels of aggressive U-boat attention. Most of this diminishing force of spare escorts were American and were the residue of a stronger United States force of escorts which had assisted in protecting North Atlantic convoys in 1942; but this had later started to be thinned out.

The best United States armed ships remaining at this stage were five US Coast Guard cutters which were, for some probably excellent reason, named after US Treasury Secretaries. The United States Navy had taken over the Coast Guard in 1941, and the cutters acquired made admirable

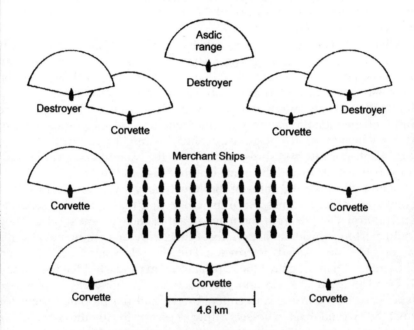

Convoy Organisation

Asdic range

Destroyer

Destroyer

Corvette

Corvette

Destroyer

Corvette

Merchant Ships

Corvette

Corvette

Corvette

Corvette

Corvette

4.6 km

Typical deployment of anti-submarine escort forces

The basic principle of the convoy is to concentrate merchant ships in large groups so that they can be protected by warships. A typical convoy of 45 ships in five-ship columns would cover an area of 13 sq km (5 sq mi.). And with the underwater detection device Asdic normally only capable of picking up submerged submarines at distances shorter than a kilometre and able to sweep in an arc of 80 degrees ahead of the vessel, only a strong escort could expect to prevent a determined mass U-Boat attack from getting through to the merchant vessels.

anti-submarine vessels. Their speed of twenty-two knots was perfectly acceptable for anti-submarine duties and their displacement of something over two thousand tons meant that they were about twice as heavy as the British destroyers used in the escort role.

The five Coast Guard cutters, by sinking three U-boats and actively assisting in the demise of a fourth in the five-month period of the winter of 1942/43, proved just how useful the availability of more vessels of this type could have been.

A look has been taken at the naval vessels which faced the U-boats during the course of a testing North Atlantic winter. The Allies were, to all intents and purposes, fighting the U-boats with escorts which were for the most part 'hand me downs' from more glamorous fields of naval warfare. Perhaps it was only later that history would look back on this phase of the Battle of the Atlantic as the most momentous, and dangerous, part of World War II at sea. To plagiarise Mahan, we might murmur that 'those far distant, storm-tossed ships, upon which the Nazi rulers never looked, stood between them and the demise of the Western World'.

Men of all ranks and rates in the Royal Navy's Western Approaches Command must, at times, have imagined that they formed a separate navy at arm's length from the mainstream of their parent service. They could exist for considerable periods of time without sighting naval ships larger than, say, Allied destroyers. The struggle waged in the, often unfriendly, Atlantic against the natural elements and a hidden foe tended to breed its own lifestyle and ground rules. In many cases, previous experience of life in the conventional navy had not prepared them for what they would meet in vessels acting as escorts to Atlantic convoys.

Regular officers were something of a rarity in warships employed in escorting Atlantic convoys. Those who did serve in the escorts tended to be commissioned gunners and engineers. Regular Royal Navy executive (what the US Navy would call deck) officers were conspicuous by their absence. Those who were to be found with convoys would normally be in command of groups, or members of a group commander's staff. A number of officers who had specialised in the TAS (Torpedo and Anti-Submarine) Board could find the fulfilment of their skills in the operations against hostile U-boats. The celebrated Captain Frederick Walker was a brilliant player in anti-submarine operations, commanded two escort groups at different times, despatched some thirty U-boats to the bottom of the ocean and carved a niche for himself in naval history. Sadly, Captain Walker died of sheer exhaustion before the end of World War II.

Another very good reason for the paucity of regular Royal Navy officers in the Atlantic lay in the fact that there were satisfactory options in the shape of Royal Naval Reserve (RNR) and Royal Naval Volunteer Reserve (RNVR) officers available.

The Royal Navy, in its wisdom, had leaned on the RNR to provide a reservoir of experienced seafaring officers. These were Merchant Navy officers who had served a statutory period with the RN in time of peace and earned commissioned rank in the Royal Naval Reserve. They were subject to recall in times of war and were paid a modest annual retainer in peacetime. Perhaps, the greatest enticement was the distinction of holding a commission in the RNR of which an officer could well be proud. In my experience, executive officers in the Royal Naval Reserve tended to produce many who were proficient in the skills of navigation, thanks to the thorough training in this art which they had received while they had served as junior officers in merchant vessels.

The Royal Naval Volunteer Reserve (RNVR) was made up of civilians from shore-side occupations, but who, for a variety of reasons, had developed an attraction for the sea. It is popular to say that the RNVR contained a large proportion of yachtsmen which is true up to a point; but probably rather exaggerated.

Well-educated 'hostilities only' naval ratings could seek their way towards, and apply for, commissions in the RNVR; and the Navy was probably the most difficult of the three armed services in which to gain a wartime commission. The average level of ability, either actual or potential, was consequently extremely high.

The Royal Navy steered large numbers of both types of reserve officer into anti-submarine escort vessels. These ships required less advanced training than a ship which was intended for working with the Fleet and in which the high level of experience of seamanship and navigation of the RNRs was of inestimable value. Lest the above be misunderstood as too sweeping a statement, I would be among the first to vouch for the fact that highly competent reserve officers were to be found serving in Fleet Destroyers and Capital Ships. RNRs were given commands as the overall naval escort force grew in number, in particular of corvettes and the older destroyers.

The Royal Naval Volunteer Reserve provided a great corps of junior officers. Initially, these had little experience and were obliged to learn many of their specific duties 'on the job'. All the same, they did find considerable gratification in practising to accept the very real responsibilities of officers who take charge of the watch in a ship at sea. This is especially important in a wartime scenario when 'snap decisions' may need to be made unexpectedly and at the shortest of notice. Seconds can make the difference between success or failure. By the year 1943, a few of the best RNVR officers were to be found in command of corvettes.

The deserved praises which have been sung about the qualities to be found among reserve officers should not be permitted to obscure the fact that the Battle of the Atlantic would have been more consistently well fought if a few more skilled regular officers had been made available in the early years of the war; but the appointing authorities undoubtedly had their hands full trying to plug the large number of holes which had resulted from the outbreak of hostilities. It should not be forgotten that the Royal Navy was fully employed from one end of the war to the other.

According to Napoleon Bonaparte: 'There is no such thing as bad troops, only bad officers.' Much depended upon the ratings who made up the bulk of the ships' companies of escort vessels. No doubt the men who served in these ships were microcosms of their wartime navies. As far as the Royal Navy was concerned, personnel went where they were told by the drafting authorities. It was a lucky man who found himself in a ship for which he had volunteered – theoretically possible, but most improbable.

The drafting authorities at the Port Divisions of Chatham, Devonport and Portsmouth produced the proportions of, ideally, trained men required for a newly-commissioning ship; and there these fortunate ratings could stay for a considerable time.

Oh! I wonder, Oh! I wonder
If the Jaunty made a blunder
When he made this 'draft chit' out for me.

Statistically, the casualty rate in escorts was pretty low and, in this respect, they suffered less than their merchant opposite numbers. Against this, merchant sailors could serve much of their time in comparatively safe regions while ships' companies of escort vessels could rarely escape the knowledge that a torpedo might strike their ship any time.

This type of apprehension can occur at pretty well any time when at sea in a wartime situation. It is, therefore, necessary to take care not to permit one's imagination to run riot. The syndrome is slightly similar to that experienced by people who would do anything to avoid flying in a commercial aircraft.

The men manning escort ships were resiliant, and young enough, to recover promptly from most untoward experiences and hardships. In general, they could appreciate, through their experience, some pride and satisfaction in the bringing of a convoy across the Atlantic (or any other convoy route) safely, and the consequent contribution towards the British war effort.

Some accounts of the Battle of the Atlantic go into detail of the shore headquarters on both sides of the ocean and of the personalities who manned these highly important organisations; but such detail is really beyond the scope of this narrative. However, the part played by aircraft in the struggles against enemy submarines must be given due attention.

Military aircraft made themselves felt at sea as a factor of great importance during the 1914–18 War. In the scouting role, aircraft could cover large ocean areas; and, due to their altitude, have a more distant view of the horizon than, say, a look-out stationed aloft in a surface ship. One of Napoleon's aphorisms was 'imagination rules the world', and human minds began to evolve more and more uses for airborne vehicles at sea, ranging from midshipmen being wafted aloft in kites, towed by capital ships, to spot 'fall of shot', sea-planes being lowered over the side by crane and being recovered by the same means; and later being catapulted and then recovered by crane using a capital ship as their home base. The fitting of radio in ship-borne and, for that matter, shore-based aircraft accelerated the speed with which directions and information could be exchanged between aircraft and ship.

The human mind also did not take long to evolve the concept of aircraft being able to carry automatic guns, bombs and depth charges in battles with surface ships and submersible craft, also to carry mines which could be laid in coastal waters such as estuaries and the approaches to harbours. The effort and expense in both manpower and money which had to be expended in sweeping these devices, which gradually became more sophisticated, was immense. A direct impact was also felt in such focal points as convoy assembly areas, coastal shipping routes and so forth. It could be frustrating, to put it mildly, to go to the effort of convoying a valuable merchant ship and its cargo over vast distances only to see it 'sit on a mine' when close to its destination in the United Kingdom.

Convoys were, basically, one of the main targets of inshore mining operations; and friendly military aircraft were used to detect minefields either visually, when the water was clear enough to enable, say, moored mines to be sighted from low-flying aircraft or by electro-magnetic means in the case of magnetic or influence mines.

Mines are a comparatively cheap form of weapon with which to deny the use of specific sea areas to an enemy. Another advantage of the mine as a weapon is that it can inflict damage where it really hurts a ship, that is, below the waterline. Surface ships tend to do their best to avoid regions which are suspected of having been the victim of hostile mine-laying activity until such time as these localities have been thoroughly searched by teams of mine counter-measures experts.

In the early days of World War II, I can well remember the news bulletins which mentioned attacks by German aircraft on shipping, including fishing vessels and convoys transiting coastal waters such as those which wash Great Britain's east coast. At that time, the Royal Air Force was desperately short of aircraft which could be spared to counter such attacks on friendly maritime activities. The situation improved greatly as the strength of the RAF increased and the expertise of such organisations as Coastal Command developed.

Other combat zones in which convoys suffered severely from the attentions of enemy aircraft included the Mediterranean, where heavy losses were suffered during the evacuation of Crete, the heroic defence of Malta GC and operations in support of the army units engaged in North Africa and, later, in Sicily and Italy. During the early campaigns, the

German Stuka dive bomber earned a reputation for being a dismaying weapon system due to its near-vertical descent upon its prey and the distinctive howl which it emitted, sometimes enhanced by artificial aids, as it dropped towards its target. The bomb carried by the Stuka was of no mean size. However, in the end, the drag of the bomb and, after release, the drop in speed as the Stuka pulled out of its dive left it vulnerable to defending fighter aircraft and the smaller calibre anti-aircraft weapons ashore or in ships. The noise of the Stuka dive bomber is somewhat reminiscent of the 'whistling arrows' used, in a previous age, by Samurai warriors to undermine the morale of the opposition.

The Casablanca Conference, which took place between Churchill and Roosevelt in mid-January 1943 can be remembered for two decisions which are pertinent to convoys. It was agreed that: 'The defeat of the U-boat must remain a first charge on the resources of the United Nations.' It was also agreed that the Allies should insist on the final 'unconditional surrender' of Germany and Japan. This was understandable at the time it was made; but historians have argued that it probably prolonged the duration of the Second World War in that it put the main enemies 'over a barrel'. The will to resist was hardened as it appeared that even when the situation had sunk to desperately low levels, Great Britain, the USA and their Allies would not contemplate any form of negotiation so there was no point in seeking an early end to hostilities.

Some five weeks after the Japanese assault on Pearl Harbor, Admiral Doenitz opened a vicious underwater attack on shipping sailing off the American east coast. This campaign was designated 'Roll of Drums' or *Paukenschlag* in German. The exercise was opened using an attacking force of a mere six U-boats. Despite its low numbers, this small group gave American shipping a horrible surprise. The submarines carried out their attacks by night; and fired their torpedoes from seaward with their target ships audaciously silhouetted against lights emanating from American towns and cities.

It seems astonishing, at this distance in time, that a blackout was not prescribed on the American east coast until the month of May 1942. Before this time, an expensive policy of 'business as usual' was adhered to; and ships were being sunk and sailors drowned in the light of places of pleasure ashore. Ships were undarkened and even lighthouses and navigation buoys were showing their appropriate characteristics. Favoured by these gifts of light and only minimally put out by ineffective anti-submarine evolutions, the German U-boats grew so bold that they started to carry out attacks in daylight. On 15 June large numbers bathing at Virginia Beach looked on in impotent dismay as a Nazi submarine torpedoed a couple of US cargo vessels. These were the six months of unrivalled success which U-boat crews called 'the happy times' and during which they disposed of the disturbing number of over 560 Allied ships. The

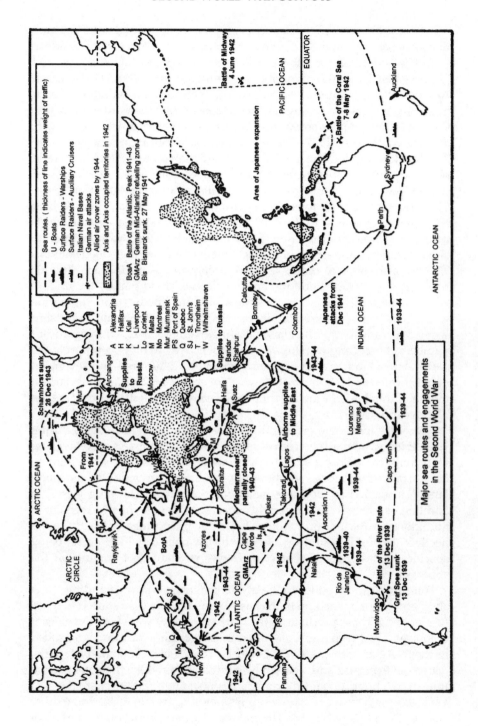

Major sea routes and engagements in the Second World War

American Chief of Staff, General George Marshall, notified Admiral King that losses of ships in the Atlantic were a threat to the American war effort.

The introduction of the convoy system for coastal shipping and improvements in anti-submarine methodology progressively decreased American losses. Admiral Doenitz and his staff did not lack flexibility or ingenuity and responded by starting to concentrate their attention on the Caribbean. Large new submarine tankers, known as 'milch cows', were introduced by July 1942. These submersibles could carry some seven hundred tons of fuel. The milch cows would make contact with U-boats at sea; and could transfer about fifty tons of fuel to a medium-sized submarine which would increase its cruising range to the Caribbean. Likewise, circa ninety tons of fuel could be passed to a bigger U-boat which might enable it to think in terms of cruising as far away from its base as the Cape of Good Hope. Toward the end of 1942, Admiral Doenitz and his staff became aware of the fact that air cover for the Allied convoys was, for a number of reasons, given at either end of the trans-Atlantic passage. There was, therefore, an unwelcome broad gap in the middle which came to be known as the 'black pit' after the German submarine wolf packs began to assemble there. Merchant ship after merchant ship seemed to vanish into 'the black pit'. In November 1942, with significant numbers of escorting warships being drawn away to play their part in the North Africa landings, the U-boats despatched a hundred and seventeen merchantmen to the bottom of the sea. November 1942 became the darkest month of the Battle of the Atlantic in the same way that 1942 became the black year in that ocean.

The Allies lost some eight million tons of shipping to U-boats during 1942. Enemy submarines were sinking merchant ships at a greater rate than America could construct replacements; and this imposed a tremendous strain upon the US shipbuilding industry, even aided by its Allies. Firstly, it needed to replace a major share of Allied shipping losses, in addition to which it was hopefully expected to double the replacement of munitions to the fighting fronts. Last, but by no means least, the US needed to build a lion's share of the warships which were being specifically designed to protect the new merchant fleet coming off the slipways.

The American response to the above challenge was outstanding. New shipyards were opened on both coasts of the US and they started to build *Liberty* ships. These products of the marine industry were far from elegant to look at. They were ugly, slow and uncomfortable for those who sailed in them. Against this, *Libertys* could be constructed amazingly rapidly. American expertise and know-how contrived to reduce the construction time of two hundred and fifty-four days taken to build the first *Liberty* in 1941, to an average of forty-two days per ship in late 1942. Some 2,700 *Libertys* were finally constructed and they carried about three-quarters of

America's cargo overseas. After *Liberty* ships came on stream, they tended to feature conspicuously in nearly all of the slower Allied convoys.

In tandem with the construction of merchantmen, brand new fleets of escort destroyers and smallish escort (aircraft) carriers were being built. These ships were designed to provide air cover in the lethal mid-Atlantic gap, known as 'the black pit', in the first instance. Each escort carrier (CVE) typically carried, say, sixteen fighters and a dozen torpedo bombers. Screened by escort destroyers, which had a good turn of speed, the CVEs became a weapon system with which to torment the U-boats which made up the German wolf packs. The fighters could strafe surfaced submarines or drop depth charges of various sizes and characteristics on their submerged equivalents, not forgetting the more conventional torpedoes. Devices, such as the Fido homing torpedo, could be launched by aircraft to add to the discomfiture of enemy submarines. In simplistic terms, Fido could be dropped in the vicinity of a U-boat's steel hull and would be attracted towards that considerable assemblage of metalwork. Assisted by a sprouting selection of sophisticated detection devices, the Allies became more adept in the art of determining the position of suspect submarines both above and below the surface of the sea.

In about the spring of 1943 squadrons of escort vessels, possibly more familiarly known as flotillas at that time, of surface escorts were formed to hunt for and, ideally, to kill the U-boats, which were then at their peak operating strength of about two hundred and thirty submarines. These units came to be known as 'hunter killer' groups. As with most innovations, there were arguments against and for the concept of hunter killer groups. For example, was this deviating from the aim of attracting submarines to the 'killing ground' for which the magnet was so often a convoy?

The proof of the pudding is in the eating. The hunter killer groups gradually began to drive the wolf packs below the surface and then started to live up to their name and to kill them off. In May 1943 some thirty U-boats met their fate at the hands of the Allies; and by June of that year losses of their merchant ships were at the lowest level since the United States added their muscle to the war. Allied bombers then added their weight to the battle against the U-boats in July 1943 by initiating regular patrols over the Bay of Biscay which helped in the destruction of an additional thirty enemy submarines in the course of that July. These sorties also added to the strain being experienced by U-boat crews who entered a combat-zone very shortly after they left harbour. On the return journey the submarine ship's company were basically in an action state until their submarine drew close to its destination on the French coast.

German shipbuilding facilities toiled desperately to replace Admiral Doenitz's losses. Rightly or wrongly, they concentrated on producing a very large submarine with the recently developed 'snorkel' breathing contraption which could enable U-boats to proceed underwater, at periscope depth; and by enabling the use of a boat's diesel engines permit higher speeds at many sea states, and permit greater distances to be covered with a submarine operating in a dived state. It was, and still is for that matter, easier to detect a snorkel ('snort' for short) than it is a periscope; but there are great advantages in having the submarine in a submerged state up until the moment of detection.

There was one priceless commodity which the German shipyards could not replace and that was trained submariners. One after another, the German U-boat aces failed to return to harbour and among those missing were Doenitz's two sons and his son-in-law.

The fall of North Africa presented Allied shipping with an invaluable bounty in that it virtually cleared the Mediterranean routes of hostile interference and it lopped about forty-five days from schedules of shipping which previously needed to be routed via the Cape. The most severe blow of all was struck with the Allied landings on the coast of France during June 1944, and the consequent follow-up operations. These resulted in the loss of the French ports to Admiral Doenitz and his submarines.

The German Admiral was not the man to give up. He was utterly confident that the latest submarines being worked on could revolutionise the war at sea and he anticipated having over three hundred of these vessels built during 1945. Shortages of specific materials needed for this most ambitious task upset his plans and, for the most part, obliged him to continue the submarine campaign employing smaller, older U-boats. However, raids by Allied bombers destroyed, or seriously damaged, many of these in their pens.

In the final event, the Battle of the Atlantic was won by the Allies; but as the great Duke of Wellington said of the Battle of Waterloo, it was at times a 'near run thing'. In a second major war, that Cinderella of the German armed forces, the submarine service, had come 'within spitting distance' of winning the conflict on its own.

It is a mark of the success of the U-boat campaign that it was not until 28 May 1945 that the British Admiralty and the United States Navy made a joint announcement to the effect that no further trade convoys need sail, that navigation lights could be burned at full brilliance and that there was no need to 'darken ship'. This was three weeks after VE Day.

The next few paragraphs are designed to be in the nature of a 'tidying up' exercise. No excuses will be made for the instances when duplication may appear to rear its head as the points at issue are important and are covered in works which consider the subject in greater detail. Should the present work stimulate interest and help to point the way for future enthusiasts, it will have achieved its aim.

The need for big ships has been disputed as far back in history as the Battle of Actium (32 BC) when Octavian, later to become the Emperor

Augustus, defeated Antony. As a matter of interest, Octavian had then given up his heavy ships for smaller, more manageable vessels. A somewhat similar state of affairs applied when the Spanish Armada was defeated by the well-handled smaller British ships commanded by Howard, with Drake as his Vice-Admiral, in late July 1588. Nowadays a number of types of submarine are assuming 'big ship' proportions.

In the Atlantic and Mediterranean and, later, in the Pacific during World War II, torpedo-carrying aircraft proved to be a key weapon system for attacking armoured ships. The torpedo itself was, originally, designed for launch from a torpedo boat, on the surface. It remains formidable in its original role; but probably had a greater influence on sea warfare after it started to be launched by aircraft or submarines. The torpedo was the major weapon used for sinking ships sailing in convoy during the two World Wars of the twentieth century.

In the Pacific, in particular, the aircraft carrier did not often have to share the credit of being capital ship with the battleship. The large spaces of the vast Pacific Ocean, with most of the climatic conditions suitable for air operations, made the greater range of a carrier's aircraft, as opposed to the range of a ship's guns, earn the aircraft carrier the title of 'Capital Ship'. Opposing battleships only met each other a couple of times and the combat between the carriers, in which strike carrier aircraft aimed at the evening carriers, decided the command of the Pacific Ocean and hence the result of the naval war in that combat zone.

While on the subject, aircraft carriers came to change the previous character of the protection of large warships. British aircraft carriers were constructed with armoured flight decks which were often a tremendous advantage, for example, when attacks by Japanese suicide pilots (kamikazes) had to be ordered. However, like their American counterparts, with their unarmoured flight decks, British carriers also depended fundamentally on the active defence provided by their anti-aircraft armament rather than the armour plate which was so much a feature of the battleship, tracing its early origins back to the sturdily built sides of the old ship of the line. More vulnerable due to the want of the passive defence provided by the use armour, aircraft carriers gained in defensive power by taking advantage of the weaponry mounted in accompanying ships. The anti-aircraft armament of destroyers stemmed from guns, which in earlier days had been mounted to combat surface torpedo boats, hence the original title 'torpedo boat destroyer'. To cope with the threat from aircraft, destroyers' guns tended to boast a high-angle capability. The British and US navies even went so far as to construct a number of anti-aircraft cruisers. In addition, aircraft carriers would include a number of fighter aircraft amongst their complement of warplanes to assist in protecting themselves, and other fleet units, from the potential attacks of hostile carrier-borne planes.

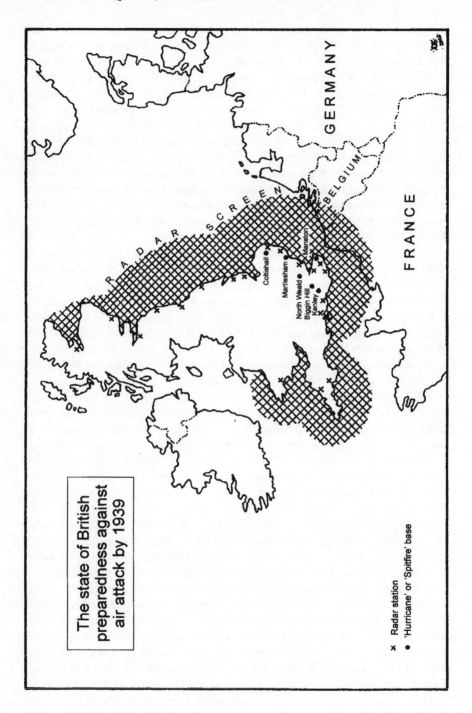

The state of British preparedness against air attack by 1939

GERMANY

BELGIUM

FRANCE

RADAR SCREEN

Coltishall
Martlesham
North Weald
Biggin Hill
Kenley
Manston

× Radar station
● 'Hurricane' or 'Spitfire' base

Aircraft, as has already been mentioned, played a major part against the submarine in the Second World War; and the submarine, as in the First World War, established that part of the naval contest in which the final result was, at times, truly in doubt. It has, on a number of occasions, been said that the World War II submarine campaigns started where those of the First World War left off. The latest asdic, or in US parlance sonar, submarine detecting devices proved themselves to be substantially better at finding and tracking submarines than the hydroplane employed in 1918.

The Germans, for their part, experienced initial problems with faulty torpedoes; but later benefited from the development of an electric torpedo which had the advantage of leaving minimal wake; and from homing torpedoes which utilised acoustic and magnetic detection/homing contrivances.

A typical German submarine of the era displaced circa five hundred tons, could dive to approximately five hundred feet, had a surface speed of about sixteen knots and a cruising range in excess of eight thousand miles.

History repeated itself to some extent. At the beginning of World War I, the Germans had had some fifty-six submarines; but not all of these were ideally suited to operations in the Atlantic and they lacked the superiority of force with which to strangle British commerce; and, of course, the British required many more escort vessels to counter the German attacks.

In the first six months of the Second World War, the Germans contrived to sink an average of more than a 140,000 tons of shipping per month. This score was about half the average monthly loss, from all causes, in 1918. It should be noted that most of the U-boat successes came in the form of single ships, i.e. those the British had seen fit to exclude from convoys due to the fact that they were either too fast to need protection or so slow that, in the interests of transport efficiency, the British Admiralty de-barred them from convoys. The same old mistakes, of sailing some ships out of convoy, were to be made again.

During the period March to late May 1940, losses of merchant vessels diminished by about sixty per cent due to the fact that the Germans allocated a significant number of their submarines to provide support to their invasion of Norway. However, in June of that year, the Germans had a force of fifty-seven U-boats available, most of which were fully replenished. These were duly sent to sea at about the same time; and ship losses rose to more than 350,000 tons. This somewhat devastating campaign owed some of its success to the new tactics introduced by Admiral Doenitz who had decided to offset the concentration of merchant ships in the defensive embrace of a convoy with a counter-concentration by the attacking submarines. This meant that when a U-boat sighted a convoy it would not attack, but would signal its position by radio. Other submarines, often ordered by Admiral Doenitz's headquarters, would assemble with the aim of attacking together. To mention but one success-ful exercise of this principle, seven German submarines sank seventeen ships out of a convoy of thirty-four merchantmen which was being escorted by a far from adequate group of four warships.

The Germans also adopted the then new tactic of attacking at night on the surface. The logic behind this method of assault was that it gave the U-boats a better opportunity to observe potential targets and the advantage of being able to use their high surface speed which was, for example, about twice the speed of the average convoy. The small size of the submarine's conning tower made the U-boat difficult to detect and its operation on the surface substantially reduced the efficacy of searching sonars. Better operating methods and better tactics resulted in the Allies losing of the order of one and a half million tons of shipping between June to late October 1940. It was during this time-frame that the Germans started to exploit the valuable long-term benefits of having bases on the French and Norwegian coasts. This permitted U-boats the convenience of having to make shorter passages between their bases and patrol areas; and, as a by-product, increased the number of German submarines on station at any one time and available for attacking merchant vessels.

The British were able to enhance the number of convoy escorts after the threat of invasion abated; and German submarines deployed in the early summer needed to return for replenishment. These factors reduced the number of sinkings. In addition, the British increased patrols by aircraft. Even low-speed, rather ungainly flying boats presented grave problems to submarines as these aeroplanes carried bombs or depth charges and the submarines were poorly armed against anti-aircraft weaponry. Frequently, an even meagrely damaged U-boat could not submerge with-out risk. Air patrols, therefore, obliged submarines to submerge and thus made it more difficult for them to track convoys.

In 1941 the U-boat war versus commerce tended to follow the pattern which had been established during late 1940. The monthly tribute exacted in 1941 amounted to something short of 200,000 tons. The Germans had only lost thirty-one submarines since the war started; but they had omitted to accelerate their building programme so that they scarcely made good the casualties they had suffered. As has been mentioned, the British were able to offset the increase in the number of German submarines in 1941 and the addition of the Italian Fleet by constructing yet more escort vessels, acquiring the fifty veteran destroyers from the American Navy and being given some direct escort aid by US naval ships. This enabled the number of escorts to be 'beefed up' and to extend the use of convoying right across the Atlantic, rather than limiting it to either end of the passage.

In 1942 Allied shipping losses to U-boats billowed to two and a half times that of the 1941 monthly averages, though they still came in about

200,000 tons short of the 700,000 tons per month that the Germans had estimated would bring them victory. The German Navy partly owed its success to an increase in the number of submarines. At the start of 1942 the Germans had 249 submarines with ninety-one in an operational state; at the end of the year they had 212 out of 393 available on paper. The building programme and training of submariners added together had spectacularly increased the German strength in submarines.

Admiral Doenitz's successful ploy of concentrating against weak points furnished the other factor which contributed to the increase in sinkings. Immediately the United States entered the war, Doenitz deployed submarines to the North American coast where they found a feast of merchant vessels trundling out of convoy. When the US got around to organising convoys, the German Admiral shifted his attention to the Caribbean and then he once again concentrated on the North Atlantic routes which had been denuded of warships to provide escorts for the tracks being frequented by the new convoys. Late in the year, the German command detached strong submarine forces to the South Atlantic, making use of some of the latest U-boats with long-range capability and capacious supply submarines which could rendezvous with the smaller attack boats to replenish the same with fuel and badly needed supplies.

The British responded to the potent German offensive by developing an advanced radar which was capable of unmasking objects as small as a submarine's conning tower. The British 'boffins' also produced radar equipment which was small and light enough to be mounted in an aircraft. These welcome advances meant that U-boats became susceptible to detection on the surface during the hours of darkness. Aircraft could also attack at night with the aid of an eighty million candlepower light which could illuminate a U-boat that had originally been discovered by radar. The Germans retaliated by fitting, in their submarines, a receiver which could detect the presence of enemy radar. This gave the U-boat the opportunity of crash-diving when in the presence of radar-equipped hostile aircraft or warships. The British, in the autumn, 'upped the stakes' with a radar which operated in a different section of the electro-magnetic spectrum. This foiled the recently produced German detector. Cruising on the surface continued to be a risky business for German submarines, particularly as the British were able to augment the number of their air patrols and the efficiency of their coverage.

The year 1943 showed promise of being a continuation of its pre-decessor as far as the Germans were concerned. They had expanded the total number of U-boats from 249 to 393 despite the fact that they had suffered the loss of eighty-seven boats. The growth in numbers denoted the fact that sufficient German commanding officers and ships' companies had endured to enhance their capabilities in spite of the great numbers of recently trained men which were needed to man a fighting force which had ballooned in size so quickly. Compared with enemy submarines, the relentlessly growing numbers of Allied escort vessels displayed skills which advanced more quickly because, compared with submarines, and ships under convoy, escorts endured somewhat negligible losses. This implies that the skill of those manning the defending ships developed, comparatively, more than that of their attacking opposite numbers.

At the start of 1943 the Germans could, not without reason, expect greater success due to the fact that they now produced some thirty submarines per month. In mid-March two Allied convoys closed a number of German submarine groups, known as wolfpacks, which together added up to more than forty U-boats. In a struggle stretching over five days, the U-boats sank twenty-one ships, or a total of 141,000 tons. In March 1943 the German submarines despatched 490,000 tons of merchant shipping in the North Atlantic. However, these devastating figures marked the peak of German success. From this time forward improved Anglo–American skills and methods employed, together with the availability of more escort vessels, meant that the Germans started to become 'overmatched'.

The British had, hitherto, carried a few aircraft in convoys by making use of the lengthy, unobstructed surfaces to be found in grain carriers or oil tankers to launch and recover a flight of, say, three to four old, slow-moving Swordfish single-engine carrier aircraft. They had, in addition, brought into service a freighter transformed into a rather ad hoc aircraft carrier as early as December 1941. The first of these carriers was called *Audacity* and could only take about a dozen aeroplanes which had to be launched with the aid of a catapult. The great thing about *Audacity* was that it gave ships in the convoy to which it was attached local air support. *Audacity* teamed up with twelve more conventional escort vessels to bring a thirty-two-ship convoy to the United Kingdom from Gibraltar. Nine U-boats attacked this convoy and sank *Audacity* and an escorting destroyer. This was the bad news. The good news was that the convoy only lost two ships; and the escorting vessels managed to sink five of the enemy submarines.

The British and Americans could field several escort carriers by April 1943, and these allowed a good many convoys to enjoy air protection even in the middle of the Atlantic where it was too far distant from land for patrol aircraft to be provided. Furthermore, as previously mentioned, the Allies had adapted the habit of forming support groups of six to eight escort vessels which, rather than defending a specific convoy, could go to the aid of any convoy suffering too close attention from a German wolfpack. The support groups gave the British and United States navies the means to employ the principle of concentration against power areas to counter Doenitz's offensive assemblies of U-boats, in the form of wolf-packs, against a single convoy.

More than twenty submarines 'had a go' at a convoy in early May 1943; but the convoy had the benefit of the addition of a support group in the vicinity. The U-boats managed to dispose of a dozen ships; but this effort was achieved at the price of losing seven submarines. The submarines next joined forces to exert their efforts against another convoy. They put paid to the careers of three ships; but lost one U-boat to aircraft operating from the escort carrier *Biter*, a second shore-based aircraft and a third to the combined exertions of an escort vessel and an aircraft operating from the shore. A concentration of submarines against a third convoy stumbled across *Biter*, which had been directed to support their convoy. The Germans only contrived to sink two ships; but sacrificed two submarines in the process with others sustaining damage. Also during May, some twelve convoys crossed the North Atlantic with the loss of only five ships; but the Germans suffered the loss of thirteen U-boats.

This picture tended to foreshadow the model of the future. Improved Anglo–American expertise, the availability of aircraft from escort carriers and shore bases, and more effective numbers of escort vessels combined to break the German offensive. The British took the step of increasing the size of convoys, and inflated the number of escort vessels in proportion. This turned out to have strengthened the defence due to the fact that the increased number of ships, which were potential targets for hostile submarines, had not, in the final event, correspondingly added to the tasks of the defenders or the opportunities presented to the attackers.

The Germans sank something less than a quarter of a million tons of shipping during May 1943, but sacrificed forty-one U-boats in the process. These are big figures; but better for the Allies than what had gone before. Afterwards, the rate of loss of merchant ships fell as it became clear that the defence had gained the upper hand. It is of interest to note that in the whole of 1943 the Germans sank scarcely two and a half million tons of shipping. This in a year during which their foes reached a rate of building ships which exceeded fourteen million tons per annum. The Germans had suffered repulse in the '*guerre de course*' in similar manner to that in which the French had suffered a couple of centuries earlier. Advances in technology played a part in World War II sea warfare which was unknown in previous conflicts. The British ability to decrypt messages encyphered by German machines also provided an advantage which it is difficult to overstate.

The Germans were also adept in a number of the disciplines which go to make a useful team with which to wage the arts of communication warfare. However, the British seem to produce people who shine at the game of code-breaking. Two hundred years, or thereabouts, previously the great Duke of Marlborough had an Oxford don in his entourage who was skilled at breaking into codes which were used by his opponents.

To return to World War II, it can truthfully be said that during the year

179

1943 German submarines were on the defensive when it came to facing airborne patrols carried out by radar-fitted carrier, or land-based aircraft which inexorably harried U-boats off the French coast, particularly in the Bay of Biscay area. The drill, briefly, was that the U-boats were found with the help of radar, then attacked with bombs or depth charges. The German submarines tried their best to run submerged except when it became essential to charge their batteries. When detected, the U-boats could either dive or fight back with an improved outfit of anti-aircraft weapons. Neither of these defensive ploys proved adequate to avoid losing fifteen submarines during a five-week period in July/August 1943.

Aircraft showed themselves to be influential weapon systems against a submersible which was not equipped with a surface warship's outfit of anti-aircraft weapons or the protection given by the surface ship's armour. Aeroplanes did not achieve their success entirely because of their speed of approach as those fitted with state of the art radar had an exceptional advantage over a vessel, in this instance a submarine, equipped with a detector which could not cope with its opponent's radar frequency.

The German response of developing the 'snort', which gave a submarine the means to operate diesel engines while submerged, was essentially a defensive step which had the disadvantages of reducing the capability of a submarine's observation capability and tending to adversely affect the morale of the boat's crew. The Germans brought into play a bigger combat U-boat, towards the end of the Second World War, which was capable of sixteen knots submerged; but this did not appear to alter the operational balance between the escorts and the submarine. The Germans had, in addition, developed a hydrogen peroxide engine for submarines which did not require a snorkel; but, perhaps fortunately for the Allies, this was at too late a stage to have an operational impact.

The advent of nuclear power has brought mankind close to the perfect submarine; but, in this case, the human beings who man these craft are the weak link. Human beings need to eat, drink, cleanse themselves and be provided with many facilities to stimulate and instruct and last, but by no means least, to provide entertainment.

The submarine suffered defeat in the Second World War for very much the same reason that it had in the First – the CONVOY.

It is well known that there are lies, damned lies and statistics; but a few figures might help to establish the splendid efficacy of the Convoy System. Germany's foes lost some 2,700 ships in World War II; but only twenty-seven per cent of these casualties were sailing in convoy when they met their fate. Submarines destroyed approximately 14,573,000 tons of shipping at a cost of 781 German and eighty-five Italian submarines. To flashback to the First World War, the Germans lost 178 U-boats and the Allies almost as many tons of merchant shipping as in the Second World War. The Germans had, therefore, exerted a greater effort, but secured proportionately smaller results. Germany's enemies had also committed greater resources to defence. Weapons for defence had improved more than those of offence. Asdic (sonar) proved to be more potent than the hydrophone. Aircraft and radar so added to the potential power of the defending forces that they could shift to the offensive against hostile submarines. Improved torpedoes and submarines could not effectively offset this.

German strategy had been correct when it had been concentrated, in succession, versus enemy areas of weakness, for example, areas of the central Atlantic when ships were not sailing in convoy, the North American seaboard, the Caribbean, the South American and African coasts, and, to some extent, the Indian Ocean. The use of the wolfpack concept to counter-balance convoys proved to be a worthwhile strategy; but it failed against stronger escorts helped by the employment of aircraft and the experienced use of radar. Later, the deployment and concentration of support groups played their part.

The part played by skill in the defeat of the submarine threat should never be discounted. The Germans lost so large a number of submarines, for example, 237 in 1943, that they constantly had to commit to active service commanding officers and ships' companies who lacked operational and combat experience. The aim of the U-boats was to sink merchant ships, rather than their escorts.

CHAPTER XV
Mediterranean Convoys in World War II

A good time to begin this chapter is the year 1920. The prospect of a future collision between Britain and Italy on the subject of who should exert control over the Middle Sea (Mediterranean) originated with the rise of Fascism in Italy during the 1920s; and to an increasing extent as time passed. Il Duce, Benito Mussolini, made it very clear that his aim was the reconstruction of the great Roman Empire in that area which he was pleased to call 'Mare Nostrum'. The Italian dictator had overthrown Abyssinia in 1936 when the only reaction of the Western Powers had been to adopt a disapproving attitude and to twist their hands. His avaricious eyes were next turned towards such places as Corsica, Tunisia and Nice. His Adriatic aspirations were mirrored in the names given to three Italian cruisers including *Trieste*. In the Balkans, Albania was swallowed up in 1939 and plotting against Greece and Yugoslavia was actively afoot.

Until the fall of France, the French were tacitly responsible for keeping a 'watching brief' on the western basin of the Mediterranean; and the Royal Navy covered the eastern region operating from Alexandria. British ships sailed, without hindrance, via the Suez Canal to and from India and the Far East. Mussolini's resolution to take Italy into World War II on the side of Germany as France was tottering to defeat, pushed the balance of maritime power in favour of the Axis and forced shipping to and from the Far East to use the long route round the Cape of Good Hope.

When France was 'removed from the board', the Italians, theoretically, had the strongest navy in the Mediterranean. Their battle fleet was built around six battleships, two of the powerful modern thirty-five thousand-ton *Littorio* class which each mounted nine 15-inch guns, two updated World War I vintage ships of the *Cavour* class with ten 12.6-inch guns, and two sisters in the throes of being modernised. In addition, they had a formidable force of nineteen cruisers, seven of them mounting 8-inch guns. They also had about a hundred and twenty destroyers and torpedo boats and about a hundred submarines, roughly twice the number with which the Germans were playing 'merry hell' in the Atlantic. Following the declaration of war, about two dozen Italian submarines moved into the Atlantic Ocean and served under German command.

The Italian Navy had not invested in aircraft carriers, and aimed to rely upon shore-based aircraft to provide air cover for the fleet. However, the air force did not own dive-bombers or torpedo planes which are the most useful aeroplanes to deploy against ships. Incidentally, the level of co-operation between the two Italian services left very much to be desired. It is probably true to say that a good air force might have worked effectively with the fleet over most of the Mediterranean as there were airfields in Italy itself, Sicily, Sardinia and the Dodecanese. In the early stages of the conflict, the British Mediterranean Fleet was stripped of ships to meet other requirements; but after the commitment of Italy to the war, work was set afoot to try to rebuild naval strength in that area. The Commander-in-Chief, Admiral Cunningham, had four battleships based on Alexandria, of which only *Warspite* had been modernised; seven 6-inch gun cruisers; twenty-two destroyers; twelve submarines; and the aircraft-carrier *Eagle,* mothering seventeen veteran Swordfish and a couple of Sea Gladiator fighters. With the exception of a handful of flying boats, the British had no land-based aircraft. Due to the apparently overpowering strength of the Italian Fleet and air potential, the Admiralty seriously thought of withdrawing its ships from the eastern Mediterranean and of concentrating British forces at Gibraltar, approximately two thousand miles distant from Alexandria. Winston Churchill blocked this proposal as it would have implied 'writing off' Malta and Egypt. The barrel was scraped to find men and ships to reinforce the Mediterranean Fleet. A by-product was that Churchill's decision to hold fast in the Mediterranean, though very hard pressed at home, made a substantial impression on the Germans and displayed confidence in the failure of any German endeavour to invade England.

Another thought which should be borne in mind is that the Italian Fleet was more powerful on paper than it was in reality. Its problem was that it was defensive rather than offensive in outlook; and its ships and tactics mirrored this state of mind. The Italian warships were sleek and graceful to behold; but the major vessels had sacrificed armoured protection to favour speed. The concept was to give, or to avoid, battle except when an engagement was on their own terms. Italian admirals usually fought when they thought that they had an overwhelming advantage. The strategy has been compared with the 'fleet-in-being' principle adopted by the German High Seas Fleet post the Battle of Jutland in World War I. A number of the Italian warships were used as high-speed troopships by the Allies after the surrender of the Italian Fleet. They were pretty looking ships to see when they visited Malta.

Italian naval personnel are prone to use the apology of poor com-munications, forgetting that the great Marconi was an Italian, as well as a lack of effective radar, sonar equipments and reliable torpedoes, again by-passing the fact that the Whitehead torpedo was developed in Italy, even though the British were quicker to appreciate the potential of that weapon in the longer term. Poor gunnery and little training in night engagements are also mentioned; but these arts are generally featured, and have been for a long time, in naval exercise programmes. Mussolini, in his wisdom, is said to have believed that the war would only last for three months and had omitted to ensure that adequate supplies of furnace fuel oil (FFO) were stockpiled. Possibly the Italian Navy's greatest error was an inferiority complex when dealing with the Royal Navy. This might sound unfair and might well have been corrected if the Italians had gained some early successes against the British, who for many years had displayed great confidence at sea. However, the Italians failed to win such laurels; and the British Admiral Cunningham was fully determined that they would not win them.

In the person of Admiral Cunningham, the Royal Navy discovered a worthy successor to Nelson, who was able to combine professional ability with that 'X factor' of charisma which could arouse the admiration of his officers and other ranks. Admiral Cunningham was guided by the fundamental principle that the enemy was there to be defeated; and that this could best happen if the fleets met and, hopefully, engaged at close range.

Admiral Cunningham was at sea with his fleet within hours of the Italian declaration of war. His aim was to confront hostile naval units and to obtain a feel for Italian military aircraft at a very early moment. The British did not succeed in drawing their hesitant adversaries out of their base at Taranto, which is sited on the heel of Italy's boot-like shape. However, Cunningham led an Anglo–French force to bombard the Libyan port of Bardia. A veteran cruiser was sunk by an Italian submarine; but the British, aided by their cryptographic experts' ability to read the Italian naval version of Enigma, captured or sank ten Italian submarines during the first month of Italy's participation in the Second World War.

The defeat of France incited the Italian Navy to increased activity. The Italians started sailing convoys to their army in Libya. This force was soon expected to advance against the woefully small British Army of the Nile which was based in Egypt. These convoys were routed within comfortable striking distance of Malta; but the conventional wisdom of pre-war strategical gurus had written off the island, planted by nature, only about fifty-six miles from the coast of Sicily, as virtually defenceless to blockade by submarines and bomber aircraft. Despite these pundits, and as the war developed, Malta grew to be the focal point of British Mediterranean strategy. The island became a staging area for British submarines, aircraft and lighter forces which harassed Italian convoys to North Africa; and great efforts were expended upon keeping the beleagured island suitably supplied with provisions and the logistical needs of the armed forces.

To put the saga of Malta in World War II very briefly, Malta resisted very severe bombing by Italian and German aircraft between 1940 and 1943 and faced a very real threat of starvation. The island was awarded the well-deserved honour of the George Cross in 1942 to give tangible recognition to the intrepid spirit of its people.

To retrace steps to the year 1940, Admiral Cunningham had another entanglement to add to his prosecution of war against Italy. This was the presence of a French naval force at Alexandria. The French ranking officer, Admiral Godoy, had obeyed the Vichy Government's directive to 'cease fire'. If Admiral Cunningham had obeyed the letter of his instructions, he could have either captured or destroyed the French warships. In the event, he was more favoured than his opposite number, Admiral Somerville at Oran, in that he was able to avoid opening fire on his recent comrades-in-arms. This fact will be long-remembered by French naval personnel. On 7 July 1940 the British Admiral was able to reach an understanding with Admiral Godoy whereby the French ships would be demilitarised for the duration of the war; and it was on that evening that Admiral Cunningham sailed to scout for the enemy.

Two days later, the first skirmish took place between the British and Italian fleets. The British Admiral's flagship, HMS *Warspite*, engaged the two Italian battleships, *Conte di Cavour* and *Giuglio Cesare*. *Warspite* was supported by torpedo-carrying Swordfish aircraft from the aircraft carrier *Eagle*. *Warspite* registered a hit on *Giuglio Cesare*. The next move was that the Italian ships withdrew behind a smoke-screen laid by their destroyers. The task of attacking British ships en route back to the Alexandria area was left to shore-based aircraft. Thirty-seven attacks were made; but not a single British ship was hit.

Whatever has been said of them, the Italian battleships posed a continuous threat to British convoys; and to the movements of the Fleet. They were together far more powerful than the three or four veterans of the First World War which Admiral Cunningham had under his command, two of which had, in fact, fought at Jutland. He had tried, in vain, to bring the Italians to battle. One form of attack remained to be attempted. That was attack by carrier-borne aircraft on ships in harbour.

There was nothing essentially new about this concept which had been studied in 1935, when the League of Nations voted sanctions against Italy at the time of the Abyssinian Crisis; when for a while it had seemed that Britain might be dragged into a conflict with the Italians. Again during the Munich Crisis in 1938, Admiral Sir Dudley Pound, Commander-in-Chief, Mediterranean, had directed Captain Lyster, commanding the aircraft-carrier *Glorious,* to prepare a plan of attack on the Italian naval base at Taranto, in the heel of Italy.

In the summer of 1940, Lyster, then a Rear-Admiral, arrived in the Mediterranean with HMS *Illustrious.* She was Britain's latest aircraft carrier, boasted an armour-plated flight-deck and was equipped with radar, a device which had not been fitted throughout Royal Navy warships at that time. She carried two flights of Swordfish aircraft which were already somewhat out-dated, but eminently capable of performing their function of firing airborne torpedoes. She also had a flight of Fulmar fighters which were pretty new and armed with eight guns.

The aircraft carrier *Eagle* was also under Admiral Lyster's command. The dust was shaken off the plan of attack on Taranto, and during the passage out from the United Kingdom, Lyster had discussed it in detail with Fleet Air Arm aircrews serving in *Illustrious*. When the ready-made plan was put to Admiral Cunningham, he was full of enthusiasm.

During the First World War, Lyster, then a young lieutenant, had spent some time acting as a liaison officer with the Italian naval squadron which was based on Taranto. He was thus well acquainted with the naval base, which consisted of an outer, or main, harbour, the Mar Grande, and a small inner harbour, the Mar Piccolo. The two were divided by a narrow tongue of land on which stood the town of Taranto. Though a canal had been cut to enable ships to pass from one harbour to the other, the battleships were, in general, secured in the eastern part of the Mar Grande, and were protected by moles and netting. However, details needed to be established to obtain a true picture for the time of the attack. Use of aircraft based on Malta was the ideal solution to the problem of scouting over the Taranto area. When Italy first decided to participate in the war, there were only three experienced old Gladiator aircraft based on Malta – aptly nicknamed by the garrison 'Faith, Hope and Charity'.

The Italian High Command had missed a 'once only' opportunity by failing to attack Malta at the very start of the war as the island was later reinforced by American Glenn Martin aircraft flown directly from Britain and with Spitfires brought by aircraft-carriers to within flying range of the island.

The earliest photographic missions over Taranto showed five battleships, eight cruisers and twenty destroyers in harbour which meant plenty of choice for the striking force. The attack was planned for the night of 21 October, not so much because it was Trafalgar Day but because there would be a full moon. The aircraft should have minimum difficulty in finding their target; and take off and landing on the flight deck would be simplified. Night attacks by carrier aircraft were still a novelty in sea-warfare.

Thirty Swordfish aircraft from *Eagle* and *Illustrious* were to deliver the attack. The two aircraft-carriers were to be positioned about forty miles west of the Greek Island of Cephalonia which is one hundred and seventy miles south-east of Taranto, at a time when the moon would have just risen in the eastern sky. The aircraft would approach their target from the west in order that the Italian battleships would be silhouetted against the moonlight. The guns were to be removed from the aircraft and extra fuel tanks fitted, to enable a round flight to be made.

'Man proposes, God disposes.' The attack had to be postponed, and modified because of a number of incidents which occurred in the meantime. A small fire broke out in *Illustrious*; and a near-miss caused some damage to *Eagle*. The attack finally went ahead on the night of 10 November; but with only twenty-one aircraft from *Illustrious*. On that evening RAF reconnaissance aircraft reported that another Italian battleship had joined the original five. Their photographs also indicated that there were now barrage-balloons in position to protect the ships.

The moon would be in its first quarter on the night of the 10th. It was decided to divide the strike aircraft into two groups, one of twelve planes and the other of nine. Each group would have six aircraft carrying torpedoes, the remainder would bomb the ships in the inner harbour and the oil storage tanks. The idea was that the resulting fires would assist the task of the torpedo-carrying aircraft. Admiral Cunningham departed from Alexandria with the fleet on 6 November. While he steamed westward with the battleships to escort a convoy en route to Malta, Lyster and his squadron tracked northwards into the Adriatic. Lyster had under his command the aircraft-carrier *Illustrious*, Captain Boyd; the cruisers *Gloucester*, *Berwick*, *Glasgow* and *York*; and the destroyers *Hyperion*, *Ilex*, *Hasty* and *Havock*. By the evening of the 10th, after an uneventful passage, he was in position off the island of Cephalonia. The night was fine, but with so light a wind that *Illustrious* had to be worked up to a speed of twenty-eight knots to permit the heavily laden aircraft to take off. The latest aerial photographs which had been flown to *Illustrious* from Malta, and reports transmitted by a Sunderland flying-boat, confirmed that six Italian battleships were still at Taranto.

The first striking force led by Lieutenant-Commander Williamson was airborne at 2040. The bombers and flare-droppers were over Taranto at 2252. The flares were released over the inner harbour and the bombing-aircraft detailed to attack the Italian ships succeeded in working on the cruisers and destroyers, despite attracting extremely heavy anti-aircraft fire. They also ignited the buildings of the seaplane base. Meanwhile, the torpedo-aircraft had gone in to attack ships in the main harbour. Williamson had split his force into two sub-flights; and they descended to near sea-level to drop their torpedoes at either end of the line of moored battleships.

At the time in question, the Italians had no radar and were consequently caught by surprise, but were soon able to put up intense anti-aircraft fire. The Swordfish might have been a joy to handle, but were very slow, which gave them time to take deliberate aim at their targets, but may have stimulated more intense fears of being picked out by searchlights and of being attacked by fighter aircraft in the light of the same. However, there was no such reaction from either of the above in this instance.

The second striking force, led by Lieutenant-Commander Hale, had been launched from the carrier about three-quarters of an hour behind the first. It numbered eight, not nine aircraft. The ninth was delayed by mechanical trouble, but flew off an hour later on its lonely bombing mission.

Two planes of the first striking force were shot down, one being Williamson's, but all of Hale's returned safely. The last landed on *Illustrious* at 0230. Three Italian seaplanes tried to shadow the British ships as they returned to Alexandria, but they were soon chased away by fighters from the aircraft-carrier.

The intrepid British pilots could only report possible hits on the enemy battleships; but the following day photographic reconnaissance by RAF aircraft from Malta revealed the full implications of the damage. A battleship of the *Littorio* class – it was, in fact *Littorio* herself – had a heavy list to starboard and her forecastle was awash. She had been hit by three torpedoes, and subsequent repairs kept her out of service until May 1941. The *Conte di Cavour* was not refloated until July, and was then towed to Trieste for repairs. She was still there when Italy asked for an armistice in September 1943.

The brilliant result of the attack on Taranto was that eleven aircraft torpedoes had put half of the Italian Battle Fleet out of action for a considerable period of time. In addition, the Italian High Commanders were apprehensive of another attack on Taranto and withdrew the remainder of the fleet to Naples, a move which gave Admiral Cunningham greater flexibility of action in his support of General Wavell's victorious advance through Libya. The special value of the successful attack on Taranto was that it came at a time when Britain's fortunes were at a low ebb.

Not long afterwards, and as a response to Mussolini's appeals, the Germans started to shift some of their air squadrons to the Mediterranean area. The Italian campaign against the Greeks was proceeding badly and the Italian army in Libya was in undignified retreat before the British Army of the Nile. On a morning in January 1941, Admiral Cunningham was escorting a Malta convoy with some of his ships when a large formation of hostile aircraft was sighted. Those who had been involved at Dunkirk in June 1940, or with patrols in the English Channel could have rapidly identified the approaching squadrons to be Stuka dive-bombers. 'We were too interested in these dive-bombing attacks, which were new to us, to have time to feel frightened . . .' Admiral Cunningham later wrote. 'We could but admire their skill and precision.'

The Stukas belonged to the German Tenth Air Corps which had recently arrived at bases on the islands of Sicily and Rhodes. The principal target of the Germans was the aircraft carrier, HMS *Illustrious*. The carrier was hit by six one thousand-pound bombs which wrecked her flight-deck, put her stearing gear out of action and started several fires. A squadron of aircraft had been launched by *Illustrious* shortly before she was attacked. They shot down eight of the enemy during the day, and continued to fight by landing at Malta to replenish fuel and ammunition. The Germans maintained relentless attacks on *Illustrious* but Captain Boyd, steering by varying the revolutions of his main engines, brought his ship into Malta that night; a highly skilled exercise in the art of ship-handling. The Luftwaffe repeatedly bombed the carrier while she was in harbour at Malta, but she was repaired and departed on 24 January 1941, to rejoin the fleet at Alexandria.

German assistance to Italy was not confined to air support. A German general arrived at Tripoli to assume command of the German–Italian army on 11 February. Erwin Rommel had already made a reputation for himself in France and he was to become an almost legendary figure at the head of his Afrika Korps. However, the safeguarding of his supplies and reinforcements was the responsibility of the Italian Fleet. The Battle of the Mediterranean was about to enter a new phase, with the British attempting to cut Rommel's supply routes between Italy and Tripolitania, and with German aircraft trying to isolate Malta.

It was at this period that Mussolini had asked for German help to defeat the gallant Greeks; and the British had sent troops, which could ill be spared, from the Army of the Nile, to lend support to the Greeks. The undertaking of protecting the flow of supplies and reinforcements to Greece put a further strain on Admiral Cunningham's badly stretched fleet.

Now the Chief of the Italian Naval Staff, Admiral Riccardi, came up with a plan to harass British communications with Greece, by mounting a reconnaissance in force as far as the island of Gaudo, off the southern coast of Crete. This was the first occasion on which the Italian Navy had displayed any flair since entering the war. An important force was to be deployed under the command of Admiral Iachino, Commander-in-Chief, and it was to operate in two battle-groups:

Group One (Admiral Iachino): *Vittorio Veneto* with a screen of four destroyers; the cruisers *Trieste*, *Trento* and *Bolzano*, commanded by Admiral Sansonetti; and three destroyers.

Group Two (Admiral Cattaneo): the cruisers *Zara*, *Pola* and *Fiume*, and four destroyers; the cruisers *Abruzzi* (Admiral Legnani) and *Garibaldi* with two destroyers.

The naval force was balanced enough for the task, but the ships' companies had little experience. The air support was dubious, for the main reason that it was not placed under the immediate orders of Admiral Iachino. He had to ask the Supermarina (the Naval High Command) for the use of the Italian seaplanes, and the Luftwaffe liaison officers on board his flagship for the employment of German aircraft. In the event, this involved chain-of-command resulted in the Italian ships being virtually without air support when they were brought to battle.

The orders given to Admiral Iachino placed a very light control over the movements of his ships. His own group was to sail on 26 March and to carry out an offensive reconnaissance to a point twenty miles south of Gaudo Island, while Admiral Cattaneo's group made a sweep some fifty miles to the north, into the Aegean Sea. They were then to return to base, having destroyed all the British convoys found proceeding to Greece.

An increase in the activity, and number, of Italian reconnaissance aircraft over-flying the Alexandria area had alerted the British to the fact that some enemy operation was likely to be approaching. It was also expected that the Germans would apply leverage on Mussolini to pursue a more active policy with his fleet – this as part of their general offensive about to be opened in Greece and North Africa. It came as no great shock when a Sunderland flying-boat from Malta reported, on 27 March, three Italian cruisers eighty miles east of Sicily steering towards Crete. At that time there was only one convoy en route to Greece, and it was still to the south of Crete. It was directed to return to Alexandria, and the convoys preparing to sail were told to delay their departure. This meant that there was little to worry about. The Italian sweep would find nothing in its path.

Despite this, Admiral Cunningham decided to put to sea when daylight started to fade and to place his battleships between the enemy and the returning convoy. This was considered to be no more than a simple security measure.

There is a pleasant anecdote that the then Japanese Consul at Alexandria was a keen golfer and a conscientious observer of British fleet movements. Whether or not he had the means (or will) to communicate this sort of information to his German and Italian friends may have been 'non proven', but it was wiser to mistrust him. Admiral Cunningham, in true Drake tradition, decided to have a round of golf while awaiting the coming of evening. The Admiral arrived at the clubhouse with a smallish pusser's (purser's) suitcase which any naval man might carry when intending to spend a night ashore; and he tried his best to ensure that his presence was noticed by the Japanese Consul. After completing his round of golf, the Admiral returned to his flagship as discreetly as he had ostentatiously gone ashore. At 1900 that evening Admiral Cunningham sailed with the battleships *Warspite*, *Barham* and *Valiant*, the new aircraft-carrier *Formidable* and a screen of flotillas of destroyers. Admiral Pridham-Wippell had already been ordered to sail from Piraeus with the cruisers *Orion*, *Perth*, *Ajax* and *Gloucester*, plus four destroyers, and to rendezvous with the Commander-in-Chief at 0630 the next morning, thirty miles south of Gaudo Island. This was almost the same geographical position as Admiral Iachino's directives would take him to at approximately the same time.

The Sunderland's report of having sighted Italian cruisers proceeding towards Crete had been intercepted, and understood, on board *Vittorio Veneto* which had sailed from Naples on the evening of the 26th. Admiral Iachino, therefore, must have realised that the chance of coming upon a British convoy to Greece had, to all intents and purposes, disappeared. There was little point in burning precious fuel-oil for nothing; far more sensible to return to base. However, the decision did not rest with the Italian Admiral. The Supermarina could well have had the same idea; but due to pressure from the Germans and for the sake of prestige in their eyes, it was decided that, at least, Iachino's battle-group would continue with the sweep as originally planned. At the same time, Cattaneo was ordered not to penetrate into the Aegean, but to rendezvous with his Commander-in-Chief at dawn on the 28th.

It was another example of naval commanders being sent cold-bloodedly to battle, with scant hope of winning, for reasons of high policy which had little, or nothing, to do with the principles of sea warfare.

At dawn on the 28th Admiral Iachino was still blissfully unaware of the fact that the British battle-fleet was at sea. He had almost reached the limit of his sweep, and he had no intention of proceeding any farther. Admiral Sansonnetti's screen of cruisers, seven miles in advance of *Vittorio Veneto*, was directed to reverse course at about 0600. At that time Cattaneo's group was ten miles to the north. A seaplane was launched from *Vittorio Veneto* and another from *Balzano* to make scouting flights over the general area. At 0642 the former reported four cruisers and four destroyers proceeding at eighteen knots on a southerly course, fifty miles east of the Italian force. Admiral Iachino cancelled his previous order to Sansonnetti and, instead, directed him to identify the ships which had been reported and to retire towards the flagship.

An hour later, *Formidable*'s reconnaissance aircraft reported three cruisers thirty miles to the south of Gaudo. They were thought, at first, to be Pridham-Wippell's; but that commander himself sighted these ships to the westward and reported them to Admiral Cunningham, adding that he was retiring towards the battleships in the hope that the enemy would follow. Admiral Cunningham was then about ninety miles to the south.

The Italian cruisers involved mounted 8-inch guns which could outrange those of Admiral Pridham-Wippell's 6-inch light cruisers. The Italians also had the legs of the British, as *Gloucester* could squeeze no more than twenty-four knots out of her engines at that juncture; and the other British cruisers were obliged to reduce speed to conform.

Admiral Sansonnetti pursued the British cruisers, instead of retiring as ordered, and at 0812 opened fire at 22,500 yards. The rear ship, *Gloucester*, was straddled three times which appeared to impart a charmed effect on her machinery as her speed of advance increased to thirty knots. This feat was appreciated by the rest of the British ships in company with her! The Italian cruisers remained out of range of their adversaries, but continued to engage them for thirty-nine minutes, then they turned away to rejoin Admiral Iachino. The latter officer reported to the High Command that his whole force was returning to base on a north-westerly course.

These were the opening moves in the action which became known as the Battle of Matapan, from the headland of that name at the southern extremity of the Peloponnese. Admiral Cunningham and his staff had felt some concern about the light cruisers; and there was a sense of relief on learning that the pursuing Italians had turned away. The British battleship *Warspite* could do no more than twenty-two knots, which meant that she would have taken the best part of four hours to reach a position where she could be of assistance to the cruisers.

When Admiral Pridham-Wippell saw that the Italians had turned away, he made the decision to follow them. At about 1100 he sighted an enemy battleship to the north which opened fire at extreme range. This was *Vittorio Veneto,* and some of her shells came uncomfortably close to the cruiser, *Orion,* Pridham-Wippell's flagship. He ordered his destroyers to lay a smoke-screen. *Vittorio Veneto,* with her speed of thirty-one knots, could easily knock out the four cruisers one by one, and still have time to retire before the British battleships arrived. This seemed to be Admiral Iachino's intention – until *Formidable*'s aircraft appeared on the scene.

Admiral Cunningham's naval career had been basically spent in surface ships, but he was undoubtedly well aware of the potential of carrier aircraft. This capability had been shown, beyond doubt, by the attack on the Italian warships at Taranto. All the same, carrier aircraft had not yet been used in strength against enemy ships at sea. The British Admiral had yet to assess their possibilities in this role. He would, no doubt, have preferred not to attack with *Formidable*'s aircraft until his battleships were within, say, fifty miles of the enemy, and so be able to bring him to battle once the carrier aircraft had reduced the speed of his capital ships. In the event, the danger that the cruisers were in from *Vittorio Veneto* forced Admiral Cunningham's hand. The only rapid means of helping Pridham-Wippell was to despatch a striking force from *Formidable* to attack the Italian battleship. This card was played at 1115. The disadvantage, as Admiral Cunningham was well aware, was that he lost all chance of bringing the enemy to battle before nightfall, because he was still sixty miles distant. The attack by torpedo-carrying aircraft would reveal to Admiral Iachino the presence of an aircraft-carrier at a distance of less than one hundred miles and, therefore, of battleships as well; and the Italian Admiral would be extremely likely to retire on a north-westerly course instead of tracking eastward towards Pridham-Wippell's cruisers.

This was precisely what did occur. When the striking force was sighted, at noon, *Vittorio Veneto* swung round. She had already discharged some eighty rounds at the British cruisers from her 15-inch guns and a number had splashed dangerously close. The air attacks were launched on the

Italian battleship without result; but at 1530 a hit was obtained by a Swordfish piloted by Commander Stead, who pressed home his attack through a tremendous barrage of gunfire and was shot down seconds after firing his torpedo at close range.

Vittorio Veneto was seen to be stopped. She got under way again at 1600, but her speed was markedly reduced. By 1700 she had managed to increase her speed to nineteen knots, but *Warspite* was then only forty-five miles distant. One more attack was made from *Formidable* and a Swordfish from Crete. A hit was obtained on the 8-inch cruiser *Pola,* bringing her to a halt.

The British had now gained the upper hand. Although the Italian battleship eventually reached Taranto safely, Admiral Cunningham had succeeded in dealing a heavy blow against Admiral Cattaneo's division, which the Italian Commander-in-Chief sent to the help of *Pola* – unaware that the British battle fleet was only some thirty-five miles away.

Admiral Cunningham had no knowledge of the injury inflicted on the Italians by his strike aircraft, but had been advised that they were tracking west at approximately fifteen knots with the damaged battleship in the middle of their formation. This situation report had been transmitted by Lieutenant-Commander Bolt whose seaplane had been launched from *Warspite*'s catapult at 1745. Admiral Cunningham ordered Pridham-Wippell to proceed at his best speed and to gain contact with the retreating enemy, from whom he was only about nine miles distant.

The British Commander-in-Chief now had to make a critical decision. The Italians could be in waters where they could be supported by land-based aircraft, by first light. Admiral Cunningham felt that the time had come to accept the hazards of a night battle, but his staff officers displayed reservations. The Admiral gave full consideration to their opinions, but as the clock had advanced to dinner time he said that he would first eat, and then see what he thought. When he returned to the bridge, the Admiral ordered the destroyers to attack, and two divisions duly proceeded at their best speed towards the enemy's estimated position. Only four destroyers were retained to screen the battleships.

This could have been a hazardous move if the Italians were to launch a similar attack, but there was little likelihood of that. Admiral Cunningham's decision was to have fortuitous consequences for the British.

Shortly after 2100 Pridham-Wippell sent an unexpected item of news. HMS *Orion*'s radar had unmasked a large ship lying motionless about five miles to port. Pridham-Wippell thought that she might well be *Vittorio Veneto,* and judged it best to leave her to the tender attentions of *Warspite,* which was not far away. There was an air of expectancy on board the British battleships. *Warspite* had no radar at that time, but *Valiant* had been fitted with the appropriate equipment prior to leaving Britain the previous summer. Her radar display painted the echo of a large vessel, estimated to be more than six hundred feet in length, immobilised six miles on the port bow.

The battleships turned forty degrees to port, towards the ship which everyone thought to be *Vittorio Veneto*. With the aid of *Valiant's* radar, all three battleships had their guns trained on the target, before she was in sight. This revolution in sea warfare, as important as the use of the aircraft-carrier, astonished the Italians when they heard of it.

Shortly before 2230 Admiral Cunningham's Chief-of-staff, Commodore Edelston, was sweeping the sea with his binoculars when he proclaimed in a matter-of-fact voice that he could see two large cruisers and a smaller one on an opposite course approximately two miles distant. One of the destroyers of *Warspite's* screen switched her searchlight onto the second ship and illuminated an enemy cruiser whose guns were trained fore and aft. The Italians had 'fallen in' with the British fleet in the darkness, and were utterly unaware of its proximity. The two large cruisers were the eight-inch *Zara* and *Fiume* of Cattaneo's division, which were tracking towards *Pola* with the aim of taking her in tow. They had even left their destroyer screen astern. The first they knew of the enemy's propinquity was the scream of incoming shells.

Warspite and *Valiant* had lost no time in firing broadsides at three thousand eight hundred yards, to all intents and purposes point-blank range. In a matter of seconds, *Zara* and *Fiume* were blown to pieces; and shortly afterwards the ships were little more than flaming torches from stem to stern.

Italian destroyers tried to intervene, and the British battleships needed to swing round to a northerly course to avoid their torpedoes. The British destroyers then rushed in, and for a time there was a general melee. *Havock* only just avoided being hit by *Warspite's* guns, and *Formidable* also almost fell victim to them. The night action had begun so quickly that the aircraft carrier had not been removed from the line of battleships. She was suddenly caught in the beam of one of *Warspite's* searchlights, and would have been the recipient of a burst from the British battleship's secondary armament if somebody on the bridge had not recognised the carrier's silhouette and rapidly gestured to the ship's gunnery officer.

Admiral Cunningham considered it judicious to steer northwards with his big ships, and to leave his destroyers to finish off the blazing cruisers. *Fiume* saved them the trouble, as she sank soon after 2300. *Zara* was despatched to the bottom by a torpedo from *Jervis* about three hours later. Two Italian destroyers which joined the fray, *Carducci* and *Alfieri*, were also sunk.

Pola, the cause of the night action, still remained. She was the large ship which had been picked up by *Orion's* radar.

Shortly after midnight *Havock*, which had pursued and sunk one of the enemy destroyers, came across a ship lying stopped. The motionless vessel was initially thought to be *Vittorio Veneto*, but was later identified as *Pola*. The *Havock*'s commanding officer, Lieutenant Watkins, was faced with a peculiar situation. *Pola* was apparently undamaged, her flag was still flying, but the utmost confusion reigned on board. Furthermore, *Havock* had expended all her torpedoes, and could not sink the cruiser with just the use of her four-inch guns. However, other British destroyers appeared on the scene and it was resolved to take off *Pola*'s ship's company by placing a destroyer alongside the cruiser. After the crew were taken off, *Pola* was sunk by torpedo.

This was the first act, at 0410 on 29 March, of the Battle of Matapan. *Vittorio Veneto* succeeded in reaching harbour; but the British had sunk three 8-inch gun cruisers and two destroyers. Admiral Iachino was ignorant of his losses when he reached Taranto at 1500 on 29 March; he only learned of them the following evening in Rome when the Italian Chief of the Naval Staff showed him a copy of the communique.

Admiral Cunningham returned to Alexandria without loss and having fought off an air attack on *Formidable* by a squadron of Junkers 88s. He had lost only two men, the gallant Commander Stead and his companion, who by their sacrifice had so markedly contributed to the victory. The Italians had lost 2,400 men, including Admiral Cattaneo. Even more would have perished if British destroyers had not returned to the scene at dawn to rescue survivors. Sadly, German aircraft appeared while there were still several hundred Italian sailors struggling in the sea, and showed every intention of attacking. The rescuing destroyers could not be exposed to heavy loss, even when engaged in such humane activity. The rescue operation was called off, but Admiral Cunningham ordained that a message should be passed to the Italian Naval Command by radio proposing that a hospital ship be sent to the scene. The *Gradisca* duly arrived and picked up a hundred and sixty Italian survivors. Incidentally, the British ships already had nine hundred of those rescued on board as captives.

Matapan was the first large-scale naval battle of the Second World War, and it marked the transition point between actions fought with guns and torpedoes, such as the Battle of the River Plate, and those fought almost entirely by carrier-borne aircraft, as was the case at the Battle of Midway. Matapan could also be described as the first in which radar was widely employed, and what a curtain raiser it had been. There can be little doubt that the Italian ships would have evaded their enemies if aircraft from *Formidable* had not been present to intervene, and that the British battleships could not have achieved such a complete surprise without the support of *Valiant*'s radar.

Admiral Iachino had received no assistance at all from Italian or German aircraft. This was applicable to both reconnaissance planes and fighter cover. Moreover, his ships' companies lacked adequate training.

Yet again, the truth of Nelson's phrase 'ships and sailors rot in harbour' was vividly illustrated. Sailors gain little experience of their profession by staying in harbour. In the eighteenth century, the French had paid dearly for being cooped up by the blockading forces of Cornwallis and Hawke. At the time of Matapan, the Italians had been kept in harbour by fuel shortages. Even short training exercises at sea involved major problems as regards supplying enough fuel-oil. The Italians were largely dependent on the Germans for the allocation of fuel supplies. The latter gave of this commodity grudgingly. Perhaps, not altogether unnaturally, they gave even less after the Italian calamity at Matapan.

The World War II Battle of the Mediterranean was still a long way from being won after Matapan. Many hard knocks still lay in store for the British Fleet. For a good two years, the efforts to fight supply convoys through to Malta were frequently just as dramatic and desperate as those of the convoys to Murmansk with supplies for the Russians. In addition, the strategic situation in the Mediterranean took quite a sudden turn for the worse towards the end of the year 1941. The British Mediterranean Fleet experienced a series of reverses, the most notable of which was due to a handful of Italian naval personnel whose daring must be remembered with great respect.

In April and May 1941 Admiral Cunningham's fleet endured serious losses from attacks by German aircraft during the evacuations of the army from Greece and Crete. Three cruisers and six destroyers were sunk during the Crete operations alone. The battleships *Warspite* and *Barham*, the aircraft-carrier *Formidable*, two cruisers and two destroyers all sustained severe damage.

The battle fleet was off the coast of Cyrenaica, in support of the army, on 25 November 1941, when the submarine U-335, commanded by Lieutenant Tiesenhausen, managed to break through the screening destroyers, and to discharge four torpedoes at HMS *Barham*. At least three struck the battleship between the funnel and after turrets. The great ship blew up and foundered in less than two minutes, throwing up an immense cloud of yellow smoke. When this dispersed, a large patch of oil mixed with debris and struggling men had changed places with *Barham*.

Some three minutes before the fatal torpedoes struck, the destroyer *Jervis* had gained a sonar contact but it was of doubtful quality and the operators had logged it as being 'non sub'. *Valiant* which was astern of *Barham*, when the latter blew up, put her wheel 'hard a-port'. Fifty seconds later U-335, lightened due to the discharge of torpedoes, broke surface about a hundred and fifty yards ahead of *Valiant*, which steered straight for the U-boat and tried to run her down. The distance was too short. The submarine slid past the battleship with less than fifty yards between the two of them, and again submerged before guns were brought to bear on her. She eventually 'got away'.

The Malta cruiser squadron met with misfortune less than a month later. The three cruisers, with four destroyers, were steaming with the aim of intercepting one of Rommel's supply convoys bound for Tripoli. During the night they tangled with a minefield which the enemy had laid in deep waters. The cruiser *Neptune* and the destroyer *Kandahar* were sunk, and the cruisers *Auror* and *Penelope* were seriously damaged. The heaviest reverse of all was being delivered in harbour at Alexandria at about the same time. In the early morning of 19 December the battleships *Queen Elizabeth* and *Valiant* were attacked and put out of service for a good many months by Italian midget submarines.

Should this success have been obtained at sea in the course of a battle, then 19 December 1941 would have counted as the date of a major Italian naval victory. Due to the fact that the assailants were so few – 'a hundred men against a fleet' in an Italian description – the achievement was not classified as a full-scale naval action. Only six penetrated the harbour defences and because the British 'hushed up' the results of the attack, little was heard of it at the time. This said, the immediate results were well nigh as serious as the destruction, a week before, of the battleship *Prince of Wales* and the battle cruiser *Repulse* by Japanese torpedo-carrying aircraft off Malaya. It was also the first successful illustration, during the Second World War, of what a party of determined men could do to a fleet in harbour.

It is interesting to ponder the fact that underwater assault was, historically, not new. As early as the Battle of Sluys (June 1340), divers armed with contemporary lances endeavoured to pierce the wooden hulls of enemy ships. Nearer to our own times, during the First World War, two Italian sailors called Paolucci and Rosetti succeeded in fixing explosive charges beneath the Austrian battleship *Viribus Unitis* which was in harbour at Pola during the night of 31 October 1918. At dawn the Austrian warship blew up and foundered.

The above feat had not been forgotten in Italy's navy; and from its personnel came the first demonstrators of the one-man and two-man submersibles. During the early stages of 1940 a research team started work in a country house not far from the naval base of La Spezia in close collaboration with the First Submarine Flotilla. This team formed the foundation of what was to become known as the Tenth Flotilla MAS (*Moscafi Anti Sommergibili*), which built and experimented with various types of assault craft. The first was the midget submarine CA, based on a model which dated from the First World War. The intention was that this should be carried close to its target by a large submarine, and could be armed with torpedoes or with mines. It was followed by the 'Maiale' (literally 'pig'); or SLC (*Siluro a lente corsa* – slow running torpedo). This might be compared to a midget submarine as a motorbike might be to a Mini car. It was, in reality, a manned underwater charge, a torpedo with two seats and a detachable warhead containing, in its turn, a delayed detonator. Several other types were developed from it, for example, the San Bartolomeo torpedo,which was never tested in an actual war scenario; and the Barchino explosive motor-boat whose one-man crew approached close to their objective, aimed the small boat and then dived overboard. When I was serving in the cruiser *Orion* in the Trieste area at the end of World War II, the ship was given one of these boats which impressed by its high speed and splendid engineering. This weapon system, also, had not been extensively tried in war conditions, but was a source of some innocent entertainment.

To return to the war, the attack on the British ships in Alexandria harbour was made by Maiale craft. These underwater charges, or propelled torpedoes, had seen action previously. The first attempt was made during August 1940. Four of these weapons were placed on board the submarine *Iride*, which was to transport them to the neighbourhood of Alexandria. A major snag occurred when the Italian submarine was sunk by Royal Air Force aircraft on 21 August while still at her moorings at Bomba. In September *Gondar* suffered a similar experience. In the meantime, *Scire*, commanded by Lieutenant-Commander Prince Valerio Borghese, had made two unsuccessful endeavours against warships at Gibraltar. The first auspicious operation came on 26 March 1941, when the cruiser *York* was severely damaged by a one-man Barchino in Suda Bay. It is ironic that when the Germans occupied Crete, they found the wrecked HMS *York* and attributed the damage inflicted on that warship to the work of the Luftwaffe. A third attempt by the *Scire* at Gibraltar ended disastrously for the Maiale teams; as did Major Tesei's attack with explosive motorboats at Malta on 26 July 1941.

Despite this the Tenth MAS persisted. On 21 September the Maiale succeeded in sinking two ships at Gibraltar. Emboldened by this, another action was mounted against shipping in the harbour at Alexandria. The submarine *Scire* was once again employed to transport the manned torpedoes to the entrance of the harbour. There were three teams allocated to the operation, the chief pilots being Lieutenant Durand de la Penne, who had taken part in the undertakings at Gibraltar, Captain Antonio Marceglia and Captain Vicenzo Martellotta, all naval officers. A reserve team was composed of Lieutenant Feltrinelli and Doctor Spaccarelli.

Scire departed from La Spezia on 3 December 1941, professedly on an exercise. When the land was out of sight, three new Maiale (SLC numbers 221, 222, and 223) were taken on board and stowed in special tubes on the submarine's deck. *Scire* then proceeded to the Dodecanese, and on 9 December reached the island of Leros. Here final preparations were carried out and up-to-date reports on the situation at Alexandria were keenly awaited.

The operation had been planned with meticulous care. Italian bombers were to attack the harbour as *Scire* approached, with the aim of creating a diversion. The submarine would then send off the three Maiali; and when these reached their goals the detachable warhead of each would be fixed to the keel of each target using special clips. Afterwards, the crews were required to strew the waters of the harbour with small incendiary devices, the idea being that the incendiary gadgets would ignite fuel-oil which could reasonably be expected to escape from the damaged ships. Another Italian submarine, *Topazio* by name, would lie off the Rosetta mouth of the Nile that night, and the night following, with the object of retrieving any survivors of this hazardous operation who might be lucky enough to reach her.

Heavy weather, and the resulting sea state, persuaded Lieutenant-Commander Borghese that he should postpone the operation for twenty-four hours, from the night of the 17th. When his submarine surfaced at 1840 the following evening, at about two thousand four hundred yards north of the mole light, the weather was admirable for the undertaking in hand. The night was moonless, with a calm sea and clear sky. The three manned torpedoes were launched and set off on their errand, while *Scire* started on the trip back to Leros. Prior to her arrival, Borghese received a message stating that reconnaissance aircraft had reported that two battleships which were in the harbour at Alexandria had been significantly damaged.

It is worth looking at the gallant deeds of the Italian teams in a little more detail. The events on the night of 18 December had been basically as follows.

The six men astride their 'sea pigs', wearing breathing apparatus and with only their heads above the water, reached the harbour entrance at a fortunate moment, that is, just as the boom had been opened to permit the entry of several destroyers returning from patrol. Lieutenant Durand de la Penne edged past the French squadron which was moored in the harbour and shortly after 0200 reached *Valiant*. He then found out that his co-pilot, Bianchi, had disappeared and that his Maiale was sinking beneath him. He dived, caught hold of the torpedo, and contrived to manhandle it to a position on the harbour bottom about ten feet below the keel of the battleship and about halfway along the ship's length. He switched on the delay detonator and swam to the surface fatigued by his exertions. He jettisoned his breathing apparatus, and the fresh air restored him; he was about to swim in the direction of the shore when shouts came from *Valiant*, and the noise of men running on the ship's decks. Search-light beams swept the waters of the harbour, and a few bursts of machine-gun fire followed. Durand de la Penne heaved himself onto *Valiant*'s mooring buoy, where to his intense astonishment, he found that his colleague, Bianchi, was already ensconced.

A launch approached, and the two Italians were taken ashore and questioned at once. They produced their military identity documents, but perfectly within international rules, declined to answer any further questions.

Admiral Cunningham had been awakened at about 0400 and apprised of the incident. He gave directions for the two prisoners to be taken on board *Valiant* and to be kept in custody in the depths of the ship; the reasoning being that if something serious was likely to occur in the near future, they might divulge information with the objective of saving their own lives.

The Italians remained silent until ten minutes to six. The detonation was timed to take place at six o'clock. Lieutenant Durand de la Penne asked to be taken to the captain and informed him that it would be advisable to abandon ship as she was due to blow up in about ten minutes' time. Captain Morgan asked him where the charges had been placed.

The Italian officer refused to answer; and was again taken below. In the darkness he attempted to cheer Bianchi up, but he received no response. This was perfectly understandable as the other Italian had managed to escape from a potentially perilous situation. After a few more tormenting moments, the charges exploded, as expected.

Lieutenant Durand de la Penne was fortunate to escape, albeit somewhat injured; and a short time later he found himself on the quarterdeck where Captain Morgan was giving directions to some of the fire-fighting parties. A few cable-lengths distant, HMS *Queen Elizabeth* was to be seen with numbers of her ship's company collected right forward. She, too, was shaken by an explosion, and was clearly observed lifting in the water. Admiral Cunningham alleged that she rose about five feet. Debris and fuel were projected out of her funnel.

This was the handiwork of Captain Marceglia and his co-pilot Schergat. Their attack had unfolded pretty well exactly as planned. The warhead had been disengaged and hung about three feet below *Queen Elizabeth*'s keel using a length of cable. The two men had then surfaced, got astride their 'sea pig' and made for the land. After sinking their craft, by setting the special device fitted for that purpose, they hid among some rocks for a time. Eventually, they reached Alexandria and caught a train out to Rosetta. Their luck then deserted them; and they never succeeded in getting out to *Topazio*. Instead, Egyptian police apprehended them as they were proceeding down to the beach.

The third Italian team, Martellotta and Marino, had been given the aircraft-carrier *Formidable* as their target. They were nearly run down by one of the destroyers while they were closing the anchorage. They then discovered that the aircraft-carrier was not at her mooring. Instead, they fixed their warhead to the hull of a large tanker, alongside which the destroyer *Jervis* was embarking fuel. The tanker duly blew up and the explosion put *Jervis* out of service for a month. The two Italians got as far as the dockyard gates before they were arrested.

It is fascinating to observe that a hundred Italian seamen, taking into account the ship's company of submarine *Scire*, had dealt the most serious damage to the British Mediterranean Fleet of anyone since the beginning of the Second World War, and this at the cost of half a dozen prisoners.

Enormous potential possibilities were offered to the Italian Navy which, at the time in question, had available to them three 35,000-ton battleships. *Vittorio Veneto* had been refitted and the new *Roma* had been commissioned. Three out of four older battleships were also in service – six Italian battleships in all; and the British had none ready for service at sea.

Luckily for the British, the Italians did not hazard the risks inherent on going over to the offensive at sea. Instead they concentrated their efforts on the approaches to Malta, and the *Rotta del Morte* as their naval personnel named the convoys supplying the needs of Rommel's troops. As time went by, the Allied landings in French North Africa, the surrender of the remains of the Afrika Korps, and the assault on Sicily knocked the heart out of the Italians. With their mainland menaced, the Italians sued for an armistice in the autumn of 1943, and the Italian Fleet sailed to Malta to surrender.

Nonetheless, those who manned the Italian 'sea pigs' set an example and their operations had not come to an end at Alexandria. Later attacks were attempted at Gibraltar and then at Algiers. Incidentally, Lieutenant-Commander Borghese was studying the feasibility of attacking shipping in New York harbour with midget submarines. The idea was that these could be transported across the Atlantic by the Italian submarine *Leonardo da Vinci*. In the final event, the armistice of 9 September 1943 put an end to the planning of this ambitious exercise.

The British were ultimately the most successful users of midget submarines as was shown by their attacks in the Gironde and against the formidable German battleship *Tirpitz* in a Norwegian fjord. However, none really surpassed the men of the Tenth MAS in terms of tenacity, ingenuity and resourcefulness. Where individual action was concerned, the Italian Navy could show itself to be as good as its contemporaries.

Should some readers query the application of midget submarines and any other of the devices mentioned above to convoys, the answers are, hopefully, obvious. Any disruption to the handling of shipping, such as the ability to turn round merchantmen promptly in port, must be 'bad news'. Charges placed by hostile divers, or those piloting manned torpedoes, can result in 'bottom searches' and the rigging of 'bottom lines'. These can be time-consuming exercises.

During World War I it was not unknown for enemies to mix a number of dud shells with live ones. It was, perhaps, difficult for recipients to sleep soundly if one, or more, unexploded shells were known to be adjacent to a dugout. World War II unexploded bombs are still found, streets evacuated and bomb disposal teams called in to help just in case the missile might be potentially lethal.

In the case of missiles, it is a difficult decision for the defence to decide which are live and which are duds being used to draw the anti-missile missiles.

CHAPTER XVI
The Far East

It is not intended to write a great deal about the activities of the Japanese Navy during the First World War, but the Japanese did send a number of destroyers to assist the Allies during that conflict. In particular, the destroyers were employed as convoy escorts in the Mediterranean. During the 1920s and 1930s, the Japanese grew to look upon the United States of America as their principal potential foe. It followed that the Japanese Navy's first aim should be to construct, and maintain, a navy which would be capable of successful engagement with the US Fleet in the Pacific.

When the sea war in the west began to 'work down' to its conclusion, when the use of the convoy system, and the employment of suitable escort vessels, had laid the groundwork of victory for the Allies, the maritime war in the east entered its final scenarios. Here the correct neglect of the use of those potent twins 'convoy' and 'escort' was one of the main causes of defeat. Japan, like Britain, was a maritime nation which had built up one of the most impressive navies on the globe. However, as others before them, neither her government, nor her navy, could acknowledge that the instrument of convoy was essential – until it was too late. Having said that, the Japanese Navy's primary task was to produce, and support, a first-line fleet. The planners favoured the theory that Japanese submarines were to be used against an enemy's warships, not to disrupt commerce. The Japanese assumed that the Americans would want to use their submarines in the same way.

Racial temperament should also have been factored into the equation. Convoy and its merits did not enthuse the aggressive samurai spirit. A comparative few historians at the Japanese Naval War College lectured the students on anti-submarine warfare, and the classes paid little serious attention. In the wider big outdoors, beyond the College, commerce protection seemed to attract a bare minimum of attention. Japanese naval students favoured the study of fleet actions, for example, their naval victories over the Chinese at the Yalu (1894) and over the Russians at Tsushima (1905) when the Russian Baltic Fleet had been sent on a seven-month voyage across the world praying that if it reached Vladivostok it might be able to regain control of the Far East seas and, as a consequence, strangle the supply of war materials to the Japanese armies in Manchuria. The First World War battles at Coronel, the Falklands and, 'top of the bill', Jutland raised the ardour of aspiring Japanese junior officers. The impact of large fleets at sea appealed to the Japanese mentality. Convoy work was deemed to be hard and often boring, which was frequently the case, and of a 'defensive nature', which was a clear misunderstanding of the convoy business.

The merchant shipping of Japan was almost invariably a weak spot. One of the primary reasons for Japan going to war was to obtain a share of the rich natural resources to be found in areas such as Malaya, Indonesia and the Philippines; and, perhaps, the greatest of these resources was 'black gold', the oil which can be the life-blood of modern military operations. Prior to the war, merchant ship construction was reduced in the interests of warship construction. Those who paid regular visits to such Japanese ports as Kure and Sasebo, in Royal Navy warships, during the Korean War could see that Japan was not likely to make this mistake again as work on large oil tankers and freighters went noisily on right round the clock.

During the 1930s, China and Russia were looked upon by the Japanese as potential enemies, and overall naval expenditure was pruned in favour of providing funds for the army. This meant that merchant shipping was allocated a smaller slice of a reduced maritime budget. In addition, the Japanese Naval Staff made a habit of repeatedly underestimating the likely wartime losses of merchant shipping. Other countries that were to become involved in maritime warfare at that time made similar errors.

Japan was even more dependent upon overseas supplies than the British Empire, yet she started the war with a merchant marine totalling little over six million gross tons, which was markedly less than one third of Britain's at the outbreak of war in 1939. Britain had approximately 9,500 ships totalling more than twenty-one million tons. Despite the lessons of the war during the two-year interval and her expansionist plots, Japan had done remarkably little to work on the problems of the protection of shipping, for example, there was no convoy system and no thought had been given to such hardware as escort-carriers. Serious efforts to set such deficiencies right were not put in train until after the number of Japanese merchant ships had been significantly reduced.

It is worth mentioning that Japanese naval bases of various capacities and sizes considered their main objectives to be the support and sustenance of the naval fleets. The protection of merchant shipping was almost completely overlooked. The impressive naval complex at Yokusuka, which was responsible for the shipping and protection of circa six hundred miles of the east coast of Honshu and the approximately seven-hundred mile route to and from Iwo Jima, sported a 'Staff Officer for Education' who was responsible for various training and educational facilities and establishments. He also seemed to be expected to take care of the protection of shipping when time allowed.

During the Korean War the United States and her allies made good use of Yokusuka, among other things as a staging point for exercises of varying degrees of complexity, for example, Hunter Killer Exercises.

To revert to World War II at sea, Japanese troopships were generally provided with escorts which were allocated from the Combined Fleet. Japan was as dependent upon imported fuel and raw materials as the United Kingdom, but there was practically no protection, no convoys, nothing at all, for the enhancement of merchant shipping. As had been the case with Britain, and other countries, Japanese merchantmen were encouraged to proceed independently to increase the speed of circulation of commercial shipping. Regulations for the control of merchant shipping, in time of emergency, did in fact exist; but these directives were produced by separate area commanders, so they varied from area to area. This confused rather than helped the masters of merchant ships.

In spite of the early Japanese wartime good fortune, the Japanese were enduring shipping losses by April 1942.

Taking these conditions into account, the consequence was that Japan's merchant shipping became a comparatively simple source of targets for American submarines. During the early phases of war in the Pacific, American torpedoes suffered from a series of defects which lessened their potential efficiency.

For example, a somewhat 'way out' incident took place during July 1943, when Lieutenant-Commander (later to become Vice-Admiral) L R Daspit, commanding the USS *Tinosa* discovered and engaged a 19,000-ton tanker. Only two torpedoes detonated from the first spread of four weapons. Eleven out of the submarine's remaining torpedoes were fired; but as the exasperated Daspit reported, 'they were all good, solid hits and ALL DUDS!'

More than eighteen months after Pearl Harbor, this was a depressing plane of technical attainment to have reached. Mercifully, Daspit displayed the initiative and sense to hold back and keep his last torpedo which was duly returned to Pearl Harbor for inspection.

By that time, Charles Lockwood, a former naval attache in London, was an admiral and in charge of the Southwest Pacific Submarine Force. Only about a month prior to *Tinosa*'s disappointing experience, Lockwood had banned the use of magnetic detonators which had been so unreliable that they bordered on inevitable failures. No one could accurately estimate how many 'good hits' had been squandered due to their faults. Suffice it to say that very few were wasted after the remedies had been implemented.

It should come as no surprise to learn that the transformation of their torpedoes into potent and effective weapons was the most significant development for American submarines; but submersible vessels were also subject to a number of other enhancements; and the philosophy of their operational use was also subject to change. In the earlier days, employment of submarines tended to verge on the cautious side. Commanding officers were only permitted to make submerged attacks in daylight without using the audible 'pings' of echo-ranging sonar equipment. The submarines themselves were progressively fitted with such items as night periscopes, periscope range finders, more elaborate radar, dependable torpedo data calculators and improved camouflage. It was noticed that light grey paint made an adequate disguise to allow night-time surface operations.

Among the leading of these was the slashing of enemy supply lines. The next (not directly combatant by nature) were photographic reconnaissance acting in a search and rescue role during air strikes, and scouting with the aim of being able to report hostile movements. Linked to the latter, they could be ready to intercept and attack emerging enemy units; and, perhaps their last, if not least, important function was to intercept, pursue and attack runaway enemy shipping fleeing from a target area or dangerous sea space.

The importance of oil supplies, or the lack of the same, was made evident by the fact that the attacks of American and Allied submarines were pointed, for a great part, in the direction of Japanese tankers. As a result the main Japanese fleet tended to be kept at Singapore with the object of being near to oil-producing areas. In Japan itself, the training of aircrews became restricted by shortages of fuel for carrying out airborne exercises.

By July 1942 the Japanese Navy had suffered its first reverse in the Coral Sea and a defeat of catastrophic proportions at Midway. Concurrently, merchant ship casualties were rising, particularly in the East China Sea. When the Second World War began, the American Navy set aside the approach of employing its submarines for attacking warships and shifted its attention to carrying out an assault on commercial shipping. It was the US submarine fleet, rather than their surface fleet, which became the scourge and most deadly antagonist of the Japanese merchant marine.

American submarines also inflicted significant losses on Japanese warships which came to nigh on a third of those which were despatched to the bottom of the sea. Two Japanese fleet carriers, *Taiho* and *Shokaku*, were sunk in the Battle of the Philippine Sea. During the later months of 1944, US submarines sank, or inflicted permanently disabling wounds on, three more aircraft-carriers as well as dealing most convincingly with the order of some thirty-five to forty destroyers.

As an antidote to the far from happy 'state of play' in the East China Sea, the Japanese formed the First Convoy Escort Fleet, a somewhat grandiose title, in July 1942, under the command of Admiral Nakajima, whose

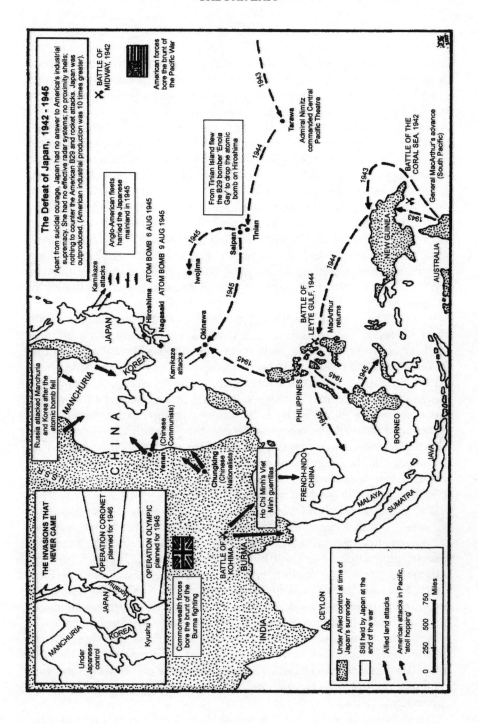

The Defeat of Japan, 1942 - 1945

Apart from suicidal courage, Japan had no answer to America's industrial supremacy. She had no effective radar systems; no proximity shells; nothing to counter the American B29 and rocket attacks. Japan was outproduced. (American industrial production was 10 times greater).

BATTLE OF MIDWAY, 1942

American forces bore the brunt of the Pacific War

Anglo-American fleets harried the Japanese mainland in 1945

Kamikaze attacks

HIROSHIMA ATOM BOMB 6 AUG 1945

NAGASAKI ATOM BOMB 9 AUG 1945

From Tinian Island flew the B29 bomber 'Enola Gay' to drop the atomic bomb on Hiroshima

Tarawa

Admiral Nimitz commanded Central Pacific Theatre

BATTLE OF THE CORAL SEA 1942

General MacArthur's advance (South Pacific)

NEW GUINEA

AUSTRALIA

Iwojima

Saipan

Tinian

Okinawa

BATTLE OF LEYTE GULF, 1944

MacArthur returns

PHILIPPINES

BORNEO

JAVA

JAPAN

KOREA

MANCHURIA

Russia attacked Manchuria and Korea after the atomic bomb fell

Kamikaze attacks

C H I N A

U.S.S.R.

Yenan (Chinese Communists)

Chungking (Chinese Nationalists)

Ho Chi Minh's Viet Minh guerrillas

FRENCH-INDO CHINA

MALAYA

SUMATRA

THE INVASIONS THAT NEVER CAME

OPERATION CORONET planned for 1946

OPERATION OLYMPIC planned for 1945

JAPAN

Honshu

Kyushu

MANCHURIA

KOREA

Under Japanese control

Commonwealth forces bore the brunt of the Burma fighting

BATTLE OF KOHIMA

BURMA

INDIA

CEYLON

Under Allied control at time of Japan's surrender

Still held by Japan at the end of the war

Allied land attacks

American attacks in Pacific, 'atoll hopping'

0 250 500 750 Miles

headquarters were sited outside the town of Takao, on the island of Formosa. The Admiral's terms of reference were to organise and escort convoys transiting the East China Sea with his force of eight rather veteran destroyers. In due course, the convoys' work was expanded to cover the Japan–Palusa route; and Nakajima's force had staff officers appointed to such places as Moji, Manila, Saigon and Singapore.

The Japanese had initiated the first move in the correct direction when the First Convoy Escort Fleet was formed. Some writers have made play with the idea that the organisation suffered from having rather an elderly flavour both in ships and men. This I would beg to dispute. People can either do a job, or they cannot – age has nothing to do with the matter. 'Old dogs for hard trails.' The septuagenarian Blucher did not do too badly during the campaign which ended with the Battle of Waterloo. In the 1943/44 era, British East Coast Convoys performed very satisfactorily with World War I 'V' and 'W' destroyers and the ex-US 'gift horses'; and merchant vessels could be found with veterans among their companies who often set a splendid example to the younger men, as mentioned in Chapter XII.

It would be a great temptation to wander off into fascinating detail about the sea-air battles of the Pacific War: the achievement of the aircraft-carrier has been fully recognised in the many books about navies in the Second World War. Battleships were used, on occasions, by the Americans during the Korean War. These factors are beyond the scope of this work. However, in the context of convoys, it would be pertinent to add that the Japanese seemed to 'miss a trick' by sailing warships of the main fleet to and from Japan on their own when they might quite effortlessly have been directed to escort a convoy for a significant part of their voyage. The argument that this might conflict with their principal task of seeking the offensive can be discarded as the vicinity of a convoy frequently provided a 'killing ground' in its own right.

The Japanese Admiral Oikawa is alleged to have advocated 'patrolled sea lanes' – a concept which has been discussed earlier in this work – somewhat to their disadvantage. The Japanese Admiral proposed safeguarding shipping en route between Japan and the Singapore area by attempting to turn the South China Sea, the Formosa Strait and the East China Sea into the equivalent of one enormous, sanitised expanse of water, more or less surrounded by land, which was secure for Japanese shipping. Gaps in the barrier could, theoretically, be plugged by such expedients as minefields and radar stations sited on shore-based positions. Similar lanes could be envisaged between, say, Kobe and Yokohama, and northward from Yokohama up the east coast of Honshu. At this time, the Sea of Japan and the Yellow Sea were still free from submarines.

The Japanese Grand Escort Command started, rather unethusiastically, to implement the plans they were given; but they were shortly to be overtaken by events. A number of mines were laid in the Formosa Strait; and two radar stations saw the light of day on Okinawa before Japanese military units were overwhelmed by Allied superiority in the air. In the meantime, the High Command was pressurising the Escort Command to free ships from such convoys as they were actually operating, even if those convoys only consisted of three or four vessels per convoy.

While the Japanese still hesitated over the introduction of the convoy principle, as a matter of habit, further blows relentlessly fell upon them. American submarines sank the best part of half a million tons of shipping in January 1944, and more than a further 256,000 tons during February. Japanese maritime confidence was obliged to endure a deadly reverse when the United States Fast Carrier Task Force attacked Truk on 17/18 February 1944, and despatched another 200,000 odd tons, mainly tankers and store ships attending to the logistic requirements of the Combined Fleet, to the bottom of the sea.

Japanese troop transports had invariably been convoyed; but even these were subject to heavy losses until late 1943. It was said at this time that 'everyone on board a transport or merchant vessel had to be resigned to the likelihood of being sunk in his travels'. In autumn 1943 the Japanese launched Operation TURTLE. The aim of this exercise was to transfer Second District Army comprising seven divisions of the Second Army and the Nineteenth Army from Manchuria, China, Korea, the Celebes, Morotai, Halmahera and Biak. Only about half the original strength remained when these military units were eventually put ashore on New Guinea. When on dry land they were in a pretty parlous state without weaponry, many lacking footwear, and considerable numbers were in a bad state of health. During February 1944 a fast convoy ferrying troops from Korea to Saipan and Guam was engaged by the American submarine *Trout*, which sank one ship which had rather more than four thousand troops embarked. More than half of them were drowned. The downside was that the escorts counter-attacked and sank *Trout*. On 3 February the tankers *Goyo Maru* and *Ariake Maru*, escorted solely by the frigate *Sado*, were sunk in the East China Sea en route to Japan. On the 19th of the same month, all five tankers making up a larger convoy with only a frigate as escort, were sunk by USS *Jack*. In each case the escorting vessel was able to achieve little more than to try to play the part of rescue ship. It now began to occur to a number of Japanese staff officers that bigger convoys with more numerous escorts might provide a more effective solution to their problems. In the meantime, the Japanese were obliged to endure more adversities. On 1 March a sizeable convoy of seven transports, eight destroyers and a special service vessel departed from Rabaul with an infantry division of more than nine thousand. Their aim was to reinforce the garrisons of Lae and Salamaua in New Guinea. Masked under a

211

thickly overcast sky that night, the convoy was detected on 2 March in the Bismarck Sea. Aircraft of the USAAF and RAAF operating from Papua initiated a series of attacks which lasted 'on and off' for about thirty-six hours. The entire convoy had been sent to the bottom, with the exception of four of the destroyer escorts, by 4 March; and more than three thousand men had been engulfed by the hungry waters.

Later in the same month of March the Japanese light cruiser *Tatsuta* and a couple of merchant vessels from a convoy transporting reinforcements to the Marianas were sunk by the American submarine *Sandlance*. A large Japanese ship, the *Meike Maru* taking 29th Infantry Regiment from Pusan to Saipan, was sent to the bottom, with a heavy death toll, just short of the entrance to the Inland Sea. This episode, probably as much as any, 'twisted arms' in the Japanese Naval General Staff to take stock of the merits and demerits of the introduction of a convoy system more thoughtfully than hitherto. During March 1944 the Japanese eventually originated what they were pleased to call a 'large convoy system'. However, as the Allies were used to operating convoys of seventy to eighty ships across the Atlantic, the Japanese convoys of between ten and twenty ships did not appear to be unduly 'large'. An Escort of Convoy Headquarters was formed, with a dedicated staff. The not uncommon apprehensions about the proficiency of the masters of merchant ships to maintain station and to communicate within the convoy were held. It was also considered hazardous to think in terms of having more than three columns of ships proceeding abreast. The ever-present shortage of escort vessels and, in the early days, the lack of convoy 'know-how' had to be taken into account.

In spite of the disadvantages, it became clear that the employment of the convoy system rapidly started to save ships. It shortly became evident that losses of ships sailing independently were two and a half times greater than those of ships proceeding in convoy. What is more, the escorts were fighting back. American submarines lost more of their company to the escorts of convoys than to aircraft, mines, patrolling surface vessels or to any other specific source.

The US submarines responded to the new challenge by adopting 'wolf-pack' tactics, for example, three or four submarines would be tasked to work together to detect, shadow and attack their targets. They would employ effective voice communications between the submarines, and be fitted with extremely good surface radar equipments. The graph of Japanese shipping losses, which had begun dropping, started to climb again.

During the month of August 1944 American submarines transferred to a base at Saipan, which was some 3,500 miles closer to the current centre of activity than was Pearl Harbor. This meant that individual submarines were given the facility to spend longer periods of time on patrol.

The Japanese continued to have a superiority in numbers, even in aircraft-carriers, after the Battle of Midway; but, as previously mentioned, they had suffered a hiccough in their offensive. The Americans proceeded to exploit their advantage cautiously at first, but with greater assurance as new ships arrived in service.

On 7 August 1942, some two months after Midway, a division of US Marines landed on Guadalcanal, in the Solomons, to attempt to dislodge the Japanese. Admiral Mikawa reacted promptly. On the night of 8 August his cruisers engaged the Allied covering force off Savo Island, and within minutes torpedoed three US cruisers, *Vincennes, Astoria* and *Quincy*, plus one Australian, the *Canberra*. The channel in which they were sunk became known by the not inappropriate name of 'Ironbottom Sound'. However, this was only the start of a long-drawn-out contest for the eastern Solomons; the Americans sank the *Ryujo* and destroyed ninety aircraft. Then on 11 October, off Cape Hope, Rear-Admiral Scott managed to 'cross the T' of the Japanese force and sink a cruiser and a destroyer. As ill luck would have it, an American destroyer was sunk as a result of coming under cross-fire.

A couple of weeks later, the scales tipped in favour of the Japanese at the Battle of Santa Cruz, where the *Hornet* was lost and *Enterprise* severely damaged. However, at the naval Battle of Guadalcanal on 14 November the battleship *Washington*, though engaging the whole Japanese squadron at one period, damaged the hostile battleship so badly that Admiral Kondo was obliged to direct that she should be scuttled.

On 30 November 1942, in a night action which became known as the Battle of Tassafarongo, eight Japanese destroyers torpedoed four American cruisers, one of which sank, for the sacrifice of only one destroyer. This engagement, which can be looked upon as a model attack by destroyers against superior forces, was the last important naval battle in the memorable struggle for Guadalcanal. On 9 February 1943 the Americans found themselves in undisputed occupancy of the island. The Japanese had retrieved their remaining troops during the course of the previous three nights using fast destroyers to evacuate them. American naval personnel called this exercise the 'Tokyo Express'.

Throughout 1943 and 1944 American and Australian operations progressed steadily in the South-West Pacific. During the course of about fifteen months the Allied forces captured the Gilbert and then the Marshall Islands, ousted the Japanese from New Guinea and on 15 June 1944 American marines and infantry landed on Saipen Island in the Marianas which was the key position in the Japanese defences. Four days later, aircraft of the rival fleets met in a furious battle.

There was a day of inconclusive combat between aircraft of Admiral Mitscher's Task Force 58 and those of Admiral Ozawa's aircraft-carriers. That evening, the American submarines *Albacore* and *Cavalla* managed to penetrate the Japanese destroyer screen and to sink the *Taiho* and the *Shokaku* in a torpedo attack. Admiral Ozawa disengaged westwards. The American Admiral Mitscher occupied most of the following day, 20 June, doing his best to locate the enemy. He was obstructed in his chase by a fresh easterly wind. This obliged his carriers to, more or less, reverse course each time their aircraft were launched or recovered.

Eventually, at 1530, the enemy was sighted, far to the west and tracking at about twenty knots. They were only just within range of the American carrier-borne aircraft. Mitscher hesitated over whether to deploy his aircraft on what would, without any doubt, be a hazardous and costly mission. However, the decision was taken and the aircraft duly launched. The first reports of success were received at 1900, namely, that the carrier *Chiyoda* had been set on fire, and the *Hiyo* was in a sinking condition.

There was no moon that night, and the returning aircraft had to land in darkness. They had scarcely any fuel left which meant that they could not circle their own carrier and await permission to be recovered. In the event, they landed to the best of their ability, on the first aircraft-carrier they sighted. The result was that there were a goodly number of accidents of varying degrees of severity. One light carrier had twice its normal complement on the flight-deck; and damaged aeroplanes were pushed over the side to make room for aircraft which were still airborne. Throughout the night, aircraft and destroyers searched the area in question. In toto, a hundred and fifty out of two hundred and nine aviators were picked up.

An impressive American force landed in the Philippines on 20 October 1944, and between the 23rd and 28th a series of naval actions, known as the Battle of Leyte Gulf, ended in the overthrow of the Japanese Fleet which was endeavouring to interfere with the landings. The engagements involved pretty well every type of ship from battleships to coastal forces. The Japanese lost three battleships, four aircraft-carriers, ten cruisers and nine destroyers. The price paid by the Americans was two light carriers and three destroyers. It was during these battles that the Japanese suicide-pilots, the kamikazes, first put in an appearance.

It is difficult for the average western mind to comprehend the mental processes of the comparatively unskilled pilots who had volunteered to make one-way flights to their deaths. They assumed the title of kamikaze after the Divine Wind which broke up the invasion fleet of the Mongols in the year 1281. Looking back into Japanese history, there are many examples of the belief that the 'way of the Samurai is found in death'. On their first appearance, the kamikaze were responsible for the destruction of the carrier *St Lo*.

The war in the Pacific lasted for a further ten months after the decisive blow to the Japanese Fleet which was inflicted during the naval actions in the Battle of Leyte Gulf. The Americans took Iwo Jima after fierce fighting in February 1945. On 1 April their navy commenced an amphibious attack to capture Okinawa, some three hundred and fifty miles south of Japan. The island was not finally conquered until mid-June, so determined was the Japanese defence. Plans to land Allied forces on the main Japanese islands were being prepared, but these were overtaken by events. An American aircraft dropped a nuclear bomb on the Japanese city of Hiroshima on 6 August 1945. This device killed or seriously injured more than a hundred and sixty people. A second bomb was dropped on Nagasaki on 9 August. The Japanese government accepted surrender terms on 14 August 1945. It is difficult to argue with the contention that the nuclear weapons saved the tens of thousands of lives that could have been lost if Japan had been invaded.

Should any readers think that detours have been made on the specific subject of convoys, this would be disputed. The 'island hopping' techniques used by the Americans and their Allies as World War II in the Pacific drew to its close required vast deployments of shipping and this shipping needed to be protected.

Useful things, convoys!

The Glorious First of June, 1794

The 'Glorious First of June' has been included both for its intrinsic interest and because it would probably never have taken place were it not for the requirement to send a badly needed supply of grain from America to France. However, there were problems.

The earnest theorists thrown up by the French Revolution had so seriously undermined the authority and emasculated the panache of the members of the French regular officer corps, who had not had the misfortune to make the acquaintance of the guillotine or been hanged from street lanterns, that about three quarters of the survivors had either emigrated or left their chosen service. In due course, the theorists abruptly woke up to the realisation that they were waging war with the two foremost naval powers of the time, namely, Britain and Holland; and that they had no one available to command and provide officers to operate the remains of Louis XVI's impressive fleet. Some thirty large ships and twenty frigates were constructed – not before time! However, who was there to lead them into active service?

There was no shortage of doughty sailors prepared to 'chance their arm' on meeting a heroic death; but sea battles are generally won by killing enemies rather than being killed oneself. With few exceptions, the new senior officers of the Republican Navy did not know much more about naval matters than how to die fighting.

In the above conditions, it was probably rather difficult to guess how the Representatives of the Republic believed that they could successfully undertake a well thought-out and planned series of naval expeditions or, for that matter, defend the French Colonies. In the year 1794 all that the French Convention could ask of its navy was to support a badly-needed grain convoy whose arrival from the Americas was awaited with some anxiety. The grain shortage in France was the result of a calamitous harvest which was caused by political troubles and internecine strife as much as by weather conditions.

One hundred and seventeen merchantmen had sailed from Chesapeake Bay on 2 April 1794, escorted by a small force of naval vessels under the operational control of Rear-Admiral Vanstabul. The escort consisted of two 74-gun ships of the line, two frigates and a brig. The original naval escort was to be joined by five ships and a number of frigates which sailed from Rochefort on 6 May under the command of Rear-Admiral Nielly. This luminary was a product of the new regime and had been a sub-lieutenant shortly before the outbreak of the Revolution. This combined French force would be far from adequate if the British appeared on the scene as it was highly likely they would.

What is not always mentioned in accounts of 'The Glorious First of June' is that the French convoy was supposed to be conveying more sugar than corn, but a significant quantity of sugar had been traded to help pay for the long French delay in harbour. What, almost certainly, most interested the Convention was that a party of rebels and witnesses of the insurrection of San Domingo were being shipped to France to make their appearance before the Revolutionary Tribunals.

By various means, the French managed to fit out twenty-five ships at Brest. The command of this force was given to one Captain Villaret de Joyeuse who was promoted to the rank of Rear-Admiral by members of the Convention who were, no doubt, usefully engaged in a mission to the Brest Naval Base. Villaret de Joyeuse 'replaced', if that is the right word, Vice-Admiral Morard de Galles, a veteran who had to his credit participated in fifteen battles and received eight wounds. This record of active service did not excuse the experienced naval officer from a prison sentence.

'General Villaret', as the new Admiral was called in the political correct-ness of the time, was closely supervised on board his flagship, the *Montagne* (120 guns) by a People's Commissary whose task it was to see that the Convention's orders were meticulously observed. Similar routines were carried out in twentieth-century Communist navies. In this instance, the emissary was a certain Jean Bon, who called himself Saint André, and had been a Calvinist minister. He took his appointment extremely seriously and hunted down Royalist and Catholic officers with a grim ferocity, which is rather typical of this kind of zealot. When the guns began to speak, however, rumour had it that his fervour noticeably shrank and he would find overwhelming reasons for descending into the deep recesses of the ship. It was obviously essential that so important a personage should be kept well away from the discharge of hostile muskets, and the trajectory of chance.

The commanding officers of the thirty-six naval vessels tasked with the protection of the inward-bound grain convoy included only one who had experienced the privilege of being captain of a ship of the line prior to 1789. The others had, until that time, officiated in such disparate roles as lieutenants or sub-lieutenants in the naval service, dockyard jobs, master mariners in the merchant service, or as officers in merchantmen engaged in the coastal trade. One of these recently hatched senior naval officers had ascended, without much training in officers' duties, from the lower deck.

Many, if not most, of the French commanding officers had gained little experience of sailing in formation with other ships and had acquired only sketchy practical knowledge of the art of 'station keeping'; no easy task in a full-rigged sailing man-of-war. The commanding officers had to learn on the job and in action. A similar situation applied to those who manned the guns of the French ships. The majority of the gunners were young and inexperienced recruits who had been drafted in from the soldiery to supplant the regular naval gunners in the aftermath of the Quiberon Revolt.

The preceding paragraphs should give an idea of the men who were sent to engage in combat with the British Channel Fleet. The British warships were under the command of Lord Howe, who was a veteran who had counted the passage of sixty-eight years and who had experienced commanding warships for about half a century. Villaret de Joyeuse had yet to see the light of day when Howe won his advancement to post-captain as a result of a successful action against a superior enemy force. All Howe's senior officers had gained distinction during the War of American Independence. Revolutionary France had, in its wisdom, divested itself of the services of the French captains who had fought, in many cases successfully, against them. The well-honed skills and background experience of the British officers meant that those who were opposing them fought under a severe handicap.

Admiral Howe had been at sea since 2 May 1794. He had departed from Spithead with a force of thirty-four ships whose aim was to ensure the safe and timely voyage down the English Channel of a large convoy whose destination was the East Indies. When this convoy was clear of the Channel, the British Admiral detached six ships to continue looking after the convoy. He then set course into the Atlantic Ocean to try to make contact with the French grain convoy. While these British movements were unfolding, Villaret de Joyeuse left Brest on 16 May. This was, in itself, in the nature of an achievement for the French. Admiral Howe spent about a week vainly looking for the enemy, but without success, until such time as he was put on the right track by an American merchant vessel. Howe eventually sighted the French on 28 May, when they were approximately four hundred miles to the west of Ushant.

At the time of meeting, each force mustered twenty-six ships. A fresh south-westerly wind was blowing. The less experienced French were, more or less, in formation in three columns on the port tack, at about 0800 on 28 May, when the British were sighted ahead and to leeward. The French Admiral had been made aware of the convoy's position, by a frigate from Nielly's division, some three days previously. Villaret had advantage of the wind and aimed to entice his opponent from the convoy's base course by steering in the opposite direction to the rendezvous area.

The French ships encountered problems in forming line of battle, in column, due to a rising wind and mounting sea state. Villaret first directed the starboard tack to be adopted, then brought the line closer to the wind and half an hour later repeated the manoeuvre to try to help matters.

The exercise for Admiral Howe was basically straightforward. He first had to attack then destroy the French naval ships. That objective having been achieved, it should, theoretically, be a comparatively simple matter to round up the virtually defenceless convoy.

The British Admiral's opening move was to detach six ships, under the tactical command of Rear-Admiral Pasle in the, later to become famous, *Bellerophon* ('Billy Ruffian' to the lower deck) to engage the French rear.

Pasle nursed the wind and duly worked his way within gunshot range of the extremity of the French line where he found the 114-gun *Revolutionnaire* (Captain Vandogen), which had been deployed by Villaret to assist the smaller ships and who was resolved to undertake his assignment beyond his senior officer's most optimistic desires. An artillery duel between *Bellerophon* and *Revolutionnaire* opened at 1800 and the two ships pounded each other with such devastating effect that the British flagship saw fit to draw off about an hour later. However, by that time five of her consorts had joined the assault on *Revolutionnaire*, which was unable to run her lower deck guns out to fire against the enemy to windward due to the heavy seas running. First, her mizzen-yard succumbed, next her foretopsail yard, and before long she was lying helplessly before the wind. Vandogen was killed at 2130, his First Lieutenant had been sorely injured, so the next senior officer, Renaudeau, was obliged to assume command. Next he too was wounded, and handed over to Lieutenant Dorre. The upper deck was strewn with dead and wounded. Fighting against such overpowering odds, the ship undoubtedly would have fallen into enemy hands but Admiral Howe signalled disengagement. Dorre managed to limp off towards the northeast with a following wind, but during the night both mizzen and main masts went. Next day he had the good fortune to stumble across two of Nielly's vessels. One of these towed him into Aix Roads, in the vicinity of Rochefort.

As far as the British were concerned *Audacious* was obliged to find shelter in the Devonport area as she was in nearly as bad a state as *Revolutionnaire*. To sum up, the first day running engagement had ended without any significant advantage to either side; but, truth to tell, neither had been fully involved in an action state. Villaret de Joyeuse was reasonably happy as his strength was, to all intents and purposes, equal to that of his enemy.

The distance between the squadrons was approximately six miles throughout the night. They were both on the starboard tack with the French still to windward. Admiral Howe resumed his attack on the French rear on the morning of 29 May. *Queen Charlotte* succeeded in breaking the French column by passing astern of *Eole*, the sixth ship from the end of the enemy line and in this manner getting to windward of her. Four other British ships followed, namely *Bellerophon, Orion, Leviathan* and *Barfleur* which cut out *Terrible, Tyrannicide* and the *Indomptable* and engaged them fiercely. The French warships offered a steadfast resistance, but received markedly more punishment than they doled out to their opponents. *Tyrannicide* and *Indomptable* were pruned to their bottom masts and needed to be escorted from the fray by two of their consorts.

The firing died away at about 1700. Villaret had lost his wind advantage through protecting the withdrawal of the crippled ships. This handicapped the French Admiral for fighting in subsequent days. However, the French manoeuvre drew the British force farther away from the convoy's track which next day passed safely through the sea area which had seen the earlier fighting.

A sea mist gave the French time to re-form and to sort themselves out on 30 May. Nielly had joined with three ships and another arrival from Cancale, which is situated in the vicinity of St Malo. The gaps left by the battle of the previous day were occupied by the newly-arrived reinforcements. On the other side of the coin, some half dozen British vessels could only be described as being in a damaged state. The sun shone radiantly on the morning of 1 June and a fresh south-westerly breeze had chased away the mist and stirred up the sea. Lord Howe, who some might have expected to show signs of weariness, poor old chap, showed the dash and ardour of his earlier years. At 0800 the British Admiral directed his whole force to sail to the attack.

Howe had briefed his captains on his aim to penetrate the centre of the French column, and he gave them complete liberty to choose the most appropriate enemy ship to engage. The British cut through their opponent's line without great trouble, and a savage close encounter followed in which the higher rate and more accurate fire of the well-trained British seamen triumphed over the efforts of the less well-trained French gun crews. It should also be noted that the British fired at the hulls of the enemy instead of at the sails and rigging. This 'shooting to sink' tactic proved to be a better policy than the French procedure of 'shooting to dismast'. While the battle was at its height in the French rear and centre, their van seemed to be unexpectedly shy of the prospect of joining action, despite repeated signals made by its Commander-in-Chief. To be charitable, the dense clouds of smoke rising from the guns of the ships of both sides could, possibly, have ensured that signals made by the French Admiral may not have been seen by the ships under his command.

At around about noon, *Montagne* contrived to disengage from the relentless attacks of *Queen Charlotte* and Villaret de Joyeuse was able to make a reassessment of the situation.

A dozen of the French ships were still engaged, even though nine of them were basically dismasted. The French Admiral oversaw the saving of five by having them towed away by frigates and corvettes. Admiral Howe then separated him from the other seven, six of which ended up being taken by the British. The seventh, *Vengeur du Peuple*, perished fighting. Her untimely end was jumped on by the French powers to originate a renowned legend. Heroic stories were as badly needed by the French as they were by the British, to boost morale on the home front. There appears to be a bit of a mystery about *Vengeur*'s exploits. The story was, perhaps not unintentionally, accepted by the French Convention and also applauded and recognised abroad to the same extent as it had been at home. In truth, *Vengeur*, commanded by Captain Renaudin, had fought a tremendous action in the form of a duel with the British *Brunswick*. *Brunswick*'s starboard anchors had become robustly hooked in her adversary's hull. The two ships were so closely grappled together that *Brunswick*'s gun crews needed to widen their gun-ports, and their French opposite numbers lacked the space to handle their ramrods. *Brunswick*'s masts succumbed one after the other, and her commanding officer was wounded.

The duel had been in progress for about three hours when the two contestants suddenly separated. However, *Vengeur* was no sooner freed from *Brunswick*'s embrace than she was attacked at close range by *Ramillies* which treated her to a broadside. Riddled with projectiles, *Vengeur* started to founder.

In the historical period under consideration, no shame was seen in surrendering when a warship was clearly lost and in no state to defend itself further. This was to enable as many as possible of the survivng members of the crew to be saved. *Vengeur* struck her colours, and forthwith attempts to save her ship's company were made by opposing ships. However, due to damage sustained by British vessels, the rescue process was a slow one. In the event, *Vengeur* went down with something of the order of over a hundred unfortunates remaining on board. Some of these shouted 'Vive la République' as they vanished beneath the surface of the sea.

The fight had indubitably been of the heroic variety and there was no requirement for fictitious details to be added, as was the case in Bareres' colourful report to the French Assembly. *Vengeur* had sunk three enemy ships before she herself went down. The whole ship's company had remained with their ship firing and with colours flying to the last. Perhaps sadly, when Captain Renaudin, who had not been one of the last to abandon his ship, returned to France from a stint, with some of his men on board English prison-hulks, he tended to be looked on as a maladroit fall-guy who had upset an elaborate theatrical stunt.

Villaret could probably have recovered the six captured ships if he had made the slightest attempt to do so. Lord Howe had eleven of his ships in a poor state and was in no position to defend or tow them. The French Admiral was prevented from making this type of move, because when the action was broken off, Jean Bon regained his composure and his authority and reminded Villaret that the grain convoy was of the first importance.

The convoy reached harbour unscathed, anchoring in Brest Roads on 7 June near Villaret's ships which had arrived the previous day. The French had, therefore, achieved their aim and could claim a victory. When Lord Howe returned with his six prizes with wild enthusiasm, the battle which is known in France as the low-key 'Fight on the Thirteenth of Prairical' is celebrated in British naval history as 'The Glorious First of June'.

Whatever one might like to call it, the engagement on this 1st of June gave the British Admiralty a great deal to think about. The French squadron had been ably controlled and handled, probably far better than might have been expected in the circumstances then predominating in France. The new Republican Navy might have had a rosy future if it had been granted the attention and support it required; but the French only had eyes for their armies. It was not long before the neglect of the French Navy was to have dismal consequences at the time of General Bonaparte's expedition to Egypt in 1798.

The 'Glorious First of June' has particular bearing upon the subject of this book as it illustrates the importance of the safe and timely arrival of a convoy to the French and the confused thinking in the British squadron which virtually ignored the existence of the French convoy in Admiral Howe's game plan for the battle.

APPENDIX II

The Battle of the Nile, 1798

To set the scene for the engagement which has become known to the British as the Battle of the Nile, it should be recalled that Admiral Jervis was elevated to the peerage by being created Earl of St Vincent and Nelson was promoted to the rank of Rear-Admiral and was made a Knight of the Bath. The new peer still had a difficult assignment ahead of him. Between April 1797 and May 1799 he was occupied in the daunting test of blockading Cádiz with his somewhat worn-out ships and spent ships' companies. The only reinforcements sent out to him tended to be ships which had been involved in the mutinies which had been taking place in the Nore and at Spithead.

Boards of Enquiry were in virtually continuous session, with the British squadron patrolling close to a hostile harbour. St Vincent stuck to his task with untiring application, but he was frequently discouraged and 'sick at heart'. The Admiral was quoted as saying: 'Why do they go on sending me these shiploads of mutineers? Do they take me for the fleet's executioner?'

St Vincent, despite his many problems, 'worked up' the dispirited British fleet into an instrument capable of triumphing over strong opponents. This fine achievement should always be remembered in any discussion of Jervis' place in the roll call of Britain's admirals. Word had reached him of French preparations at Toulon. The Royal Navy for the past couple of years or so had been pushed from one Mediterranean base to another in the wake of Napoleon's conquests in Italy. The British Admiral made the lonely decision to send a dozen British warships into the 'Middle Sea'; and he appointed the young Rear-Admiral whose right eye had been seriously damaged during the siege of Calvi in 1794 and who had lost his right arm in the attack on Santa Cruz in the Canary Islands in July 1797, to command this squadron: an officer short of one arm and one eye, but most certainly not wanting in zeal, enthusiasm and moral backbone. This commander was soon to gain a victory which would recover naval dominance in the Mediterranean for his country, and which Britain was to maintain until the Second World War.

The enterprise being worked on at Toulon has been dubbed by some historians the 'most astonishing and rash of which Napoleon's fertile imagination had been the creator'. He had given up the plan of invading the British Isles due to the lack of available hardware needed to provide the leverage of adequate naval power. Instead, he was building up a force of some thirty thousand plus military effectives with the aim of invading Egypt; and after that, assailing British interests east of Suez. His soaring visions are commonly believed to have nourished the feasibility of leading French forces to the sub-continent of India.

Napoleon set aside all difficulties and protests. Transports were to be commandeered in defeated Italy. Escort vessels could be furnished by the Eastern Mediterranean Squadron, or the few, that is, which had evaded being badly mauled at Toulon by the British in December 1793, and from those vessels in harbours along the Italian Riviera. The total added up to thirteen ships of the line and half a dozen frigates described as being 'old and rotting, not even able to support the firing of their own guns if it became at all heavy'. In the final event, some of the guns needed to be unshipped as it was doubtful whether the decks could be relied upon to continue to bear their weight. The ships' companies were in only marginally better condition than the ships they served in. A French officer's report penned shortly before the battle, while the fleet was moored in Aboukir Bay, said that 'on the whole our ships are very poorly manned, and in my opinion it needs much courage to command such an ill-prepared fleet'.

The sailors of the French Republic were poorly fed, badly paid and lacked even a change of clothing. Admiral Secey, writing in 1796, grieved that his men had to go naked while they washed their garments. Similar conditions were still in existence some five years later. In 1801 the commanding officer of *Sans Pareille* excused the poor performance of his men in action, saying that 'they were all wet through after twenty-eight hours with nothing to change into, for I could only get ten lots of spare clothes for the whole crew'.

The French force sailed on 19 May with the warships mentioned above escorting four hundred transports which was, by any stretch of the imagination, a large convoy.

The French sailed to Malta, en route to their final destination, and captured that island within a few days. Valetta still had its magnificent battlements which even now provide a lesson in the art of the military engineers of the age in which they were built, such as the great Vauban. However, the Knights of St John had grown effete and did not display their forefathers' enthusiasm in defending the curtains, fleches, counterscarps, etc. with whose protection their Order had been entrusted for several hundred years. In addition, the French Knights were unwilling to fight fellow Frenchmen.

The lucky man who was appointed to command the Toulon Squadron was Pierre Martin, then 40 years of age. He had been a naval officer without much of a future when elected Rear-Admiral by the People's Representative at Fort National (Fort de France), the capital of Martinique. The Paris Convention had not made a poor selection in choosing him, for he was not lacking in steadiness and skill, and had held his own against a British squadron off Corsica in 1795. With the wisdom of hindsight, it was a mischance for France that he had failed to intercept four British ships in the Gulf of Genoa that same year. One of the four was the 64-gun ship *Agamemnon* commanded by Captain Horatio Nelson.

Human nature can produce unexpected results. Pierre Martin was not liked by Truguet, the new French Minister of Marine who had recently been selected by the Directory. Martin was relieved of his post and replaced by François Paul Brueys d'Argalliers. The new Very Important Person had been a lowly lieutenant in 1789; but the scarcity of naval officers, thanks to the Revolution, had brought promotion to flag rank. Although recently elevated, the Admiral was in no sense qualified to lead a squadron particularly against an officer of Nelson's calibre, even though his personal courage was equal to that of the Englishman, as was to be shown by his gallant death in action. Brueys had come to the attention of the young General Bonaparte at Ragusa during the Italian campaign. The General had praised him to the Directory and advancement had followed.

Brueys must have been no mean organiser, as he master-minded the accomplishment of ensuring the safe arrival of four hundred troop transports to Egypt. Brueys' convoy just missed being sighted by Nelson's squadron which was searching for him all over the eastern Mediterranean – neither side knew that they had been so close at the time in question. The French convoy arrived at Alexandria on 1 July. Nelson had looked into that port two days previously, then left to seek the French in the direction of Constantinople.

At last, on 28 July, Nelson heard that the French had disembarked in Egypt. Another speedy passage resulted and on 1 August the British came in sight of Alexandria again. There they found the merchant ships, but no warships.

Napoleon won the Battle of the Pyramids about three weeks after he had landed in Egypt (on 21 July) but, being a 'land animal', he failed to see the high importance which any sort of effective fleet could be to his plans. In fact, Napoleon seemed to give no further thought to his warships, other than to direct Brueys to make his way back to Alexandria. The execution of this order was left entirely to the Admiral.

Brueys was obsessed by the fear of running aground. There should have been little danger of this eventuality as his biggest ship only drew about twenty-two feet, and it was difficult to find anywhere in the harbour of Alexandria with a depth of less than twenty-seven feet. However, with his fetish about striking the bottom, Brueys preferred to think in terms of the anchorage at Aboukir (Abu Qir) which is about twenty-seven miles east of

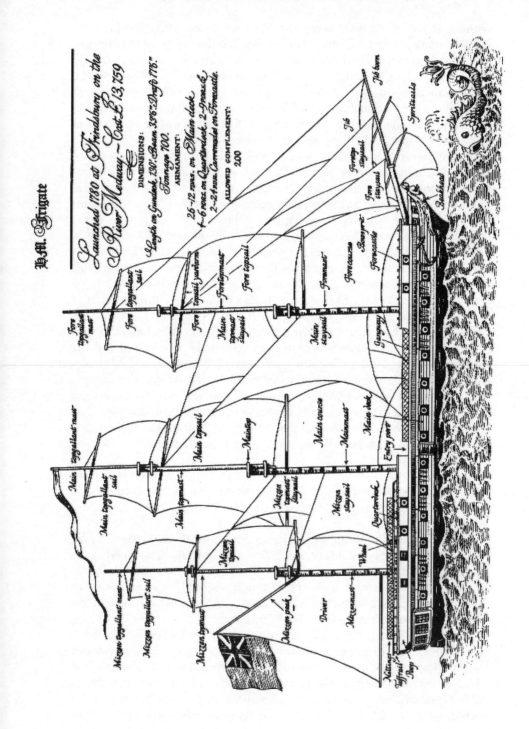

H.M. Frigate

Launched 1780 at Frindsbury on the River Medway — Cost £13,759

DIMENSIONS:
Length on Gundeck 130'; Beam 35'6"; Draft 17'6".
Tonnage 700.

ARMAMENT:
26-12 guns. on Main deck
+6 guns. on Quarterdeck. 2-guns. &
2-24-guns. Carronades on Forecastle.

ALLOWED COMPLEMENT:
200

the Nile. Here the shore shelves very slowly which meant that Brueys needed to moor his squadron three miles from the shore. The only protection provided by nature was the small island of Aboukir which is situated a few cable-lengths off the western point of the bay, together with some rocks and sandbanks.

The French squadron anchored in a single column while the van headed towards Aboukir Island with the 74-gun ships *Guerrier*, *Conquerant*, *Spartiale*, *Peuple*, *Souverain* and *Aquilon* forming the van with the 80-gun *Franklin* flying the flag of Rear-Admiral Blanquet du Chayla. Next in the line came Brueys' flagship, the powerful 120-gun *Orient*, seventh in the line of thirteen, followed by the 80-gun *Tonnant* and the 74-gun ships *Heureux* and *Mercure*. Four frigates of 36 to 40 guns, commanded by Rear-Admiral Decres were moored inshore of the bigger warships.

Brueys, thanks to his phobia about running aground, gave himself a handsome margin of error – far too generous, as later events were to prove. For example, *Guerrier* could have been much closer to the island and, indeed, the entire French line could have been half a nautical mile closer to the land with some advantage. All the same, the French seemed to have deployed a strong position.

As might have been anticipated, it was not very long before Nelson obtained knowledge of the French landing in Egypt. Brueys was fully aware that the British Admiral would not indulge in a moment's relaxation until he had discovered the whereabouts of his enemy's ships of war, even if the exercise involved surveying every harbour along the suspect coastline. It appeared that all that Brueys could reasonably do was to arrange to give the British an appropriate reception.

This said, the French senior officers could not achieve agreement among themselves. Councils of War, unless the presiding senior officer is a strong and decisive chairman, can be disastrous and can be used as an excuse to spread the blame if things should go awry. Perhaps these practices are reminiscent of the adage that 'a camel is a horse put together by a committee'. In this instance, the council convened by Brueys can be said to have been similar to that indulged in by Quieret, Behuchet and Barbavera shortly before the Battle of Sluys, many years earlier.

Brueys, who had no experience of commanding a force of warships in action, failed to sense that his best opportunity was to seize the initiative rather than to await quiescently in the bay. Chayla pressed on him the advantages of selecting the time and place of engagement, of doing his best to take the enemy by surprise and working his ships with the aim of trying to ensure that the wind direction would be in their favour. Du Chayla could be counted as one of the most experienced officers in the French fleet. He had twenty-three years of experience at sea behind him, had participated in some thirteen battles and suffered from wounds on several occasions. He advised: 'Our only chance is to fight under sail.' The commanding officer of *Tonnant* supported him: 'We have no hope if we wait for Nelson in this awkward situation. We must weigh at once!'

Brueys was in a quandary. His Chief-of-Staff, Ganteaume, held an entirely contradictory point of view. He pointed out the poor state of the French ships and that it was not realistic to fight in the open sea, which was probably true enough. In the final event, Brueys decided to remain on the defensive. If fighting there had to be, it would be with French ships at anchor; they would be prepared for, but would not seek, battle.

Given this state of affairs, it might be imagined that the French would set up some shore batteries, or, at the very least, turn Aboukir Island into a strong point. However, all that was done was to mount some five or six pounders and a couple of mortars on the island, which was not sufficient to command the channel between it and *Guerrier* which was lying at the head of the French column.

The days passed rapidly for the French. However, their squadron lay so far offshore that furnishing the ships with necessary supplies presented a number of problems, for example, boats needed to act as ferries between the warships and the shore in the endless quest for food and drinking water. The better part of half Brueys' ships' companies were busy ashore digging wells or skirmishing, in the naval sense, for food. The working parties often went as far afield as Rosetta in their search for sources of provender.

The inevitable befell at 1300 on 1 August 1798, when the lookout on board *Heureux* reported a dozen sails to the north-north-west. This was the British squadron sailing majestically in column under a full spread of canvas and with a following wind. The afternoon was a fine and sunny one, and the sea was calm, scarcely disturbed by the freshening wind.

Brueys dispatched two gun boats on a scouting exercise, but it was somewhat late to think of that. Incidentally, no duty frigates had been sent to sea for the past three weeks. Brueys rapidly saw that the hawsers were rigged between his ships to discourage the enemy from trying to break through the French line. Boats were sent away to bring back as many as possible from the working parties on shore. However, it has been estimated that over four thousand men did not return to their ships in time to participate in the engagement. They must have been sorely missed.

Some writers have made much of the fact that neither Nelson nor his captains were well acquainted with the coast,and the charts they held were not very good. Captain Foley, who has been given the credit for running a well-found and taut ship, had the latest chart in the British squadron which was twenty years old. The age of a chart does not necessarily matter. A number of modern charts are based upon surveys carried out during the nineteenth century, but, of course, mariners rely upon the fact that the Hydrographic Department keeps them up-to-date and issues corrections in the form of such media as Notices to Mariners.

This said, Nelson displayed great confidence in the ability of his captains and himself by running into the attack. The reasoning was that where there was room for a French ship to swing when at single anchor, there would be room for a British ship to pass on either side. It may be construed as a bit of luck that Brueys' ships had anchored only by the bow. This left gaps between the ships which made the French defensive line less strong than might have been the case. The second piece of luck was that the wind was blowing ideally for entrance into Aboukir Bay.

Hood in *Zealous* headed the line and kept taking soundings as he worked his way in. *Goliath* passed between Aboukir Island and *Guerrier*. In *Goliath*, Foley took the logic of being able to pass farther on either side of the French and with the exercise of inspired initiative, turned his ship around and inside the French line; a manoeuvre which hardly anyone expected, least of all, Brueys. On his landward side, his ships' ports were closed and the big guns were cluttered with unwanted bric-a-brac, such as barrels, items of furniture and pots of paint. *Goliath* was followed to an inshore position by *Zealous* and *Theseus*.

Audacious penetrated the French line from seaward, passing between the first two ships of the French van. Nelson's *Vanguard* engaged the French from their seaward side. He was trailed by the rest of the squadron with the exception of *Culloden* which now ran aground, to the chagrin of her commanding officer, Captain Troubridge. On the credit side, it has been argued that *Culloden* acted as a beacon and might well have saved other vessels from suffering a similar mishap. Troubridge, of course, was devastated at being out of the battle as he did not contrive to refloat his ship until the following morning.

It is a temptation to go into more detail about the Battle of the Nile, but that is beyond the scope of this work. To summarise: the French van was vanquished by the application of superior numbers and firepower at a limited part of the enemy squadron. Nelson's adage of 'only numbers will annihilate' was seen being exerted with masterful skill. The wind was blowing down the French line which meant that their rearmost warships could do nothing to assist their compatriots. Those in the rear could really do nothing but wait helplessly as the focal point of the engagement edged inexorably in their direction.

Admiral Brueys' flagship was stationed in a fairly conventional position at about the centre of the French column. The flagship was the, by those days, vast *L'Orient*, armed with a hundred and twenty pieces of ordnance. At about 2100 she had started to succumb to that dreaded enemy of the wooden ship, fire; and, depite the courageous efforts of her ship's company, the flames were soon taking control of the proceedings. The French Admiral was, by this time, fatally wounded, and Commodore Casabianca, the Captain of the Fleet, was also severely injured. The young Casabianca was with his father, whom he flatly refused to abandon. The gallant lad inspired the poem 'The boy stood on the burning deck' which it was almost mandatory to learn verbatim when I was at school. Apart from any intrinsic merit of the poetry, the story was, no doubt, intended to instil virtues such as loyalty and bravery into the subconscious minds of those who had to commit the blessed lines to memory.

Shortly after 2200 the fire reached *L'Orient*'s magazine and the great ship blew up with an immense detonation which was heard a good ten miles away by French contingents in Rosetta and its neighbourhood. All fighting stopped for a moment, and a bewildered silence settled over Aboukir Bay for a brief time. *L'Orient* took with her all the spoils of Malta which had been stored on board.

At this time, all the ships making up the French van had been effectively dealt with; and the tiring British were starting to progress towards the rear of the French line.

Nelson had received a severe wound as he had been hit on the forehead by a piece of broken roundshot which resulted in a flap of skin hanging over his good eye. This temporarily blinded him, and provided one of the occasions when the Admiral thought that he had received a mortal injury. He staggered into his flag captain's arms saying that he was killed and asked to be remembered to his wife. The wound was messy, but not lethal, and within the hour he had begun to work on his dispatch. Nelson wrote: 'Victory is not a name strong enough for such a scene.'

The light of dawn on the following day revealed that he and his ships had gained a spectacular victory over their opponents. The Battle of the Nile was a great naval triumph for the British, but it could well be asked that some thought be given to the relevance of convoys to the overall picture.

In the first instance, the 35,000-odd French troops which were landed in Egypt were carried there in four hundred transports sailing in convoy and escorted by the French naval vessels which later became Nelson's prey in Aboukir Bay. The concept of this evolution was perfectly correct: but matters went wrong when the French escorting force was taken apart by Nelson's ships in Aboukir Bay.

Perhaps one of the main results of the Battle of the Nile was that an army was bottled up in Egypt until finally defeated by General Sir Ralph Abercromby, whose army disposed of the remains of Napoleon's garrison of Egypt on 1 March 1801. Sadly, Abercromby himself was killed during this engagement.

The French did not have the ability to gather together a suitable convoy and escort to retrieve the force which had been left in Egypt. Napoleon himself managed to engineer an escape to France in the *Muiron* during the second half of August 1799. His somewhat contrived justification for sailing off did not impress the men he had left behind who, on the whole, considered that they had been left in the lurch.

Another side effect of the Battle of the Nile was that it showed other countries that the French were not invincible; and it encouraged the belief that, given the right circumstances, they could be defeated.

The Battle of the Nile also put paid to French ambitions to look farther towards the rising sun, in particular, to dabble in Indian affairs, after they had, say, made a move into Turkey, the Levant or, of course, Egypt. France had a diligent ally in the person of Tippoo Sahib who could probably help to support their ambitions directed towards the sub-continent and to the disservice of Britannia.

Thanks to the British success in Aboukir Bay, the need to keep open the all-important sea-trade which provided life-giving funds to stimulate and nourish the country's war effort, the movement of convoys and shipping in general in the Mediterranean was simplified and army units had a freedom of movement which was not available to land powers, however formidable the size of their armies.

APPENDIX III

The Thoughts of an American Admiral

To: Secretary of the Navy.
Through Admiralty. From Queenstown.
Sent: June 28, 1917.
Admiralty for Secretary Navy Washington, providing it meets
Admiralty's full approval.
From Admiral Sims.

Referring to the Department's opinion, reported in last two cables, to the effect that adequate armament and trained crews constitute one of the most effective defensive anti-submarine measures, I again submit with all possible stress the following based on extended [Allied] war experience. The measures demanded, if enemy defeat in time is to be assured, are not defensive but offensive defensive. The merchantman's inherent weakness is lack of speed and protection. Guns are no defense against torpedo attack without warning, which is necessarily the enemy method of attack against armed ships. In this area alone during the last six weeks thirty armed ships were sunk by torpedoes without submarine being seen, although three of these were escorted, each by a single destroyer. The result would of course have been the same no matter how many guns these ships carried or what their caliber. Three mystery ships, heavily manned by expert naval crews with much previous experience with submarine attack, have recently been torpedoed without warning. Another case within the month of mystery ship engaging submarine with gunfire at six thousand yards but submarine submerged and approached unseen and torpedoed ship at close range. The ineffectiveness of heaviest batteries against submarine attack is conclusively shown by Admiralty's practise always sending destroyers to escort their men-of-war. The comparative immunity of the relatively small number American ships, especially liners, is believed here to be due to the enemy's hopes that the pacifist movement will succeed. Cases are on record of submarines making successful gun attacks from advantageous sun position against armed ships without ship being able to see submarine. I submit that if submarine campaign is to be defeated it must be by offensive measures. The enemy submarine mission must be destruction of shipping and avoidance of anti-submarine craft. Enemy submarines are now using for their final approach an auxiliary periscope less than two inches in diameter. This information just acquired. All of the experience in this submarine campaign to date demonstrates that it would be a seriously dangerous misapprehension to base our action on the assumption that any armament on merchantman is any protection against submarines which are willing to use their torpedoes. The British have now definitely decided the adoption, to the maximum practicable extent, convoys from sixteen to twenty ships. This is an offensive measure against submarines, as the latter will be subject to the attack of our anti-submarine craft whenever they come within torpedoing distance of convoyed merchantmen. Moreover it permits of concentrated attack by our forces and obliges the enemy to disperse his forces to cover the various routes of approach.

Concerning Department's reference to a scheme for protection of merchant shipping which will not interfere with present escort duties, I submit that the time element alone prevents utilization of any new anti-submarine invention. The campaign may easily be lost before any such schemes can come into effective operation. The enemy is certainly counting on maximum effort being exerted before long nights and bad weather of autumn, that is, in next three months. Heaviest effort may be anticipated in July and August. I again submit that protection of our coastlines and of Allied shipping must necessarily be carried out in field of enemy activity if it is to be effective. The mission of the Allies must be to force submarines to give battle. Hence no operations in home waters should take precedence over, or be allowed to diminish, the maximum effort we can exert in area in which enemy is operating, and must continue to operate in order to succeed.

SIMS.

APPENDIX IV

The Advantages of the Convoy System

London,
June 29, 1917.

From: Commander U.S. Naval Forces operating in European Waters.
To: Secretary of the Navy (Operations).
Subject: General report concerning military situation

1. I feel that there is little to add to my recent cable despatches which, in view of the importance of the time element, have been made full and detailed.

2. To sum up my despatches briefly, I would repeat that I consider that the military situation is very grave indeed on account of the success of the enemy submarine campaign.

If the shipping losses continue as they have during the past four months, it is submitted that the Allies will be forced to dire straits indeed, if they will not actually be forced into an unsatisfactory peace.

The present rate of destruction is very much greater than the rate of building, and the shortage of tonnage is already so great that the efficiency of the naval forces is already reduced by lack of oil. Orders have just been given to use three-fifths speed, except in cases of emergency. This simply means that the enemy is winning the war.

3. My reasons for being so insistent in my cable despatches have been because of my conviction that measures of co-operation which we may take will be inefficient if they are not put into operation immediately, that is, within a month.

There is every reason to believe that the maximum enemy submarine effort will occur between now and the first of November, reaching its height probably during the latter part of July, if not earlier.

4. There is certainly no sovereign solution for the submarine menace except through well-established methods of warfare based upon fundamental military principles.

5. It is submitted that the cardinal principle of concentration of effort is at present being pursued by the enemy and not by the Allies.

6. We are dispersing our forces while the enemy is concentrating his. The enemy's submarine mission is and must continue to be the destruction of merchant shipping. The limitations of submarines and the distances over which they must operate prevent them from attacking our naval forces, that is, anti-submarine craft. They cannot afford to engage anti-submarine craft with guns; they must use torpedoes. If they should do so to any considerable extent their limited supply would greatly reduce their period of operation away from base, and the number of merchant-men they could destroy. Their object is to avoid contact with anti-submarine craft. This they can almost always do, as the submarine can see the surface craft at many times the distance the surface craft can see the periscope, particularly one less than two inches in diameter.

Moreover, the submarine greatly fears the anti-submarine craft because of the great danger of the depth charges. Our tactics should therefore be such as to force the submarine to incur this danger in order to get within range of merchantmen.

7. It therefore seems to go without question that the only course for us to pursue is to revert to the ancient practice of convoy. This will be purely an offensive measure, because if we concentrate our shipping into convoys and protect it with our naval forces we will thereby force the enemy, in order to carry out his mission, to encounter naval forces which are not embarrassed with valuable cargoes, and which are a great danger to the submarine. At present our naval forces are wearing down their personnel and material in an attempted combination of escorting single ships, when they can be picked up, and also of attempting to seek and offensively engage an enemy whose object is to avoid such encounters. With the convoy system the conditions can be reversed. Although the enemy may easily know when our convoys sail, he can never know the course they will pursue or the route of approach to their destinations. Our escorting forces will thus be able to work on a deliberate prearranged plan, preserving their oil supplies and energy, while the enemy will be forced to disperse his forces and seek us. In a word, the handicap we now labor under will be shifted to the enemy: we will have adopted the essential principle of concentration while the enemy will lose it.

8. The most careful and thorough study of the convoy system made by the British Admiralty shows clearly that while we may have some losses under this system, owing to lack of adequate number of anti-submarine craft, they nevertheless will not be critical as they are at present.

9. I again submit that if the Allied campaign is to be viewed as a whole, there is no necessity for any high sea protection on our coast. The submarine as a type of war vessel possesses no unusual characteristics different from those of other naval craft, with the single exception of its ability to submerge for a limited time. The difficulty of maintaining distant bases is the same for the submarine as it is for other craft. As long

as we maintain control of the sea as far as surface craft are concerned, there can be no fear of the enemy establishing submarine bases in the Western Hemisphere.

10. To take an extreme illustration, if the enemy could be led or forced into diverting part of his submarine effort to the United States coast, or to any other area distant from the critical area surrounding the coast of France and the United Kingdom, the anti-submarine campaign would at once be won. The enemy labors under severe difficulties in carrying out his campaign, even in this restricted area, owing to the material limitations and the distances they must operate from their bases, through extremely dangerous localities. The extent of the United States coastline and the distances between its principal commercial ports preclude the possibility of any submarine effort in that part of the world except limited operations of diversion designed to affect public opinion, and thereby hold our forces from the vital field of action.

11. The difficulties confronting the convoy system are, of course, considerable. They are primarily involved in the widely dispersed ports of origin of merchant shipping; the difficulty of communication by cable; the time involved by communications by mail; and the difficulties of obtaining a co-operation and co-ordination between Allied Governments.

As reported by cable despatch, the British Government has definitely reached the decision to put the convoy system into operation as far as its ability goes. Convoys from Hampton Roads, Canada, Mediterranean, and Scandinavian countries are already in operation. Convoys from New York will be put in operation as soon as ships are available. The British navy is already strained beyond its capacity, and I therefore urgently recommend that we co-operate, at least to the extent of handling convoys from New York.

12. The dangers to convoys from high sea raiders is remote, but, of course, must be provided against, and hence the necessity for escorting cruisers or reserve battleships. The necessity is even greater, however, for anti-submarine craft in the submarine war zone.

13. As stated in my despatches, the arming of merchantmen is not a solution of the submarine menace, it serves the single purpose of forcing the submarine to use torpedoes instead of guns and bombs. The facts that men-of-war cannot proceed safely at sea without escort, and that in the Queenstown avenue of approach alone in the past six weeks there have been thirty armed merchantmen sunk, without having seen the submarine at all before the attack, seem to be conclusive evidence. A great mass of other evidence and war experience could be collected in support of the above.

14. The week ending June 19th has been one of great submarine activity. Evidence indicates that fifteen to nineteen of the largest and latest submarines have been operating, of which ten to thirteen were operating

in the critical area to the west and south-west of the British Isles. The above numbers are exclusive of the smaller and earlier type of submarines, and submarines carrying mines alone. Two submarines are working to the westward of the Straits of Gibraltar. A feature of the week was the sinking of ships as far west as nineteen degrees. Three merchant ship convoys are en route from Hampton Roads, the last one,consisting of eighteen ships, having sailed on the 19th of June. One hundred and sixteen moored mines have been swept up during the week.

Twenty-two reports of encounters with enemy submarines in waters surrounding the United Kingdom have been reported during the week – three by destroyers, two by cruisers, two by mystery ships, one by French gunboat, three by submarines, nine by auxiliary patrol vessels, one by seaplane, and one by merchant vessel.

(Signed) Wm. S. Sims

APPENDIX V

Monthly Losses from Enemy Action
February 1917–October 1918

During the twenty-one months of unrestricted submarine warfare from February 1917 to October 1918 inclusive, 3,843 merchant vessels (British fishing vessels included) of a total gross tonnage of 8,478,947 have been sunk by enemy action, a monthly average of 183 vessels totalling 403,760 gross tons. The October tonnage losses show a decrease from this average of 291,333 tons or 72 per cent.

The following table gives the tonnage losses by months from February 1917 to October 1918 inclusive:

Month	British Merchant Vessels	Other Allied Merchant Vessels	Neutral Merchant Vessels	British Fishing Vessels	Total
1917					
February	313,486	84,820	135,090	3,478	536,334
March	353,478	81,151	165,225	3,586	603,440
April	545,282	134,448	189,373	5,920	875,023
May	352,289	102,960	137,957	1,448	594,654
June	417,925	126,171	139,229	1,342	684,667
July	364,858	111,683	70,370	2,736	549,647
August	329,810	128,489	53,018	242	511,559
September	196,212	119,086	29,941	245	345,484
October	276,132	127,932	54,432	227	458,723
November	173,560	87,646	31,476	87	292,769
December	253,087	86,981	54,047	413	394,528
1918					
January	179,973	87,078	35,037	375	302,463
February	226,896	54,904	36,374	686	318,860
March	199,458	94,321	51,035	293	345,107
April	215,453	50,879	11,361	241	277,934
May	192,436	80,826	20,757	504	294,523

June	162,990	51,173	38,474	639	253,276
July	165,449	70,900	23,552	555	260,456
August	145,721	91,209	41,946	1,455	280,331
September	136,864	39,343	10,393	142	186,742
October	57,607	41,308	13,512	—	112,427

APPENDIX VI

Tonnage constructed by Allied and Neutral Nations since August 1914

Construction of merchant shipping is shown in the following table, which gives tonnage completed since the beginning of the war for the United Kingdom, United States and for other Allied and Neutral Nations

Period	United Kingdom Gross tons	United States Gross tons	Other Allied and Neutral Gross tons	World Total Gross tons
1914	675,610	120,000*	217,310	1,012,920
1915	650,919	225,122	325,929	1,202,000
1916	541,552	325,413	821,036	1,688,000
1917	1,163,474	1,034,296	505,585	2,703,355
1918 1st ¼	320,280	328,541	220,496	869,317
1918 2nd „	442,966	559,939	240,369	1,243,274
1918 3rd „	411,395	834,250	232,127	1,477,772
1918 October	136,100	357,532	50,000	543,632
1918 (10 mths)	1,310,741	2,080,262	742,992	4,133,995

* estimated.

APPENDIX VII

The Clyde Escort Force and Clyde Area

A large part of the material upon which this Appendix is based was taken from notes made by the late Lieutenant Commander Gordon Davies MBE, RNVR. Gordon Davies served for a significant part of the Second World War in the then new headquarters in Liverpool.

The up-to-date operations centre for the Western Approaches was opened in Derby House on 7 February 1941. Admiral Sir Percy Noble was appointed Commander-in-Chief Western Approaches on 17 February 1941. The directive to Admiral Noble from the Admiralty sounded disarmingly simple. He was to be responsible for the protection of trade, the routeing and control of outward and homebound convoys, ocean convoys, and measures to deal with attacks on convoys by U-boats or hostile aircraft within his command. There was also the vitally important need to maintain close contact with Air-Vice Marshal J M Robb, RAF (and his staff) commanding 15 Group Coastal Command, responsible for air operations in the north-western approaches.

To return more closely to the Clyde, the Twelfth Destroyer Flotilla was formed in August 1940 and the idea was that it should be attached to the Home Fleet. Captain D K Bain RN was in charge serving as Captain D12 in the destroyer HMS *Keppel*. As a matter of passing interest, *Keppel* sailed from Greenock to Scapa Flow, then returned to the Clyde as her boilers needed to be re-tubed. Captain 'D' and his staff moved ashore to St Enoch's Hotel while the re-tubing exercise was being carried out.

The Twelfth Destroyer Flotilla at this time was made up of a 'mixed bag' of a number of 'A' Class destroyers and some 'V's and 'W's of World War I vintage.

At this period convoys were only escorted to about twelve degrees west and the group system, as it was later to be known, had not seen the light of day. Circa mid-October 1940, Captain D12 shifted to shore offices at Greenock; the address being Navy House, Clarence Street, to administer the destroyers working with convoys.

In April 1941 a number of the ex-American Town Class destroyers arrived in the Clyde and came under the administrative umbrella of Captain D12, who later assumed the title of Captain 'D', Greenock.

Escort Groups were organised during early 1941 and were made up of destroyers of both British and American origin, corvettes and trawlers. There were no special 'convoy instructions' until the end of 1940 as the only ships engaged in this activity were Fleet Destroyers which meant a certain level of uniformity.

The increase in the number of types of ship employed in the work of escorting convoys led the Commander-in-Chief Western Approaches, who was based at Plymouth during the earlier days of World War II, to issue a document which rejoiced in the abbreviated name of WACIs (Western Approaches Convoy Instructions). The first issue of these directives consisted of a few typewritten pages of instructions with some diagrams, as appropriate.

The Clyde Escort Force was made up, by the beginning of 1941, of ships belonging to the British, Canadian, French and Polish navies; and the types of ship were essentially destroyers, corvettes and trawlers. By mid-1941 the Canadian destroyers had left Greenock and had crossed the Atlantic to be based at Canadian ports.

The destroyer depot ship, stationed at Greenock during the earlier period of the war, was HMS *Hecla*. *Hecla* departed from Greenock in July 1941, and was relieved by the repair ship *Greenwich*, followed, shortly afterwards, by *Sandhurst*.

The two main groups of naval ships based on Greenock during the year 1941 were the Third Escort Group of twenty-two ships consisting of seven destroyers, nine corvettes and six trawlers; and the Fourth Escort Group composed of twenty-one ships including seven destroyers, ten corvettes and four trawlers. A fairly steady stream of new corvettes arrived during the year to join the Clyde Escort Force.

The B3 Group was organised in February 1942. This Group remained in being until the Invasion of Normandy began in June 1944. The B3 Group was a three-nation outfit formed of British, Polish and French ships. The Senior Officer of the Group was, in turn, Commander H P Henderson (later Captain Henderson), Commander A A Tait (lost when HMS *Harvester* was torpedoed in April 1943) and Commander Evans who left the Group shortly before the Normandy Invasion and who later became the Training Captain, Western Approaches.

Convoys to North Russia became a regular commitment to Greenock-based ships during 1942. Ships from the Clyde took part in practically all the North Russian convoys until the end of World War II in Europe.

The late summer of 1942 was particularly notable for the extremely large number of escort vessels which were sent to the Clyde to screen ships earmarked to cover the North Africa invasion. The code name given to this major operation was Operation TORCH. This was to inflict upon Greenock the most hectic peak of activity which, as an escort base, it has possibly ever known, in that all the escorts for the first convoys destined for North Africa sailed from the Clyde. I use the word 'possibly' with intent as I was a serving teenage midshipman in the battleship *Warspite* when a most impressive armada of ships left the Clyde in early June 1944, destination Normandy.

Few, if any, would attempt to deny that Greenock was one of the main ports of departure for ships of many shapes and sizes which left the Clyde area for major naval operations in the Second World War, whether fighting the *Bismarck* or *Scharnhorst* or pitched battles with U-boats in the Atlantic and northern Russian seas.

APPENDIX VIII
The Russian Convoys
The Torture of Convoy PQ17

The military prowess of the Axis powers seemed to be victorious practically everywhere in July 1942. Rommel was advancing on Alexandria so expeditiously that the British Fleet was giving serious consideration to the wisdom of withdrawal from that port. The Germans appeared all too likely to be capable of reaching the Suez Canal. To shift attention to the Russian front, Sebastopol, for long having had the reputation of being the most impregnable fortified area in the world, fell to the Germans in July after putting up a dogged resistance for twenty-five days. The German Army was building itself up for the great summer offensive to reach Stalingrad and the Volga river by autumn 1942.

At about the same time, the Germans gained a most decisive triumph at sea by sinking twenty-two out of the thirty-three merchant ships in a convoy to Russia. PQ17 was the largest of the convoys which had then been despatched via that often ghastly route to Murmansk. A very strong escort group had been provided; and a strong force of capital ships had been sailed out of Scapa Flow to cover the convoy's passage. To add to the potential joys of a summer get-together in northern waters, German heavy ships were diverted to put to sea. In the final event, there was no clash between the opposing capital ships, perhaps due to the fact that neither side appeared to be too enthusiastic at the prospect of risking them. Whatever the reason, the Germans scored a tactical success all the same.

When the British Admiralty were made aware that the German heavy warships were at sea, the order was given for the convoy to 'scatter'. The result of this was that the merchant ships, from the dispersing convoy, were exposed to appalling attacks by German submarines and aircraft. Many were lost.

The time has come to switch attention to the 'raison d'être' for the forming of Russia-bound convoys at this point in World War II. The only practicable route for the supply of Anglo–American war material to Russia was via the Arctic, in particular to Murmansk. Russia was separated from her allies by land. The Baltic and the Black Seas were both blocked by the enemy.

Authors covering the problems which arose when it was decided to supply the Russians with war material generally write a few words saying that there was an overland supply route from the Persian Gulf. However, communications with Russian industrial areas were under threat from the enemy until quite late in the war, and, in any case, were of indifferent quality and extremely lengthy. The same criteria applied to the supply of goods via Vladivostok in the Far East.

Problems of supplying the Russians also occurred during World War I. The port of Archangel had been the principal place of entry at that time. Murmansk was little more than a fishing village. It owed its expansion to the description of 'port' to the fact that it is ice-free throughout the year, while Archangel tends to be frozen over for rather more than six months per annum.

The early Russian convoys were sailed from Britain during the summer of the year 1941 and initially made their way through with very little if any difficulty. Some one hundred and eleven ships had arrived at Archangel or Murmansk by 1 March 1942, and seventy-eight had got back to Britain. This for the loss of one merchantman and one escorting vessel. So far, so good; but German counter-measures were not very long a'coming.

The German Naval Command had started to move large warships to fjords in northern Norway during January 1942. The very new battleship *Tirpitz* made her first appearance on 6 March, when Convoy PQ12 was en route to Murmansk and Convoy P8 was tracking westward from Russia. The great ship's appearance was only of the fleeting variety, and no engagement occurred. One vessel in the west-bound convoy, the Russian *Liora*, which was straggling in the rear, was 'snapped up' by *Frederick Ihn*, which was a member of *Tirpitz*'s destroyer screen. This was a cautionary notice of what might be in store for future Allied convoys.

Thirteen ships, sailing in Convoy PQ13, were lost in April, thanks to the combined efforts of German destroyers and dive-bombers stationed in northern Norway. Admiral Doenitz recalled a number of German submarines from the Atlantic; and during the long hours of daylight in the northern summer the Russian convoys were uncovered to air attacks, raids by surface warships and onslaughts from submarines with no hours of darkness to bring spells of relief.

In May 1942 Convoy PQ16 was the object of simultaneous assaults by a pack of some half a dozen U-boats and several squadrons of aircraft – making a total deployment of over three hundred military aircraft. In this instance, the U-boats were repulsed; but the aircraft managed to sink seven merchantmen from a convoy of thirty-four vessels being escorted.

The above figures were bad enough; but considerably worse was to follow. The Nazi Naval Command proposed the employment of all the naval might which could be made available against the next British convoy destined for Russia. By the month of June 1942, *Tirpitz* had been reinforced by the presence of the heavy cruiser *Admiral Hipper;* and the two pocket-battleships *Lutzow* (formerly *Deutschland*) and *Admiral Scheer* were based on Narvik. Together with half a dozen large destroyers, the Germans had assembled something in the nature of a battle fleet.

The Eleventh U-boat Flotilla (about a dozen units) was based on Bergen, and the Fifth Luftflotte (Fleet Air Arm equivalent), with in excess of three hundred aircraft, was at the air bases of Barderfoss, between Narvik and Tromso, and Banak, a shortish distance east of North Cape. The co-ordinated manoeuvering of these units was assigned the code-name 'Rosselsprung' ('Knight's move' in the game of chess), and the overall control put under the command of Admiral Carls, who was responsible for the northern theatre of operations and whose command headquarters was situated at Kiel. The Admiral's desires were focused on heartfelt wishes to gain a notable victory which would compare favourably with the Army's triumphs. This should lift the morale of those who manned the capital ships whose inactivity had, without doubt, given rise to something of an inferiority complex with regard to the exploits of U-boats and air crews.

Unfortunately for the Germans, there were unwelcome complications in the chain of command. The Luftflotte squadrons were not under the direct orders of Admiral Carls. The Admiral had a liaison officer attached to the staff of Colonel-General Stumpf, the commander of the air squadrons, but Stumpf came under the control of Goering. Admiral Schniewind, commander of the naval forces, wearing his flag in *Tirpitz,* was under Carls' orders, but above was Grand-Admiral Raeder and one Adolf Hitler. The potential snags arising from this hierarchy are worth a moment's study.

Admiral Raeder was definitely not one to create difficulties over the planned use of surface warships; nor was Admiral Doenitz in the case of submarines. Sadly for the Germans, Hitler was Commander-in-Chief of all the Nazi armed forces; and he made a habit of continually interfering with and hampering the naval effort throughout World War II. For example, *Tirpitz* could not be moved by so much as a cable-length without his consent. He was responsible for the directions which could have turned Operation ROSSELSPRUNG into a complete 'pot mess', to use a naval phrase. The fact that the opposite was the case can, in no way, be credited to the Führer's naval leadership ability.

Admiral Carls sought an increased level of air reconnaissance in early June, but he was unable to impress the Fifth Luftflotte with the importance of giving 'early warning' of the sailing of an Allied convoy. Stumpf's officers appeared to be so proud of their success against the previous convoy that they wished to hold their bombers in readiness to attack the next. Carls, therefore, was obliged to rely upon U-boats for the informa-tion he required. Three submarines set out on 10 June to patrol the route which was normally favoured by the enemy convoys. Two more followed on 16 June, and by the time convoy PQ17 sailed from Iceland about ten U-boats were on the prowl along its route.

The British Admiralty was aware of the increasing strength of the hostile forces based on Norway and provided strong cover for convoy PQ17. The close escort, under Commander Broome in the destroyer *Keppel*, was made up of six destroyers, two anti-aircraft vessels, two submarines and eleven armed trawlers, minesweepers and corvettes. Four cruisers commanded by Rear-Admiral Dalrymple-Hamilton steamed one hundred miles ahead of the convoy to afford a more distant escort facility. Admiral Tovey, Commander-in-Chief, Home Fleet, sailed from Scapa Flow with the battleship *Duke of York*, the United States battleship *Washington*, the aircraft carrier *Victorious*, three cruisers and a number of destroyers. The aim of this force was to cover the passage of the convoy as far as Bear Island, ready to interfere in the event of the German battle fleet putting in an appearance. In addition, nine submarines were on patrol north-west of North Cape. Four or five Russian submarines were stationed off the entrance to the fjords in which the German capital ships were anchored. The total number of warships engaged in covering convoy PQ17 was appreciably greater than that of the merchant vessels making up the convoy. Taking into account the call upon Allied resources by the Battle of the Atlantic, the contest in the Mediterranean and war in the Pacific, this must be looked upon as quite an astonishing 'tour de force' of organisation.

Twenty-two of the ships in the convoy were United States freighters, and two were Soviet tankers. Also present were one British tanker and three rescue ships. The convoy assembled off Iceland observing the usual procedures. Some of the ships steamed round from Reykjavik and through the Denmark Strait in the direction of Jan Mayen Island, while the others departed from Seydisfjord on the east coast of Iceland and joined up forty-eight hours later.

Matters did not pan out well from the beginning. One merchant vessel took to the ground while getting away from Reykjavik; another was severely damaged by ice floes and was obliged to return to harbour. This meant that there were only thirty-three ships in the convoy when the commanding officer of U-255, Lieutenant Reinhard Reche, transmitted a signal to report that he had sighted the ships of PQ17 some sixty miles east of Jan Mayen Island. The U-408 confirmed this report a short time later. No messages had been received from German aircraft. Admiral Carls' immediate action was to direct the U-boat pack to attack and to maintain contact with the convoy. This was on 2 July when the convoy was five days out. The weather was bad, but the escorting destroyers were at 'full alert' and the hostile submarines scored no successes. Later in the day, at about 1815, the first dive bombers put in an appearance. The Fifth

Luftflotte maintained its attacks for an hour and a half, but were kept at bay by well-directed anti-aircraft fire.

The next day the convoy reached a position north-west of Bear Island and altered to an easterly course. For Russian convoys this was invariably a most dangerous section of the voyage because convoys were then at their nearest to the German air bases. An added complication was that the ice-cap prevented ships from keeping more to the northward.

This stretch of the voyage was especially perilous for convoy PQ17 due to the fact that the covering force was soon withdrawn. Admiral Tovey's ships were some distance from the convoy and were not visible to the merchant vessels; but their presence was known which acted as a source of some comfort.

The British Admiralty's assessment of the situation seems to have been that should the German capital ships make an appearance while the convoy was still to the west of Bear Island, the engagement would be fought in favourable conditions, due to the fact that the area was out of the range of the German air bases. On the reverse side of the coin, if the German warships did not appear, Admiral Tovey would retire westwards in the hope that the German battle fleet might be drawn in pursuit. In either of the above eventualities the convoy would escape attack by the big German surface ships. It would have the U-boats and the bombers to cope with; but these were not the main business of Admiral Tovey's large warships.

Admiral Dalrymple-Hamilton's cruisers were directed not to proceed farther than longitude twenty-five degrees east (that of North Cape). If *Tirpitz* then turned up, contrary to expectations, the convoy would need to 'scatter' and to make for Novaya Zemlya, or try to reach Archangel on an independent basis. In the final event, Admiral Dalrymple-Hamilton exceeded his orders and proceeded as far east as longitude thirty, before being ordered to return. It was at this stage that disaster fell upon the convoy.

In the meantime on the side of the Germans, the two battleships and the two cruisers had left their bases late on 2 July with the aim of concentrating in Altenfjord, closer to North Cape. *Lutzow,* however, scraped her bottom while making her way down the Tjelle-Sund in a thick mist, and had to return to Narvik. A similar accident the following day damaged three destroyers in a fjord in the Lofoten Islands. Continuous fog was impeding German plans. Air surveillance was impracticable; and for thirty-six hours the convoy had been advancing without any intervention by the enemy. The Germans did not consider that the Allies would prevent their heavy ships from approaching within range of Stumpf's dive-bombers, a conviction which was absolutely correct. This implied that *Tirpitz* could put to sea and attack on 4 or 5 July without much risk to herself.

Hitler, as previously mentioned, would not tolerate losses. He had expressly forbidden an attack by *Tirpitz,* if an aircraft carrier should be in the locality, if superiority should be uncertain, if, if, if . . . It is well nigh impossible to wage effective war in the face of such constraints.

The fog lifted on the morning of 4 July. The first air attack on the convoy came when it was north of Bear Island. A torpedo-carrying aircraft found a break in the cloud and obtained a hit on the seven thousand-ton US cargo ship *Christopher Newport,* which was laden with tanks, and badly damaged her. A U-boat sank her the following day.

The convoy continued on its way unassailed until the evening when there were low clouds, a calm sea and virtually no wind. This was when enemy aircraft next appeared at 1800. They met with a warm reception. The US destroyer *Wainwright* in particular put up a fine volume of fire well worthy of Independence Day (4 July). Two hours later, though, the convoy was attacked by twenty-five dive-bombers and three more ships were sunk. Four of the attacking aircraft were shot down, one by *Wainwright* which definitely deserved the success. The three rescue vessels carried out excellent work in the execution of their prime function.

Human nature being what it is, the German aviators became so engrossed with their attacks that they omitted to transmit information about the convoy. Admiral Schniewind (in *Tirpitz*) was eagerly awaiting such details as position, course and speed, but of such data-information came there none. On the credit side, for the Nazis, he was aware of the fact that Admiral Tovey's force had altered course westward at 0615 that morning. He had also received a report from the air base in the Lofoten Islands that a patrol between longitudes fourteen and twenty-six had detected nothing unusual.

The above information was relayed to Admiral Carls who, in his turn, requested permission for capital ships to be sailed. Admiral Raeder referred the request to the Führer. This was tantamount to 'kicking for touch'.

Meanwhile, Convoy PQ17 was about to lose the cover provided by the British cruisers. The U-boats, so far, had not been successful. The convoy would be vulnerable to air attack for a further twenty-four hours, being within two hundred and fifty miles of the German airfields during that period of time. However, the guns' crews in both merchant vessels and escorting ships had displayed great tenacity and persistence; and there were sanguine hopes of being able to make Archangel without undue further losses. Rear-Admiral Dalrymple-Hamilton had remained in the area of the convoy until the evening of the 4th; but at about 2110 a message from the Admiralty directed him to return to the west at his best speed. About twelve minutes later instructions were received ordering the convoy to 'scatter'.

The reason for this directive was that no information about *Tirpitz* had been received for thirty-six hours. It was believed that she must be somewhere at sea. From soon after midnight the British heavy ships were expected to be in action with the Germans.

In fact, *Tirpitz* was still in Altenfjord. Sailing orders were not received until 1140 on 5 July; and it was not before 1300 that *Tirpitz* and the other German warships were clearing the entrance to the fjord and setting course towards the north-east with the aim of intercepting Convoy PQ17 which was then spread widely over the Barents Sea. No Allied capital ship was within about four hundred miles of North Cape.

Admiral Schniewind did not sail very far with his squadron. Not all that long after the Führer had authorised the sailing, he sent for Admiral Raeder and reiterated that, in no event, was *Tirpitz* to be exposed to risk, especially if an enemy aircraft carrier was within operational range.

At 1700 on that memorable day a radio message was intercepted, urgently reporting, in English, the position and course of two large enemy warships and eight destroyers. The report identified Admiral Schniewind's squadron. This confirmed that *Tirpitz* had been sighted; and Admiral Tovey's force could be expected to alter course and proceed towards their prey at their best speed, with the aircraft carrier *Victorious* under his command. Hitler could, therefore, no longer be reassured that his splendid new battleship was in no peril. Admiral Raeder, now heart-sick, put an end to the operation.

At 2100 approximately, on the bridge of *Admiral Scheer*, Admiral Kummetz, his Chief-of-Staff and the ship's navigating officer were deliberating the current situation and leaning over the chart table. Suddenly, a signal was flown by *Tirpitz* ordering the German force to reverse course. The order appeared to be unthinkable, and needed to be repeated before it was understood by the recipients.

At 1130 the following morning, 6 July, the German squadron anchored in Kaa Fjord. The ships' companies were filled with consternation and bitterly mortified.

The reason for the withdrawal of the German warships was down to the commanding officer of the Russian submarine, Lieutenant Lunin. Soon after 1600 on 5 July this officer had sighted *Tirpitz* and discharged a torpedo at her. He thought that this weapon had found its target. Lieutenant Lunin was later awarded the decoration of 'Hero of the Soviet Union' for his achievement. However, nobody in *Tirpitz* had been conscious of the attack, let alone its purported success. Despite this, the effort of K-21's report exerted considerable leverage. Admiral Tovey did alter course to the east again. He had little or no hope of bringing the German squadron to action, as he was then about four hundred and fifty miles distant from the same; but he believed, with justification, that if his movements filtered through to the enemy, they might at least discourage the Germans from continuing. As is now known, the German intercept of the warning signal sufficed to trigger the recall of the German squadron.

The battleship *Tirpitz* and her group of ships may never have sighted the convoy they were intended to assault, but the mere foreboding of their interference had had a great effect. Convoy PQ17 had scattered and the merchant vessels were stripped of the cover which was, normally, part of the protection to be expected of being part of a convoy. The dispersed units soon became the subject of violent attacks by enemy submarines and aircraft. The mighty *Tirpitz* had not fired a single shot, but had contributed indirectly to a noteworthy German victory at sea.

Fourteen of the convoy ships were sunk on 5 July alone! The first sacrifice was one of the devoted rescue ships, *Zaafaran*, which was despatched by dive-bombers. Her survivors were rescued by *Zamalek*. The next to go was *Carlton* torpedoed by U-334. Later, six merchantmen were sunk by aircraft, and soon after noon six by U-boats, one of which, the *River Afton*, was carrying the Commodore of the convoy. The US *Daniel Morgan* was noteworthy for putting up a splendid struggle against successive waves of aircraft. Her gunners shot down two enemy bombers and fought on for twenty-eight hours before the ship finally succumbed. The ship's company members who survived suffered and struggled for four days in lifeboats, battling against snowstorms and desperation. They finally reached the 'horrible, icy regions of Novaya Zamlya', as a report worded this feat of endurance and fortitude.

The following day, 6 July, saw two more ships sunk, one by aircraft and the other by submarine. Two more were sunk by U-boats on 7 July and *Olopano* fell to a torpedo attack on 8 July. The captain had refused to take the survivors of a sinking vessel on board, three days before, as he was worried that there was unlikely to be sufficient room in the lifeboats for his own men. Late on 9 July bombers sank the USS *Hoosier* and the Panama registered *El Capitan* when they were within about fifty miles of the White Sea and the crew members thought that they might be reaching safety.

The first ship to reach Archangel was the rescue vessel *Rathlin* on 9 July. She was soon followed by two merchant ships. The remaining vessels, which had succeeded in gaining refuge along the black coast of Novaya Zamlya or in the Matookin Straits, arrived one after another, the last getting in near the end of the month. These arrivals totalled no more than eleven of the thirty-three which had sailed in the inauspicious convoy. Only seventy thousand tons of the two hundred thousand tons of war supplies being transported reached Russia.

The decimation of convoy PQ17 was a great success for Germany and a bitter blow for the Allies. An exceptional circumstance was that a majority of the merchant ships lost were American, i.e. fourteen out of twenty-two ships. The cause of the disaster was, with little doubt, the instruction to the convoy to 'scatter'. This was, in the event, an error of judgment. The German aircraft and U-boat were handed an opportunity to operate freely and with practically equal success. U-344, as a matter of interest, was attacked, in error, and obliged to return to her base at Kirkenes. Her commanding officer was successful, nonetheless, in sinking the *Carlton*, making a prisoner of this ship's master.

The utterly cynical and offhand manner of the Russian leader must have disheartened and revolted the Allied ships' companies. Stalin was alleged to have refused to believe that there had been thirty-three ships in the convoy and suggested that there could not have been more than fifteen! Enough said on that particular subject.

The gallant personnel of the Allied merchant ships persevered in running supplies to Russia through the dangerous, frozen wastes of water.

Convoy PQ18 departed from Iceland in early September 1942. This convoy consisted of thirty-nine ships, and was allocated a strong escort which included, for the first time, one of the new 'Mickey Mouse' escort carriers with twelve fighters on board. Her name was *Avenger*. Despite this strong escort, twelve ships of the convoy were lost to aircraft and submarine attacks.

There were no convoys to Russia during the next three months, due to precedence being given to the needs arising from the Allied North Africa landings. However, convoys were resumed towards the end of December; and the Germans put in a similar operation to the previous ROSSELSPRUNG Admiral Kummetz sailed with *Hipper*, *Lutzow* and a number of destroyers; but in a succession of sharp engagements they were driven away from the convoy by destroyers and two six-inch cruisers, namely *Jamaica* and *Sheffield*, under the command of Rear-Admiral Burnett. The convoy reached its destination without loss, much to Hitler's exasperation. The next convoy, in January 1943, repeated the performance of its predecessor.

Scharnhorst was despatched in March 1943 to join the Norway-based German ships, but it was not until September that the big German ships again appeared in the Arctic Sea. *Tirpitz* and *Scharnhorst*, screened by ten destroyers, carried out a raid on the meteorological office at Spitzbergen. Not long after their return to Altenfjord, *Tirpitz* was severely damaged as the consequence of a brave attack by British midget submarines during the night of 21 September. Lieutenant Place RN and Lieutenant Cameron RNR were awarded the Victoria Cross for their daring and gallant feat. The German battleship was repaired, but was attacked and damaged again by Fleet Air aircraft during April 1944. *Tirpitz* was finally sunk on 12 November, when at Tromsoe, by Royal Air Force Lancaster bombers employing extremely heavy bombs.

The German Naval Command made the decision to risk *Scharnhorst* in an attack on a convoy (JW55B) destined for Russia which had been detected by the Luftwaffe. *Scharnhorst* tried to close the convoy on the morning of 26 December, but was repulsed by the escort of cruisers under the command of Rear-Admiral Burnett. That afternoon the battleship *Duke of York* was moving up at high speed with the aim of intercepting the well-armed German attacker. Together with the cruiser *Jamaica* and four destroyers under the direction of Admiral Sir Bruce Fraser, she was providing distant protection for the threatened convoy. The destroyers heroically faced up to *Scharnhorst*'s formidable armament to deliver a torpedo attack, and obtained hits which succeeded in reducing the big ship's speed. This permitted *Duke of York* to close the range. *Scharnhorst* fought a lonely battle to the end versus the British battleship, four cruisers and eight destroyers. She was set on fire by heavy salvoes from the *Duke of York*'s main armament and finally despatched by a torpedo fired by the cruiser *Jamaica*. *Scharnhorst* went down by the bows as her predecessor had done at the Battle of the Falkland Islands in 1914. She turned over and the last seen of her was her three propellers, still revolving.

The British ships found only thirty-six survivors from *Scharnhorst*'s complement of nineteen hundred men, to rescue from the freezing, turbulent waters. Rear-Admiral Bey, Captain Hintze and all her officers were among those unaccounted for.

This would seem to be a suitable point to conclude this brief study of the Arctic Convoys. The principle of the convoy system was endorsed in the Arctic. Whether the Arctic Convoys were justified, as a maritime undertaking, either morally or politically will, doubtless, be debated for years to come.

Bibliography

Selected works
Clowes, William Laird, *The Royal Navy. A History from Earliest Times to 1900*, (7 volumes), London 1897–1903, reprinted 1996
Jones, Archer, *The Art of War in the Western World*, New York, 1987
    Has sections on naval warfare
Keegan, John, *Battle at Sea from Man of War to Submarine*, Pimlico, 1993
    Originally published under the title *The Price of Admiralty*
Kennedy, Paul, *The Rise and Fall of British Naval History*, London, 1989
Liddell Hart, B H, *The Strategy of Indirect Approach*, London, 1929
Mahan, A T, *The Influence of Sea Power upon History 1660–1783*, Boston, 1890
    For general principles of naval warfare
Winton, John, *Convoy: The Defence of Sea Trade 1890–1990*, London, 1983

The French Revolution and the Napoleonic Wars
Bryant, Arthur, *The Years of Endurance 1793–1802*, London, 1942
_____ *The Years of Victory 1802–1812*, London, 1944
Pope, Dudley, *England Expects*, London, 1959
Schom, Alan, *Trafalgar: Countdown to Battle*, London, 1990
Terraine, John, *Trafalgar*, London, 1975

Nelson
Bennett, Geoffrey, *Nelson the Commander*, London, 1972
Browne, G Latham, *Nelson. The Public and Private Life*, London, 1891, reprinted 1999
Hibbert, Chrisopher, *Nelson: A Personal History*, London, 1994
Howarth, David and Stephen, *Nelson. The Immortal Memory*, London, 1988
Kennedy, Ludovic, *Nelson's Band of Brothers*, London, 1951
Mahan, A T, *The Life of Nelson*, Boston, 1943
Oman, Carola, *Nelson*, London, 1947
Pocock, Tom, *Horatio Nelson*, London, 1987
Southey, Robert, *The Life of Horatio Nelson*, 2 volumes, London, 1813
    Virtually mandatory reading during the 1930s and 1940s

First World War

Auten, Harold, *Q-boat Adventures*, London, nd

Bennett, Geoffrey, *Naval Battles of the First World War*, London, 1968

Campbell, Gordon, *My Mystery Ships*, London, 1928

Chatterton, E Keble, *The Sea Raiders*, London, 1923

_____ *Danger Zone. The Story of the Queenstown Command*, London, 1934

_____ *Q-ships and their Story*, London, 1923

    The classic study that first alerted the public to their existence

Second World War

Costello, John, *The Pacific War*, London, 1985

Howarth, Stephen and Law, Derek (eds), *The Battle of the Atlantic 1939–1945*

    The 50th Anniversary International Conference

Jane's Naval History of World War II, London, 1998

Keegan, John, *The Second World War*, London, 1997

Leckie, Robert, *Delivered from Evil. The Saga of World War II*, New York, 1987

Liddell Hart, *History of the Second World War*, London, 1973

Middlebrook, Martin, *Convoy*, London 1978

Mohr, Ulrich and Sellwood AV, *Atlantis – Story of a German Surface Raider*, London, 1955

Padfield, Peter, *Doenitz, the Last Führer*, London, 1984

Roskill, Stephen, *The Navy at War 1939–1945*, London, 1960

van der Vat, Dan, *The Atlantic Campaign. The Great Struggle at Sea 1939–1945*, London, 1988

Winston, John (ed.), *The War at Sea 1939–1945*, London, 1967

Index

Abercromby, General Sir Ralph: 232

Aberdeen, Scotland: 83

Aboukir 227, 229–33

Aboukir, HMS: 24, 84

Abruzzi: 190

Abyssinia, Mussolini's invasion of, 1935: 183, 186

Achilles, HMS: 140, 141, 142

Actium, Battle of 32BC: 172–3

Aden: 34, 128

Admiral Graf Spee see *Graf Spee*

Admiral Hipper: 145–56, 251

Admiral Scheer: 39, 139, 144–5, 251, 255

Admiralty, British: xv, xvi, xvii–xviii, 4, 31–2, 39–40, 55, 84, 89, 98, 109, 125, 139, 172, 175, 184, 223, 249, 252, 253, 254

Adriatic Sea: 83, 188

Aegean Sea: 191, 192

Agamemnon, HMS: 227

Africa: 54, 67, 112, 115, 119, 167, 181, 191

Africa, HMS: 117–18

Africa Shell, SS: 139

African Prince, SS see *Lambridge*, HMS

Afrika Korps: 190, 202

Agrippine, SS: 57–58

Aircraft, deployment of: 51, 166–7, 172, 175, 176, 178, 180, 185, 188, 190, 196–7

Ajax, HMS: 88, 140, 141, 142, 144, 191

Alabama, CSS: 52, 55–62

Albacare, USS: 213–14

Albania, Mussolini's invasion of: 183

Albemarle HMS: 86, 87

Alexandria, Egypt: 183, 184, 186, 190, 196, 199–202, 227

Alfieri: 195

Algiers: 202

Alsation, HMS: 84

Altenfjord, Norway: 253, 255, 257

Altmark: 139

Amazon river: 121

America *see* United States

American Civil War: 54–62, 70

American Navy *see* United States Navy

Amphion, HMS: 80

Anna Jans, SS: 70

Antwerp, SS: 24

Appam, SS: 119, 120, 123, 124

Aquilon: 229

Aquitania, RMS: 78

Arabic, SS: 26

Archangel, USSR: 82, 87, 250, 253, 254, 256

Archimede: 24

Argentina 140, 143

Ariadne, SS: 119

Ariake Maru, SS: 211

Ariel, SS: 58–9